An Advanced Guide to Coin Collecting

By the same author
Beginner's Guide to Coin Collecting

An Advanced Guide to Coin Collecting

HOWARD LINECAR

PELHAM BOOKS

First published in Great Britain by
PELHAM BOOKS LTD
52 Bedford Square
London, W.C.1
1970

7207 0224 0

Printed in Great Britain
by Ebenezer Baylis and Son, Ltd
The Trinity Press, Worcester, and London
and bound by James Burn at Esher

For Rhoda

Contents

Illustrations

MILLED COINAGE PHASE ONE *1662–1816*

THE SCOTTISH COINAGE

Line Drawings

Acknowledgements

In compiling this book I have been more than usually fortunate in having permission, most generously given, to use a considerable amount of the original work of other writers. Commander R. P. Mack who has studied the Ancient British series all his life, allowed me to use much of the fruits of his study, *The Coinage of Ancient Britain.* Mr. J. J. North, author of *English Hammered Coinage,* two volumes, not only allowed me a free hand with his work but also the use of as many of his maps, original drawings and illustrations as I thought might be useful in this book. He also most kindly read the proofs of the section on hammered coinage. Without this help many errors might have occurred.

In the milled gold and silver series I had the advantage of *The Milled Coinage of England,* and am grateful to its publisher, Spink & Son, for the use of the fine illustrations which the original edition of this book contained. In the copper and bronze series I had the kind permission of Mr. Wilson Peck to quote from his monumental catalogue, *English Copper, Tin and Bronze Coins in the British Museum, 1558–1958,* published by the Museum Trustees.

The account of the Scottish coinage is based on the works mentioned in Chapter 8. After the text of this book had been completed Patrick Finn virtually rewrote it, in the light of *The Guide Book to the Coinage of Ireland,* of which he was co-author with Anthony Dowle. This work is mentioned under its tentative title on page 266: it was still being written.

Wherever the illustrations of coins have been taken from, whether the Cotswold Colotype plates of Mack and North, from the Milled Coinage, or from original plaster casts, it is true to say that the basic origin of them all was the work of the British Museum Department of Coins and Medals. Over many years they have never failed to provide the thousands of casts of coins needed for the many books which I have seen through the press as part of my duties with Spink & Son, and for other books which I have written in the past, as well as for those to come. This kindness extends not only to the facility to use coins from the British Museum collection, but to willingness to cast coins in many private cabinets.

To all who have helped to make this book possible my sincere thanks. My only doubt is that it may not be worthy of their kindness.

Howard Linecar

Introduction

As its title suggests and as is frequently repeated in its pages, this book is a guide to help the collector who, advanced a little beyond the beginner stage, looks around for further help. This help he may possibly need before his theme of collecting begins to crystalize. Conversely his collecting pattern may begin to become apparent and in it he looks for further guidance.

There are plenty of guides for the beginner. A more advanced guide may fall between these and the standard works to which all serious collectors must refer. That is the intention of this book.

In Britain coins have been in use in various forms for close on 2,000 years. As a result British coinage will not fit snugly into any one system of presentation. No set forms can be laid down and followed through all the changes our coinage encounters. The effects of history on British coinage and coinage on British history are such that no sterile compartments can be devised into which the whole coinage of Britain will fit.

As a great nation struggled to birth through extra-mural and civil wars; solidified; threw out colonial extensions; declined and then began to develop to meet the challenge of a science-ruled age, much money has been coined to mark its progress. So many names have been given to its denominations, so much history has been written that our subject, the coinages of Great Britain, will have to be presented in what seems the best way, bearing in mind each and every coinage period which it will encounter.

It cannot be too clearly stated that this book makes no pretence at original research. It is based, with due acknowledgement, on the work of many students in the numismatic field. It tries, perhaps not very successfully, to sift the work of others. From this sifting it attempts to give a guide as to possible collecting themes. More especially it directs the attention of its readers to the standard works upon which it is based. In the main these are the latest works in any particular numismatic field or, where no very recent work is available, to catalogues and other publications which the collector will find reasonably simple to use if he pursues the subject further. As a whole the number of works on which this guide is based has been kept to an absolute minimum. If, as is frequently recommended, the collector consults these works, they will usually be found to contain their own bibliographies. No bibliography of any size is, therefore, published herein.

The coinage of the British Isles divides itself into a number of broad groups. First is the Ancient British coinage. This is followed by that of the Roman occupation, ending with a small series of British imitations of Roman coins, some of which are thought to be contemporary. About the Romano-British coins we shall have little more to say. While representative pieces belong in any cabinet of British coins they are really a part of the study of Roman coinage as a whole, a subject outside this work. With the departure of the Romans all coinage in this country is thought to have ceased.

After an interval the early Anglo-Saxon hammered coins begin to emerge, around A.D. 575. By about 765 the silver Penny, a denomination which alone was to serve the country for some 500 years, made its debut. Since this denomination went on being issued continuously from its inception till the present day, taking on various forms as it developed, it has been given a good deal of space as a collecting theme; one among so many that British coinage offers.

Plate 1

1 An example of so-called 'tin' money, actually made of speculum. **2** Little of the intended Apollo/bull design now remains, the device having become a geometric pattern. **3** Gold Stater of Philip II of Macedon. On this was founded many of the Ancient British coin designs. **4** Gold Stater of the Bellovaci, the design based on the previous coin. **5** Westerham type gold Stater. On the obverse there are still traces of parts of a face and head. What looks like a sprig of leaves crossing the coin diagonally is part of the wreath. In front a ɑ shape is probably an ear and in front of it all that remains of an eye. On the reverse the horse has become an arrangement of lines and dots. **6** Clacton type gold Stater. On the obverse the wreath is still fairly plain but it is difficult to find traces of human features in the remainder of the design. The horse on the reverse, however, is a much better representation. **7** Gold Stater of Tincommius. **8** A similar piece, not so well executed. **9** Gold Stater found at Whaddon Chase, which gives its name to the type. **10** Gold Stater of Tasciovanus. **11** Gold Stater of Cunobeline, struck at Camulodunum (Colchester). **12** Cast bronze coin of the Durotriges. All the above taken from Mack, *The Coinage of Ancient Britain*.

1

2

3

4

5

6

7

8

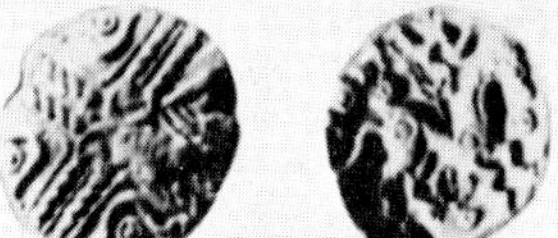

9

10

11

12

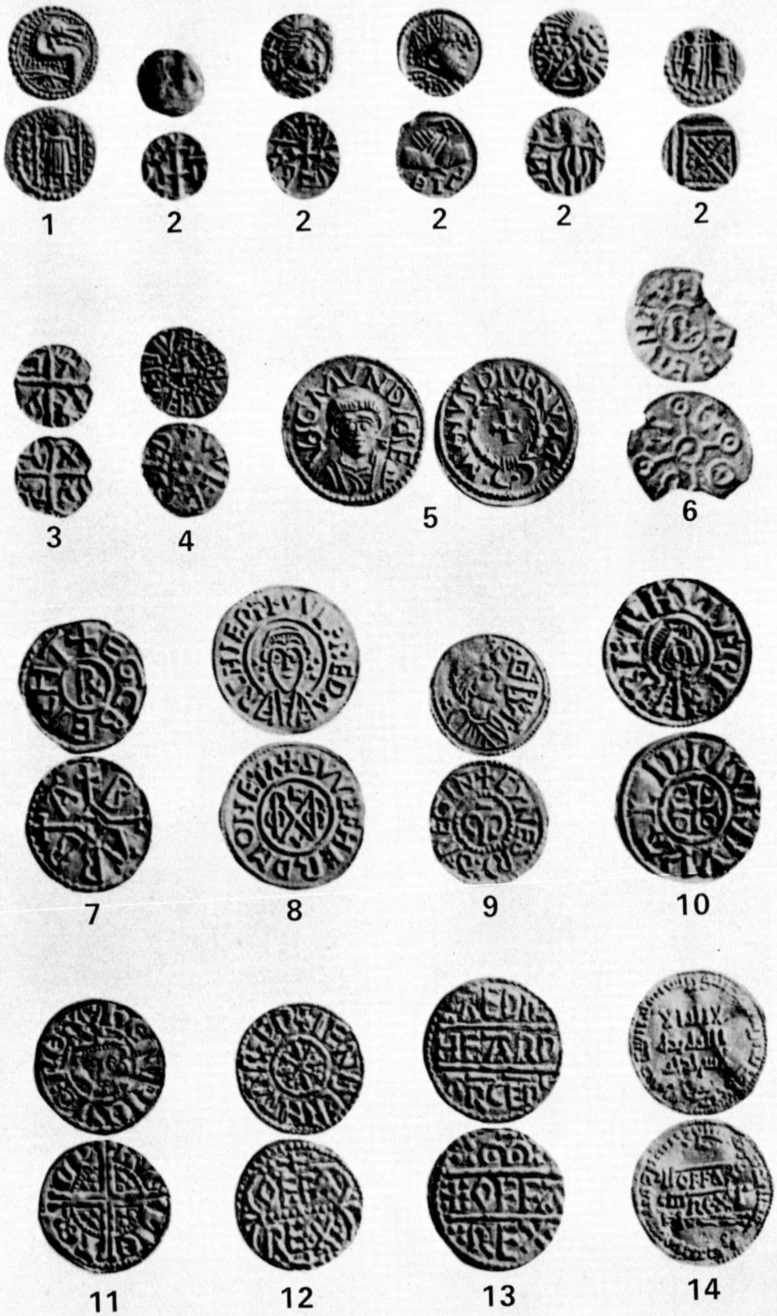
1 2 2 2 2 2
3 4 5 6
7 8 9 10
11 12 13 14

The Norman invasion brought the Anglo-Saxon issues to a close and by about 1344, (Edward III), the coinage denominations began to expand. This expansion will be seen to continue till the end of the hammered period of our coinage. Then follows the first period of the total use of milled coins, from 1662 till 1813, referred to in this book as Milled Coinage, phase one. It was followed by the second milled series, from 1816 till the present time; Milled Coinage, phase two.

It should be mentioned that till the Act of Union of 1707, which brought the kingdoms of England and Scotland into a single realm, (Queen Anne, 1702–1714), the term 'English coinage' will have to be used to distinguish those issues from the separate coinage of Scotland. A further division, from the collector's point of view, is thus formed by the coinage of Scotland. This coinage will be dealt with after the end of the story of English/British coinage. The story of the Scottish coinage takes us back to the hammered series again and continues through the Scottish milled issues.

Plate 2

1 Silver 'Sceatta', London series. Obverse, a dragon; reverse, a man. **2** Further examples of silver 'Sceattas'. **3** Gold Anglo-Saxon Tremissis. **4** Copper Styca of Wulfhere, Archbishop of York. **5** Gold Solidus of Wigmund, Archbishop of York. Note the excellent portrait, bearing in mind the date of the piece, *circa* A.D. 840–50. **6** The only known issue of Heabert (or Headberth), King of Kent, possibly struck at Canterbury. **7** Silver. One of the first Pennies ever struck, in the reign of Ecgberht, *circa* A.D. 765–780. This coin, probably struck at Canterbury, was one of those which gave its name to a denomination that was to survive 1,200 years. Reign by reign the Penny has continued to be struck and, as a denominational name, has come down to us from the remote past. Even decimalization has failed to kill the Penny. **8** Portraits. A full-face, simply constructed from a number of lines. Note the moneyer's name, DOROBERNIA in monogram on the reverse. Silver, Penny of Wulfred, Archbishop of Canterbury, struck in that town. **9** Portraits. A profile, good, but by no means the best at this period. Silver, Penny of Cynethrith, King of Mercia, possibly struck at Canterbury. **10** Portraits (?). Not a very successful profile of Berhtwulf, King of Mercia. Silver Penny, possibly struck at Canterbury. **11** Portraits and crosses. Full-face of Henry III, made up of dots, curves and lines. Probably no resemblance, but at least a human face. Silver Penny, Long-cross type, struck in London. **12** Silver Penny of Jaenberht, Archbishop of Canterbury, with Offa as overlord: whose name appears on the reverse. **13** Silver Penny of Aethelheard, Archbishop of Canterbury, with Offa as overlord: whose name appears on the reverse. **14** Gold Dinar of Offa, King of Mercia. Copied from a Southern French imitation of a Dinar of El-Mansoor, the piece has an unusual look beside its contemporaries. All the above taken from North, *English Hammered Coinage*, volume 1.

Similarly with the coinage of Ireland. This series again has its hammered and milled issues, till Ireland forms itself into two, and the Republic of Ireland is born.

Thus the main pattern of our story.

A book which attempts to cover so much ground has the disadvantage that it may tend to defeat its own purpose. Looking at it casually the potential reader may feel that it contains a great deal of material which is of no interest to him, while not offering enough on his own particular collecting interest. Unfortunately this is unavoidable but the author hopes, most sincerely, that his casual reader may find himself interested in coinages outside his particular field and thus consider expanding his collection. Brief background histories given from time to time in these pages may be of some help in such stimulation of collecting interest.

Let us make a beginning. For the centuries-long story we return to the remote past, to times before the Roman occupation, to see something of such money as there was in Ancient Britain.

CHAPTER ONE

Ancient British Coinage

The coinage which has come to be known as Ancient British reached these islands through a number of invasions from Belgic Gaul, that is, the mainland of Europe close to our shores. Prior to Julius Caesar's 'invasions' in 55 and 54 B.C. the Belgic people had brought in their train firstly a rough type of coin, often referred to as Tin coinage, believed to have originated in Central Gaul. In fact this was made of a metal known as speculum, an alloy of tin and bronze which, when new probably had a shiny silver-like appearance. These coins were cast in strips and later separated, and are found from time to time in the area now known as Kent and along the Thames basin. A find of such pieces was made at Sunbury-on-Thames some years ago.

As well as these speculum coins, which were mainly locally manufactured since the Belgae are stated not to have made such pieces themselves, the invaders brought with them and established in Britain gold coins known as Staters, Half and Quarter Staters, as well as some silver pieces similarly named, and a number of bronze coins. Such pieces were probably in use in Britain as early as the second century B.C., while the 'tin' coins probably cover a period from about 50 B.C. to A.D. 50. Many of the invaders were probably refugees from Belgic Gaul, flying before the German invasion across the Rhine.

It will be remembered that the two expeditions under the leadership of Julius Caesar did not establish a permanent Roman settlement in Britain. They arose in part from the fact that the Britons had been assisting the inhabitants of northern Gaul in their fight against the Romans, who were steadily extending their domination over more and more of southern and middle Europe.

Caesar therefore undertook two so-called 'invasions', to attempt to prevent the Britons from continuing to oppose the extending Roman influence over Europe, and accordingly landed in August 55 B.C. and in the spring of the next year. During the second invasion he crossed the Thames, pushing on into what is now

Hertfordshire. His armies broke up the forces of the various British tribes who opposed him, but were under constant pressure from them in what would now be called guerrilla warfare. Partly because of this Caesar returned to the mainland in September, 54 B.C. and, as events fell out, did not again return to Britain. It was left to Claudius, in A.D. 43, to achieve the Roman conquest of Britain. Much of this can be followed up in Caesar's commentaries, which give the earliest reliable historical facts concerning the state of that part of Britain which he saw and of its people.

With the departure of Caesar came a further Gallo-Belgic influx of refugees, after his final campaigns in Gaul in 52 B.C.

The people whom Caesar found in Britain: local inhabitants, reinforced by the waves of refugees, constituted some nine tribes or collections of people. Their geographical distribution was loose in the extreme, no boundaries being known for the various tribal areas. These nine tribes have, partly through finds of their coins, been found to be distributed throughout Britain roughly as follows.

The Cantii occupied what is now known as Kent, with probably a small part of East Sussex as their western boundary, their northern limits being defined by the Thames. The Regni, south-west of the Cantii, occupied the rest of Sussex and parts of Hampshire, their probable western limits being defined by the Hampshire Avon, while to their north lay the lands of the Atrebates, whose eastern boundary marched with the Cantii and their northern with the upper Thames valley, perhaps extending almost to the upper Severn estuary. The land to the west of the Hampshire Avon and to the east of the River Exe was occupied by the Durotriges, their northern and southern boundaries being the Bristol and English Channels respectively.

North of the Thames the area around Essex and Suffolk, probably a fairly wide coastal strip, was occupied by the Trinovantes, while to the north of them were the Icini, occupying the 'bulge' of Norfolk as far as the south-east of the Wash, their area possibly bounded inland by the Great Ouse. It must be remembered that in these remote times the Ouse and the other rivers that flowed into the Wash soaked their way through vast areas of swamp and low ground, which were probably almost uninhabitable, save in isolated places, such as the 'isle' of Ely, the 'soake' of Peterborough, and so forth.

The distribution of the tribes in Britain. (By courtesy of R. P. Mack)

South of the Icini and west of the Trinovantes were the Catuvellauni, whose area extended to the north bank of the upper Thames, while to their west, based between the far upper Thames and the Severn estuary were the Dobunni.

North of the Warwickshire Avon and the eastern-flowing river Nene lay the area of the Coritani. Their territory probably extended into parts of the West Riding of Yorkshire.

The 'tin' coins which were manufactured locally and are also present in continental finds of coins in excavations are very crude pieces. It takes some imagination to see in the lines of the obverse the head of Apollo and in those of the reverse a charging bull. As a whole the pieces are considered as local money. While it is not known when the idea of their manufacture was brought into this country from Central Gaul, it is considered that these coins were not made by the invading Belgic tribes. Finds of such pieces would have us deduce that they were in use long before the coming of Caesar, who makes some reference to the coins which he found in Britain, and to a type which were probably these speculum pieces.

Though the speculum coins can be classified into two main classes, partly by size and weight and partly by design, the basic idea is the same throughout. On the early types Apollo and the bull are much as shown in the illustration. In the later types the design gets more and more crude till it is difficult to see more than a geometric pattern.

The Ancient British gold coins are a more interesting series. They are thought to have had their origins in the gold staters of Philip II of Macedon, for whom these pieces were being struck around the middle of the fourth century B.C. These staters were handsome pieces, with the head of Apollo on the obverse and a two-horse chariot, known as a biga, complete with charioteer on the reverse. In the exergue appears the name of Philip.

Once in Gaul it was natural enough that these pieces should migrate to Britain with the Belgic invasions, and as they were copied and re-copied to become more and more crude in design. What has not been finally decided is the way in which they reached Gaul. One school of thought gives the route as a slow progress through the Danube countries and what is now Switzerland, while another, that they reached Gaul by way of Rome. The first method of migration would be in the course of gradually expanding Greek trade. It is suggested by Brooke that the Romans in about the early part of the second century B.C. brought back with them from their conquests large quantities of these Macedonian pieces, and even used them as their own money.

In a series of important studies Derek Allen has shown the routes by which these pieces and their cruder imitations reached Britain. Our illustrations show how the type developed. The artists of the period could not produce anything as fine as the Greek original, but the gold stater of the Bellovaci is a remarkably fine piece of work. The head is well executed and though the chariot has disappeared, the horse remains.

How far this head and horse came to be run down can be seen. Among the early British pieces one, of the Southern district, known as the Westerham type, the first of them having been found there, still bears a portion of the face and head though the horse has become very crude. On other types it is difficult to see anything recognizable as a head or face, but the horse is quite clear. A stater from the Eastern district shows further degeneration of the head. The dot with smaller dots round it below the horse frequently occurs in the many types in a variety of ways. Sometimes it is just a single dot, sometimes a group. Occasionally it looks like a flaming sun, and quite frequently a wheel, presumably the last remnant of the chariot.

Tincommius (circa 20 B.C. to A.D. 5) appears to have dispensed with the remains of the head on some of his coins and to have attempted to replace it with his name. Its length, however, appears to have defeated the engraver, so that pieces with TINC and COME appear. It will be noted on the reverse of the first piece how finely the horse and rider are shown, and one is reminded of the St. George of Pistrucci on modern Sovereigns, as well as of the controversy concerning the possible date of the invention of the stirrup.

Finds of staters at Whaddon Chase in 1849 and at Wonersh in 1848 gave their names to certain types of stater. On some of these it is almost impossible to read anything into the crude design while on others in the latter find the horse and rider, the latter waving a carnyx, are once more well struck.

Probably of all the ancient British tribal rulers or chiefs Cunobeline is the most familiar to us, having been preserved through Shakespeare's character Cymbeline. (Boadicea was the widow of a ruler, not necessarily a ruler in her own right.) The staters, halves and quarters of Cunobeline (circa A.D. 10–40) are often of better striking than many that had preceded them, with an ear of wheat frequently appearing on the obverse, and a horse, sometimes with part of the ruler's name under it, occupying the reverse. The letters on the obverse CA MU stand for the mint at Camulodunum (Colchester) at which they were struck and are our first instance of a mint name appearing on a coin. We shall see this practice appearing with increasing frequency.

It is not true to say that the design of Ancient British coins started at a certain level and gradually deteriorated as time went on. In some cases designs improved, some tribal areas producing quite remarkable pieces. On the other hand some tribes, such as the Durotriges, produced some very rough pieces, with little more than dots and lines by way of design. Incidentally this tribe produced some base metal coins, usually classified as bronze. The tribe also

The following nine plates are devoted to a pictorial study of the silver Penny. By taking a cross-section of the many types in use over a long period it is hoped that the collector may be able to see something of the various parts and the names of parts which go to make up the Penny designs, as well as something of the general development of the coin.

All the illustrations are taken from North, *English Hammered Coinage*, volume 1, by kind permission of the author.

Plate 3

1 Before starting on the study of the Penny the second gold piece attributed to Offa, King of Mercia should be shown. It bears many resemblances to a Roman coin, from which it was derived. **2** Now to our study of the Penny. This example struck for Offa at Canterbury. Note the cross botonnée on both obverse and reverse. **3** A further Canterbury piece, with the king's name across the upper part of the field. **4** Another Canterbury piece of the same king with a lozenge centre containing an annulet and pellet. **5** Portraits. A profile of Offa on a Canterbury Penny. **6** Portraits. A further profile of Offa, again on a Canterbury piece, with the name of the kingdom, MERCIORM, clearly stated. On the reverse the lozenge contains a flower of four petals and four trefoil-headed sceptres. **7** Portraits. Yet another profile of Offa, on a coin from the same mint. The reverse device is a serpent or snake, not quite so obvious as that on Plate 2, no. 1. **8** No portrait of Offa on this Canterbury piece, but his name across the obverse. For want of a clearer description the object on the reverse is called a double-lobed 'dumbell' ornament. **9** Portraits and crosses. Penny of Coenwulf, King of Mercia, probably struck at Canterbury. Note the cross on the reverse, with oval open limbs with a small cross pommée beneath it. **10** Portraits. Coenwulf, on a Penny probably struck at an East Anglian mint. On the reverse a large quatrefoil with a leaf made up of pellets within each angle. Within leaf the moneyer's name, LUL, a cross in the first leaf. **11** Portraits. Rather a rough representation of Coelwulf I, King of Mercia, on a Penny possibly struck at Rochester. On the reverse are four crescents in the form of a cross. The formation of the lettering, particularly on the reverse, is interesting. It reads EANVVLF MONET. **12** Portraits. Beornwulf, King of Mercia, on one of his Pennies, possibly struck at an East Anglian mint. Here again the letter-forms are of interest. They read, Obv., BEORNWVLF REX; note how the bust cuts through between RE and X. Rev., WERBALD MONE. In both cases note the Δ, apparently used any way round, as W, and the tree-like form used for M. **13** Lettering. Ludica, King of Mercia, possibly struck at an East Anglian mint. Note the very clear lettering achieved on this piece. **14** Berhtwulf, King of Mercia jointly with Æthelwulf of Wessex. Not so clearly struck, the legends read, obv., BERHVLF REX, rev., AETHELVLF REX. **15** Portraits. Berhtwulf, possibly struck at Canterbury. Note the cross on the reverse, built up of four lines with annulets in the angles. **16** Portraits. Burgred, King of Mercia. The moneyer's name on the reverse is divided by lines known as lunettes.

1

2

3

4

5

6

7

8

9

10

11

12

13

14

15

16

1

2

3

4

5

6

7

8

9

10

11

12

13

14

15

16

produced silver coins, and their pieces were sometimes struck and sometimes cast.

The whole of the Ancient British series is one of great fluidity, the coins being struck by the tribes at various times over the long period circa 125 B.C. to circa A.D. 40–50. Calculated back from the present this span of years takes us to about 1790 and the reign of George III. As has been seen, it is only possible to classify the coins in various large groups, some having the name of the tribe which struck them or the tribal area in which they are found, others taking type names from the places in which they were first discovered.

Finds of Ancient British coins have been very numerous. Sometimes only single specimens have come to light, while in other cases hoards of various sizes have been unearthed. Probably the largest of such hoards was that already mentioned as being found at Whaddon Chase, Buckinghamshire, (in Catuvellaunian territory), in 1849. This hoard consisted of some 2,000 gold staters and it has been suggested that so large an amount of money formed part of an annual payment of tribute money by the Britons to the Roman Commonwealth. Mack lists 78 hoards which have come to light, some consisting of as few as four or five pieces, and found in places as far apart as Cairnmuir, Peeblesshire, and Jersey, Channel Islands. While, in view of the Belgic invasions, hoards in Jersey

Plate 4

1 Ceolwulf II, King of Mercia. Interest here not only in the diademed bust but in the reverse design. This consists of a cross crosslet with lozenge centre, in which a small cross. **2** Æthelberht Lul, King of East Anglia. Here the legend is partly in runes. Note the wolf and twins, the legendary founders of Rome, in a frame of pellets on the reverse. **3** Portraits. Æthelstan I, King of East Anglia. A simple cross crosslet in the centre of the reverse. **4** The same king, but with no portrait. The reverse has a cross pattée over a cross saltire. **5** Æthelweard, King of East Anglia. Obv. Note the cross pattée with a crescent in each angle and, rev., a similar cross with wedges. **6** Eadmund, King of East Anglia. A similar piece. **7** A copy by the Viking Invaders of a London Penny of Ælfred. Note the word LONDON in monogram on the reverse. **8** Penny of the St. Eadmund memorial coinage. The obverse legend, which is often blundered, should read SC EADMVND REX. **9–11** Pennies of the Viking Invaders, of the Sievert-Siefred-Cnut group. **12** Halfpenny of the same group. **13, 14, 15** Hiberno-Norse Kings of York. Pennies of (13), Sihtric 1, (14) Anlaf Guthfrithsson with a raven on the obverse, (15) Anlaf Quaran Sihtricsson with a trefoil-shaped shield on the obverse and a Danish standard on the reverse. **16** Penny of the memorial coinage of St. Peter of York, struck about A.D. 905, late in the Viking Invaders series.

are not unexpected, that as far north as Scotland gives certain food for thought, in a country in which at this time travel in the accepted sense of the word was almost a physical impossibility.

A glance at the eighteen maps in *The Coinage of Ancient Britain* showing the numerous finds is most illuminating. While it can be seen that the principal finds of tribal coin types are found in or reasonably near the tribal areas, in practically every case there are stray finds of many types far from their official location. Very broadly speaking the main finds have all been concentrated in an area bounded in the north by the Humber and the Mersey, the main bulk being roughly in south-east England, with the Severn valley coming second. But again and again the odd find, by ruler or by type, is made, far from the 'home' ground.

Thus the broadly designated Ancient British series is one which can be treated as a collecting theme. The pieces are not inexpensive to collect nor are they, by numismatic standards, considered common. They are full of interest and full of problems and speculation. More specimens and hoards will be found in the future, thus adding something to the knowledge already gained.

The principal work of research on the series has been carried out by the late Sir John Evans, by D. F. Allen and by Commander R. P. Mack and records of finds and other pertinent matter occur in the pages of the *Numismatic Chronicle* and similar numismatic publications and in the archaeological journals. To this source material those interested are directed and in particular to the concise working-book by Commander Mack.

Bibliography

EVANS, SIR JOHN *The Coins of the Ancient Britons.*

ALLEN, D. F. *The Belgic Dynasties of Britain and their coins.* In Archaeologia, Vol. XC, 1944.

ALLEN, D. F. *Belgic coins as illustrations of Life in the late Pre-Roman Iron Age of Britain.* Proceedings of the Prehistoric Society for 1958, Vol. XXIV.

ALLEN, D. F. *The Origins of Coinage in Britain, A Re-appraisal.* Problems of the Iron Age in Southern Britain, 1958.

ALLEN, D. F. *Sylloge of Coins of the British Isles. The Coins of the Coritani*, 1963. Oxford University Press and Spink & Son.

MACK, R. P. *The Coinage of Ancient Britain.* Second edition, 1964. Spink & Son and B. A. Seaby Ltd.

Ordnance Survey Map of Southern Britain in the Iron Age, 1962. H.M.S.O.

For a general description of an Ancient British site, coins and material found and similar matters of background reading,

Reports of the Research Committee of the Society of Antiquaries of London. No. III, Excavations at Hengistbury Head, Hampshire in 1911–1912, by J. P. Bushe-Fox, with appendices by G. F. Hill and Professor W. Gowland, 1915.

CHAPTER TWO

Interim, the Dark Ages and the Anglo-Saxon Kingdoms

From the point of view of the collector the coinage of England from the withdrawal of the Roman Legions till the establishment of the

Plate 5

1 Kings of Wessex. Penny of Beorhtric. On this well-struck piece the device in the centre of the obverse is an Alpha-Omega monogram. That on the reverse is the Mercian M (which was noted before), now inverted and thus standing for Omega. **2** Ecgberht Penny, struck at Canterbury with portrait on the obverse and a clear example of a cross crosslet in the centre of the reverse. **3** A further Penny of the same king, classified by numismatists as Group II; struck at Canterbury. **4** The same king once more, type, Group III, with a rough portrait on the obverse. **5** Another, of Group IV, possibly struck at Rochester. The portrait has degenerated in a somewhat similar manner to the face on certain Ancient British coins which were illustrated earlier. **6** Penny of Æthelwulf, possibly struck at Rochester. In the centre of the reverse the Alpha-Omega monogram. Type, phase I. **7** Of the same king, type, phase II, possibly struck at Canterbury. The portrait dominates the obverse. The cross on the reverse is of interest, having two limbs pattée and two moline. **8** Again the same king, type, phase III, struck at Canterbury. The design looks complicated but is an interesting study. The obverse legend, ETHELVVLF REX is often blundered. The centre is occupied by a monogram of CANT. The apparently jumbled letters in the centre of the reverse read DORIB. **9** The last portrait issue of Æthelwulf, type, phase IV, possibly struck at Canterbury. A large cross, composed of beads, dominates the reverse and contains the moneyer's name. **10** Penny of Eanred. Though he may be classified as an 'uncertain king' his portrait is firm enough. On the reverse another example of the cross crosslet/cross moline type. **11** Penny of Æthelberht. This well-struck piece has a good portrait and a fine example of a floriated cross with a leaf in each angle on the reverse. **12** Penny of Æthelred I. The portrait has a hair-style that resembles a judge wearing the traditional legal wig. The reverse has the moneyer's name in three lines in and between two lunettes. **13** Penny of the first coinage of Ælfred. **14** A further example, second coinage, the bust dominating the obverse. The rather fussy reverse design is made up of a cross pattée within a lozenge, superimposed on a beaded long cross. **15** Penny of Ælfred's third coinage. The obverse legend reads ÆLFRED REX ANGLOX. The unusual reverse shows two emperors, seated facing, while above them hovers a Victory with extended wings. This design, which gives the name 'two Emporers' to the type, resembles certain Byzantine coins. **16** Ælfred's fourth coinage, the piece possibly struck in London. Neat, but very plain by comparison with the previous pieces.

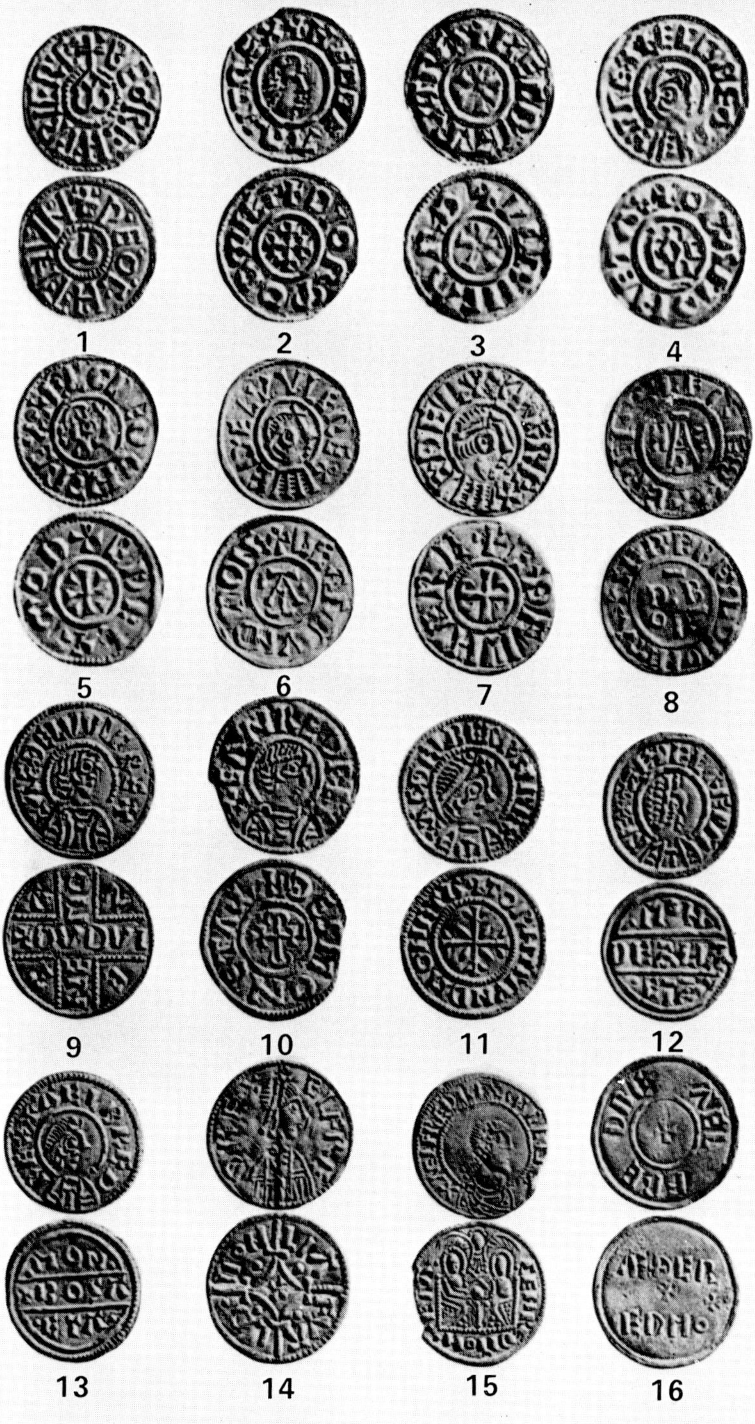
1
2
3
4
5
6
7
8
9
10
11
12
13
14
15
16

1

2

3

4

5

6

7

8

9

10

11

12

13

14

silver Penny can be compressed into one chapter. For the numismatic condition in Britain at this time we can do no better than quote North, who says:

'The cessation of supplies of Roman coins late in the fourth century caused currency and precious metals to become increasingly scarce in this country. Although the remaining coins continued to circulate for several decades, those of gold and silver were soon hoarded as bullion and the country was reduced to a mono-metallic system of worn and clipped copper coins. Two schools of thought have long existed about the question of coinage during the Dark Ages. On the one hand it is maintained that a coinage of clipped copper and barbarous copies continued to be struck in England until the seventh century, whilst the other view is that no coins ever circulated as such after the middle of the fifth century.'

This latter view is advanced by Dr. J. P. C. Kent of the

Plate 6

1 Still with Ælfred, a Penny possibly struck about the middle of the reign, at the Gloucester mint. The reverse legend reads AET GLEAWA. The T-shaped device is described as a long cross with only three limbs. **2** Now to Edward the Elder, a Penny known as the 'two-line' type. **3** The same king, this time a portrait type. Unlike so many portraits shown, here Edward faces left. **4** The Hand of Providence type of Edward the Elder silver Penny. **5** The same king, this time with an attempt to show a church tower on the reverse. **6** Again the same king, this piece with a flower on the reverse. **7** Finally the Minster type. Edward's die sinkers and engravers appear to have shown both interest and initiative in producing what must, at this period, have seemed unconventional designs. One wonders what the public reaction was to these deviations from convention. **Kings of All England,** whose dates will now be included. **8** Æthelstan, *924–939*. Design, for a period, seems to have reverted to the no-portrait, two-line type. Over 90 moneyers are recorded as being engaged in producing this type of Penny. With all England to be provided with the money of one king for the first time, a simple design was, no doubt, considered to have the most utility, as well as probably giving longer die life. **9** The same king: Penny of the Circumscription type, i.e., on 'all round' legend. Possibly another simple, utility type. **10** But Æthelstan was not to forego the portrait type, of which this is a particularly good example, showing the king wearing his crown. Struck in London. **11** A Tower type Penny of Æthelstan, struck at York. The name of the town, EB OR/AC AE, is divided by the tower, which stands firmly on a ground-line, with the moneyer's name below. There had been a Christian church of importance on the site of the present York Minster since the 7th century. This had been burned down in 741 and rebuilt. This little tower may well have been intended to represent that of the church as rebuilt. **12** Eadwig, *955–959*. A Three Line type, struck at Oxford. **13** Eadgar, *959–975*. A Circumscription Cross type. **14** An early portrait type of Eadgar, struck at Hertford.

Department of Coins and Medals, British Museum, and the general opinion among numismatic scholars is now strongly in favour.

The early Anglo-Saxon coinage which emerged circa A.D. 600–750 is one of great interest, but its complexities are such that one hesitates to offer it as a collecting theme at this stage in the reader's numismatic studies. The silver coins, known as Sceattas, show strong Saxon, Merovingian and Frisian art influence, while a part of the series which has been classified as the 'standard' series shows strong Roman inspiration. Byzantine art also influences these so-called Sceattas, and the series as a whole is one which it is suggested might well be returned to by the collector at a later date, if his interest in Anglo-Saxon coins merits such a course.

There were also gold coins at this time, with such names as Tremissis, Solidus and Triens, catalogued as a group of 'Thrymsas etc.'. The whole series is one which is studied at very advanced level in the science of numismatics, and to attempt to give a precis of the series and its problems in a book of this type might well daunt rather than encourage the collector who is advancing beyond the beginner standard.

Problems apart, the coins have considerable interest. Many of them have their own legends written in the Runic alphabet, a system of writing long since forgotten by all but historians. While we have suggested that the more advanced collector may not feel like dealing with the problems of this particular series of coins at this point in his collecting career, perhaps we might deal with a point or two which might stimulate interest later in the collector's life. For example the Runic alphabet.

'The origin of the runic writing,' says Chambers's Encyclopaedia, 'has been a matter of prolonged controversy. The runes were formally supposed to have originated out of the Phoenician or the Latin letters, but it is now generally agreed that they must have been derived about the sixth century B.C., from an early form of the Greek alphabet which was employed by the Milesian traders and colonists of Olbia and other towns on the northern shores of the Black Sea. These traders, as we know from Herodotus, penetrated to the north by the trade route of the Dnieper, as far probably as the territory occupied by the Goths on the head-waters of the Vistula. This conjecture is confirmed by the fact that Greek coins struck in the fifth century B.C. have been found in the region of the Baltic. The oldest runic inscriptions being retrograde, the Goths must have obtained the art of writing from the Greeks at a time when Greek was still written in the retrograde direction from right to left, which gives us a date earlier than the fifth century, but after the new letters *omega* and *chi* had been evolved, and while H retained the value both of *h*, which it has in the Latin alphabet and of *e* which it has in the Greek, and before *koppa* which became Q in Latin fell into disuse among the Greeks. From these and similar data it appears that the runic writing must have been obtained from the Greeks after the seventh and earlier than the fifteenth century B.C.'

The form, number and value of the runic letters changed considerably during the many centuries they were in use. At one period they seemed to have crystalized into a form that could be used as a 'secret writing', rather like Samuel Pepys' personal shorthand. Some years ago the writer amused himself by converting personal notes into runic script, but found it too slow and cumbersome for such a use. A reasonably facile alphabet did evolve, as shown here.

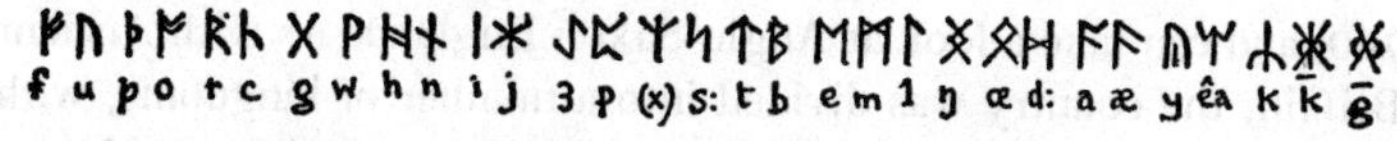

The Runic alphabet (By courtesy of J. J. North)

From the pictorial point of view these very early coins hold much of interest. The obverses frequently showed busts or faces, often firmly drawn and showing, bearing in mind the primitive minting methods of so remote a time, a reasonable likeness to the subject, long before portraits in any other form became common in Britain. The reverses of these remote coins frequently showed various animals. Consider for a moment the illustration on plate 2, no 1. The obverse shows a snake-like creature classified as a dragon. One could deduce from this that dragons, fearful dream-like creatures, have haunted the imagination of man from the most remote times. They are probably a survival from the remote times when primitive man on his way up to civilization met such creatures as the brontosaurus on its way to extinction. Over the centuries which we are about to consider the dragon motif frequently occurs, usually as the personification of evil till, so far as British coinage is concerned, we find him being finally slaughtered by St. George in Pistrucci's St. George and dragon reverse, as shown on the Crowns and Sovereigns of George III (1760–1820). Various types of design on our coinage have shown this idea over the centuries but the final representation, at least for the moment, still appears on the reverse of our gold Sovereigns: the design 'after' Pistrucci. For how many centuries has the 'dragon' terrified mankind? Are not most men more feared of large spiders: and women of mice?

The reverse of the same coin shows a man. A man such as a child might draw. In these remote times this was, apart from the possible portraits mentioned above, about all that the coin die engraver could achieve in his representation of 'a man'. Looking at some of the modern sculpture now offered to us as masterpieces, have not these remote artists give us a more understandable figure of a man (or a woman) than, say, Henry Moore?

All this is remote from our main theme, that of coin collecting. It may show, however, into what divergations the collector's interest may be turned. As we have said, this coinage of almost the 'Dark Ages' is a subject for the real specialist.

We have now arrived, give or take a year or two, at about A.D. 700, and can take a look at Anglo-Saxon England. As with Ancient Britain, the country was divided into a number of kingdoms, with no very sure boundaries, and in these kingdoms numismatic history was being made.

First to the kingdoms themselves. Around A.D. 775 the kingdom of Northumbria occupied, roughly, the land north of the Humber and the Mersey rivers to a point around Bamburgh, with York as its ancient city. North of this was Scotland, whose southern limits were to change from time to time over the centuries to come. On the east, Lindsey occupied very roughly the land between the south shore of the Humber, the north bank of the Witham, which flows into the north-east corner of the Wash, and the river Trent, with Lincoln as its principal city. The centre of England from the Wash to the borders of Wales, and from the south shore of the Mersey to the upper reaches of the Thames and Severn in the west and south and to the shores of the Ouse in the east lay the kingdom of Mercia. The ancient kingdom of Wales, soon to be shut off by Offa's Dyke, the Berlin Wall of the period copied from the Roman walls further

The Anglo-Saxon Kingdoms about A.D. 775 (By courtesy of J. J. North)

north which, more or less, held back the Scots, contained the mountains and valleys into which so many had fled, and into whose security so many would still retreat to find sanctuary from invading forces.

The 'bulge' of England, now Norfolk, Suffolk and Essex, contained the kingdom of East Anglia, with Thetford and Norwich as local points, while the land immediately to the south of the Thames was the kingdom of Kent. In close touch with the mainland of Europe, we have seen how this ancient kingdom was, as now, the gateway to the Continent, through which flowed people, trade, ideas and coinage. London, by virtue of its place on the principal navigable river opposite the mainland was always there, almost a kingdom in itself.

To the west of Kent and bounded roughly by the south bank of the Thames, by the Severn and the Tamar, lay the kingdom of Wessex, with Winchester as its great city, at one time rivalling both London and Canterbury in importance.

Beyond the Tamar, Cornwall, never a recognized ancient kingdom but a land full of legend; rocky and sparsely populated but with an almost sub-tropical climate; filled with stories of a lost continent between the Lizard and the Isles of Scilly and beyond, and with stories of contacts with Phoenician traders who bargained for Cornwall's tin, and with the legends of King Arthur.

The *Handbook of Dates* gives two other kingdoms, Deira and Bernicia, but as they apparently produced no coinage they do not concern us, and are not shown on the map.

For the purpose of our story we, therefore, are concerned with the kingdoms of Northumbria, Lindsey, Mercia, East Anglia, Wessex and Kent. In these kingdoms coins were issued, sometimes by the rulers and sometimes by the Archbishops, in whom was vested for a time the privilege to strike money.

NORTHUMBRIA

Between 737 and 867 Northumbria was ruled by the following Kings:

Eadberht, 737–757/8
Alhred, 765–774
Æthelred I, first reign, 774–778/9
Ælfwald, 778/9–788
Æthelred I, second reign, 790–796
Eanred, 806/8–840/1
Æthelred II, first reign, 840/1–844
Redwulf, 844
Æthelred II, second reign, 844–848/50
Osberht, 848/50–867

A moment's consideration of the list of kings will show gaps and doubts as to exact dates. The knowledge which we have of this kingdom in these remote times is full of such gaps. Guesses and theories could possibly fill these gaps, but the historian is not interested in guesses, and takes a guarded view of theories. Thus, the list given above concerns only those kings for whom coins are known. In fact the *Handbook of Dates* gives a total of some twenty-nine kings who ruled Northumbria, tracing them back to 592/3, but not all these rulers issued coins, and the coins of previous rulers sometimes served later kings. In fact the *Handbook* shows four kings after Osberht, the last recorded King of Northumbria, much of which kingdom came under the rule of Scandinavian Kings of York as its history progressed.

Our list of kings, therefore, shows, as stated, only those who are known to have issued coins. Of these Eadberht (737–758), Alhred (765–774), Æthelred I, (first reign 774–779, second reign 789–796), and Ælfwald (779–788), issued small silver coins now known as Sceats.

As will be seen, these little pieces were obviously descended from the Sceattas by way of legend. In point of design they were somewhat the poorer. Attempts were made to show animals but in the main these little pieces were covered with lettering.

When Eanred (810–841) became king of Northumbria a debasement of the coinage obviously took place. In his name, and in those of his successors, Æthelred II, Redwulf and Osberht, debased silver and copper coins, called Stycas, were issued. This particular name, Styca, has been given to these coins by numismatists, on the understanding that it is most unlikely to have been the real name. Lacking actual knowledge an identification label had to be given, if only for the purpose of classification.

In this series we begin to get probably for the first time the name of the Moneyers on the coins. These Moneyers either struck the coins or, more often, were the persons who were vested with the right of striking coins, a right always carefully guarded, and given only after due consideration.

In the ancient city of York, part of Northumbria according to the map, but like London, almost a kingdom in itself, the Archbishops had the privilege of coining money. At this period there were four such Archbishops:

Ecgberht, 732/4–766
Eanbald II, 796–circa 830
Wigmund, 837–854(?)
Wulfhere, 854–900(?)

During the reign of Eadberht of Northumbria, Archbishop Ecgberht (732/4–766) issued silver Sceats, and a further issue appeared during the reign of Alhred. Archbishop Eanbald (796–circa 830) made an issue of Stycas in base silver, while Wigmund (837–854?) and Wulfhere (854–900?) issued similar pieces in copper. Sometimes parts of the legends on these pieces, as on those of the Kings of Northumbria, are retrograde, that is reading anti-clockwise.

In Wigmund's time there was struck a gold Solidus whose authenticity was long doubted by numismatists. As will be seen, this fine piece carried a 'portrait', and its authenticity was vindicated by the President of the Royal Numismatic Society in 1960 in his Presidential address, later published in the *Numismatic Chronicle*.

With one or two exceptions we now come to the period when the long history of the coin called the Penny started. The piece made its first appearance in the reigns of Heabert and Ecgberht of Kent, somewhere about the year 780. From that time till the present no reign has passed without silver pennies being issued. As we shall see, for many centuries it was the only coin struck, together with its half, and it survives today as a silver piece among the Maundy money, of which more in its place. It branched out into a copper and later a bronze piece, also still in daily use, and this branching also we shall see in due time. The Penny is therefore Britain's most ancient coin, having been in continuous use for 1188 years. In spite of coming changes in our coinage its name will survive, in the form of the New Penny, a decimal denomination. This is as it should be. So ancient a coin ought not to be lightly extinguished.

KENT

As stated above, the first Penny is credited to Ecgberht, King of Kent, whose line of kings was as follows:

Heabert, circa 764
Ecgberht, circa 765–circa 780 or later
Cuthred, 798–807
Baldred, expelled 825

For Heabert (circa 764) only one issue of coinage is known. It was only authenticated quite recently by Christopher Blunt and as will be seen from the illustration of probably the only specimen known, it is a small piece, not well preserved and not quite so large in size as the Penny which we shall soon be considering, though the illustration is slightly smaller than the actual coin. Enough remains, however, for the king's name HEABERHT to be read, while in the centre is the word REX in monogram. The reverse contains the word EOBA.

We will pass on to the next stage: coins which can more easily be appreciated by the reasonably advanced collector. For those who might be stimulated into studying the 'Thrymsas' etc., and the 'Silver Sceattas' the following works will provide some further very serious reading.

Bibliography

BONSOR, W. *Anglo-Saxon and Celtic Bibliography*. Oxford, 1957.

CREEKE, A. B. *Regal Sceatta and Styca Series of Northumbria.* British Numismatic Journal, 1.

CREEKE, A. B. *Sceatta and Styca Coinage of the Early Archbishops of York.* B.N.J. 2.

HILL, P. V. *Saxon Sceattas and their problems.* B.N.J. XXVI.

HILL, P. V. *The 'Standard' and London Series of Anglo-Saxon Sceattas.* B.N.J. XXVI.

HILL, P. V. *The Animal, 'Anglo-Merovingian' and Miscellaneous Series of Anglo-Saxon Sceattas.* B.N.J. XXVII.

LYON, C. S. S. *A Reappriasal of the Sceatta and Styca Coinage of Northumbria.* B.N.J. XXVIII.

RIGOLD, S. E. *The Two Primary Series of Sceattas.* B.N.J. XXX.

SUTHERLAND, C. H. V. *Anglo-Saxon Gold Coinage in the Light of the Crondall Hoard.*

CHAPTER THREE

The Early Hammered Coinage
The Penny

From the point of view of the more advanced student of English coinage this would appear to be an unlikely spot at which to start a new chapter. From the point of view of the collector it could be considered as a turning-point in that, as stated above, we have now arrived at the time when the Penny makes its appearance. It and its halves and quarters were to serve England for some 500 years before multiples of the Penny began to appear and the denominations themselves to multiply.

We have tried to clear the decks, as it were, for the introduction of the Penny by dealing with the various ancient coins in use before its appearance. Many have specialised in the collection of Pennies in use in England in Anglo-Saxon and later times. The early silver Penny, with its sub-divisions, is a collecting theme, and as such we will treat it.

KENT

We start, then, by taking up our story with the Kings of Kent, listing them again for convenience. As was said, in the reigns of Heabert and Ecgberht, Kings of Kent around 765–780 the Penny first appeared.

Kings of Kent
Heabert, circa 764
Ecgberht, circa 765–circa 780 or later
Cuthred, 798–807
Baldred, expelled 825

Some general characteristics of the piece may be helpful. It was to serve as the main coin of the realm from its introduction till the time of Edward III (1327–1377), when two larger silver coins the Groat, equal to four Pennies, and the Half Groat, equal to twopence were added to the silver coinage and a gold coinage became established. Of all this more in its place.

The Silver Penny, which varied slightly in size from time to time was, in the main, of a size between that of our modern Sixpence and Shilling. It was struck on a thin flan of silver from handmade dies. This silver flan was usually cut from a sheet of metal and trimmed for size and weight, though in some instances it is said that the flan was obtained by cutting it from circular silver bars. During the 500 odd years in which it was the staple coin of the country, the devices which appear on it are legion. Portraits come and go, some of them quite remarkable, others little more than a hopeful outline of human features.

The cross in every and any form frequently appeared. Adopted as the Christian symbol, it does not follow that it was always used in this context when shown on a coin. It offered a convenient way of dividing up the circle of the coin into four sections, in which various devices, mainly lettering by way of legend, could be placed. Until quite recently the linial descendant of the cross motif on the Penny was still in use. By 1662, when milled coinage was introduced, it took the form of the various royal arms, set cruciform. Such cruciform arms continued to appear on our coins at intervals till the reign of George V, (1910–1935).

Sometimes the cross appeared quite small, in the centre of the Penny, surrounded by the legend, with or without circular lines to define its limits. Alternately it became so large that it reached from edge to edge of the Penny. Such pence are later, for purpose of classification, known as the 'Long Cross' type. By then, temp Henry III (1216–1272), it had been realized that the cross motif, if voided and brought to the very edges of the coin, would indicate how the coin could legally be cut into two (Halfpence) or four (Farthing) pieces. Additionally it would show if the coin had been clipped. If the ends of the cross were missing, someone had been tampering with the coin.

Only a large number of illustrations could show the many devices on the Penny apart from the cross motif. Sometimes the flan was divided into three sections by two parallel lines, or lines of dots, placed across it from East to West. Lettering filled the three spaces so left. Only reference to the numerous catalogues of the piece can show the collector how diverse and interesting they are. It will be appreciated that with five centuries of Pennies before us a lot of historical background will have to be covered.

Within Kent lay Canterbury, the Jerusalem of England, a town of such ecclesiastical importance that its Archbishops had for a considerable period the privilege of striking Pennies. We have seen this privilege granted to York, and we shall come across other instances of ecclesiastical mints, at least till the time of Cardinal Wolsey.

Thus, within the kingdom of Kent the following Archbishops struck Pennies:

Jaenberht, 766–792
Æthelheard, 793–805
Wulfred, 805–832
Ceolnoth, 833–870
Æthered, 870–889
Plegmund, 890–914

The names of the Archbishops usually appear on their coinage, but among the early issues another name appears, OFFA REX. Offa, officially King of Mercia from 757 till 796, was doing some of the 'spade work' that was, centuries ahead, to unify the kingdoms into one. It is too early yet to see this even dimly, but in his own time Offa was a considerable force in the land. His contribution to history should be followed in the many histories of England.

He was overlord of the kingdom of Kent during the times when Archbishops Jaenberht (766–792), and Æthelheard (793–805) were striking their Pennies. Thus, his name appears on them. Offa's successor as King of Mercia, Coenwulf (796–821), was also overlord of Kent. His name therefore appears on the last (third) issue of Pennies struck by Archbishop Æthelheard (793–805).

By the time Archbishops Wulfred (805–832), Ceolnoth (833–870), Æthered (870–889), and Plegmund (890–914) were striking Pennies at the ecclesiastical mint of Canterbury, both Offa and Coenwulf had passed from the scene of history. The name of the Archbishop therefore appears alone on his coinage.

MERCIA

The coinage of the kingdom of Mercia at this period has been the subject of much study. Eminent numismatists have divided it up in various ways. First, though, the Kings,

Offa, 757–796
Coenwulf, 796–821
Coelwulf I, 821–823
Beornwulf, 823–825
Ludica, 825–827
Wiglaf, 827–829, 830–840
Berhtwulf, 840–852
Burgred, 852–874
Coelwulf II, 874–877?

Two remarkable gold coins are attributed to Offa. The first is usually known as the gold Dinar of Offa, and Christopher Blunt has authenticated this remarkable piece, describing the only known specimen in a paper in the *British Numismatic Journal*. The piece is copied from a Southern French imitation of a dinar of El-Mansoor dated A.H. 157. This date is equivalent to A.D. 774, the middle of Offa's reign. The second gold piece is derived from a Roman prototype, and has again been the subject of considerable research by Mr. Blunt.

Of the silver Pennies there are many interesting varieties among which Mr. Blunt has also carried out much original research, dividing them into main groups and sub-dividing them into moneyers. His researches are published in *Anglo-Saxon Coinage*. The classifications which follow are not those of Mr. Blunt, but are taken from North, *English Hammered Coinage*, vol. 1, where they were adapted to conform with the general method of classification used by the author throughout that book.

First are the coins struck at the Canterbury mint. It will be remembered that during the time of Archbishops Jaenberht (766–792) and Æthelheard (793–805) Pennies were struck at Canterbury with Offa as overlord, till 796. It will be noted how these dates fit with the groups of coins about to be described as struck at the Canterbury mint, but classified under Offa. The significant difference between the two types of pence is that these Pennies are Offa's, while those mentioned above rightly belong to the Archbishops, whose names appear on the obverses. Offa's appearing on the reverse.

The first group (Group I) of the Offa coins struck at Canterbury were produced from about 784 to 787. Offa was by then complete overlord of Ecgberht and in control of the mint. They are subdivided by North into obverse types having (i) a plain cross, (ii) a cross on saltire, that is a cross botonnée on a saltire botonnée, (iii) crosslet and (iv) a standard obverse. The types of cross described appeared as follows:

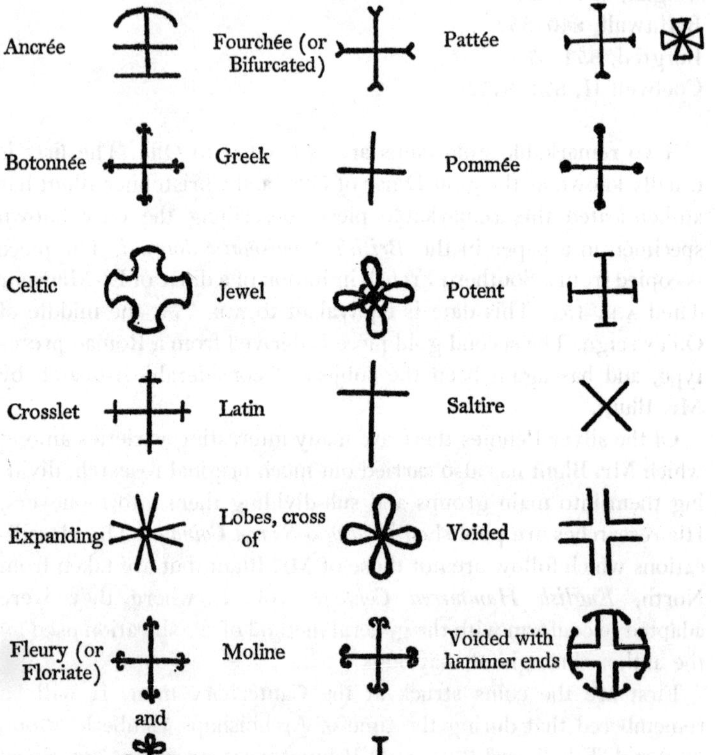

Various types of cross, referred to here and elsewhere in the text (By courtesy of J. J. North)

The second group (Group II) of Offa's Canterbury coins were struck from about 787 to 792, and fall first into two main divisions, those without a portrait and those with.

The first of these divisions is then subdivided into obverse types, having (i) a Celtic cross, (ii) a cross and saltire of lobes, (iii) a cross crosslet, (iv) a cross of lobes, (v) with lozenge obverses, (vi) with the King's name across the field and (vii) with annulet and pellet, an annulet being a small ring and a pellet a dot.

The second of these divisions of Pennies of the Canterbury mint have six quite distinct types of bust or portrait, with more than a dozen slight varieties. To continue with the classifications by the type of cross used, they now being on the reverse, the types are as follows. (i) Celtic cross, (ii) cross of lobes, (iii) floriate cross, with lozenge centre, (iv) cross crosslet with lozenge centre, (v) plain cross, Pennies in group (vi) have lozenge reverses, those of group (vii) have flowers and other devices in an inner circle, and the final group (viii) have serpent reverses.

The final Canterbury coins which form Group III were struck from about 792 to 796. They are all slightly larger in size than those described above and all have a similar obverse design. This consists of the name OFFA placed between two plain or beaded lines across the centre of the coin, with REX below and the letter M above.

The final Pennies issued during Offa's reign were probably struck in East Anglia. They come under the Group II period, namely 787–792 and Group III period, 792–796.

Finally, Cynethrith, the wife of Offa, is credited with striking two types of Pennies during the Group II period, 787–792.

It will be remembered that Coenwulf, who succeeded Offa as King of Mercia in 796 and reigned till 821, was also overlord of Kent, and that his name appears on some of the Archbishop's coins. He too issued Pennies at Canterbury in his own name. These issues are classified as the Early coinage, probably from 800–809, the Middle coinage, probably struck from about 805–810, and the Late coinage struck after 810. Since the Canterbury and East Anglia mints were denied to Coenwulf during the first two years of his reign, the Early coins were struck at another mint, probably London, while in the Middle and Late coinages it is almost certain that some of the pieces were struck in London and Rochester, since the moneyers whose names appear on the coins were known to have been working at these mints. Thus, with one particular Penny we get examples struck by the moneyers Coelheard, of London, Dealla, of Canterbury, Dun, of Rochester and Ealhstan, of Rochester.

The remaining Pennies of the reign of Coenwulf were probably struck in East Anglia. There are about fourteen varieties, all rare pieces.

Ceolwulf I (821–823), probably had his Pennies struck at the Rochester mint and at a mint in East Anglia. Here again with the Rochester group we get the probability arising, from the known location of the moneyer, of coins in the group being struck in London and Canterbury.

The Pennies of both the next two Kings of Mercia, Beornwulf (823–825) and Ludica (825–827) were probably struck in the East Anglian mint, while those of both the first and second reigns of Wiglaf (827–829 and 830–840) were probably struck in London. The coins of all three reigns are extremely rare, and do not fall into large numbers of classifications.

The Pennies of Berhtwulf (840–852) are a little more complex again. The first type were struck jointly with Æthelwulf of Wessex

Plate 7

1 Edward the Martyr, 975–978, Penny struck at Hertford. **2** Æthelred II, 978–1016. Penny of the First Hand type, struck at Southampton. The Hand of Providence issues from clouds, with A W to left and right. **3** The Second Hand type of the same king, struck at Barnstaple. **4** A further Hand type. The hand is now of the Latin Benediction type, with two fingers folded down. The coin was struck at Rochester. **5** Known as the Crux type this Penny of Æthelred II takes its type-name from the letters CRVX in the angles of the short voided cross on the reverse. Note that on this and the two previous coins shown the king is holding a sceptre. This piece struck at Wareham. **6** Long Cross type Penny of the same king, struck at Milborne Port, north of Dorchester in Dorset. **7** Cnut, 1016–1035, Penny struck at Lydford in Devonshire. The use of a quatrefoil to enclose the bust and decorate the voided cross on the reverse has given its name to this type of coin. Note that the ends of the cross are decorated with crescents. **8** The pointed helmet type of Cnut Penny, this example struck at Bruton in Somerset. Note how the bust extends right to the edge of the coin. **9** The short cross type, struck at Crewkerne. Note how Cnut's bust and sceptre take up a considerable amount of the obverse. **10** The jewel cross type, struck in London. **11** Harold I, 1035–1040, struck at Dover, also the jewel cross type. **12** The Fleur-de-lis type, struck at Leicester. Note the fleurs in the angles of the long voided cross. **13** Harthacnut, 1035–1042. (Harold I and Harthacnut reigned jointly from 1035–1037 and as sole kings from 1037–1040 and 1040–1042 respectively.) Second jewel cross type struck at Axbridge. **14** Arm and sceptre type of Harthacnut, struck at Nottingham. Note the arm and hand at the base of the obverse. **15** Edward the Confessor, 1042–1066, struck at Taunton. Known as the PACX type, the letters being in the angles of the long voided cross on the reverse. **16** The radiate-small cross type, struck at Gloucester. Note the radiate crown on the king's head.

1

2

3

4

5

6

7

8

9

10

11

12

13

14

15

16

1

2

3

4

5

6

7

8

9

10

11

12

13

14

15

16

about 843. Both King's names appear, one on each side of the coin. The remaining coins then fall into the non-portrait and portrait issues, the portrait type being classified into two date groups, Group I, about 843–848 and Group II, about 848–851. In the first group there are six varieties of bust, and in the second some five minor varieties with a number of sub-varieties of arrangement, not

Plate 8
1 Edward the Confessor, 1042–1066. Struck at Berkeley and known as the trefoil-quadrilateral type. The quadrilateral is the device at the centre of the short voided cross on the reverse. **2** Expanding cross type, of the same king, struck at Dorchester. Notice how the sizes vary. **3** The pointed helmet type, struck at Hythe in Kent. Note how Edward is shown as an old man with beard; also the decorated ends of the short voided cross on the reverse. Also, as a general note, there was not yet any rule or custom as to which way the king should face on his coinage. **4** The Sovereign-Eagles type, struck at Horndon; a very detailed piece of die-work. Edward is shown seated on a throne, holding sceptre and orb. Since this is how the king was shown on the first gold Sovereigns issued by Henry VII, 1485–1509, numismatists have given the name Sovereign type to this style of obverse. The reverse has eagles in the angles of the short voided cross on the reverse. **5** The hammer cross type, struck at Bedwyn, so called on account of the ends of the short voided cross on the reverse. **6** The facing bust-small cross type, struck at Hastings. **7** The pyramids type, so called on account of the small pointed devices between the angles of the voided cross on the reverse. **8** The eve of the battle. Penny of Harold II, 1066. The word PAX across the field on the reverse was perhaps a little overhopeful. **Norman Kings. 9** William I, 1066–1087. Penny struck at Ilchester and known as the profile-cross fleury type. A good example of a really flowery cross. **10** The canopy type, struck at Taunton. The king is either standing before a canopy, such as is still erected when, say, royalty goes to the theatre, or, possibly, is seated on a high-backed throne. The reverse device is described as a double-quadrilateral, fleury at the angles. The annulet in the centre makes a focusing-point for the eye. **11** The two sceptres type, this example struck at Malmsbury. Note the sceptres on either side of the king: possibly the artist wanted a balanced effect. The interesting reverse device is a cross fleury with an annulet in the centre, over a saltire botonnée cross. **12** The two stars type, this example struck at Cricklade. The reverse design is made up of a cross botonnée, with an annulet in the centre, superimposed on a quadrilateral. **13** Sword type. The king is now holding a large sword in place of a sceptre. Reverse much as the last but the cross pattée is over a fleured quadrilateral. **14** The profile-cross type, this specimen struck at Oxford. The whole design is interesting. On the obverse is a profile portrait bust to right, as opposed to the more usual facing bust of William. The reverse has a cross pattée with an annulet in the centre and is embellished in each angle with a voided trefoil. **15** The PAXS type, this example struck at Rhuddlan in North Wales. The type-name is taken from the letters in the angles of the cross potent on the reverse. **16** William II, 1087–1100. The cross in quatrefoil type, from the Salisbury mint.

affecting the actual five different faces. Again, these are all very rare pieces.

Of the Kings of Mercia there now remain but two, Burgred (852–874) and Ceolwulf II (874–877?). The Pennies of the former are not anything like so rare, save for one type, as are those we have been considering. The King's bust appears on the obverse, the main differences being in the appearance of the five reverse types, which consist of the moneyer's name across the centre with MON ETA (moneta; moneyer) divided top and bottom, as indicated. The greater extent numerically of Burgred's issues may be gleaned from the fact that some fifty-two moneyers' names appear.

The two types of the final King are both extremely rare, and only five moneyers were engaged in their production.

EAST ANGLIA

The coinage, Pennies once again, of the Kings of East Anglia, is neither as extensive nor complicated as that of the Kings of Mercia. Again most coins are very rare, except the majority of those of the last King. The Kings are:

Beonna, circa 758
 Æthelberht Lul, accession unknown, died 794
Eadwald, circa 796
Æthelstan I, circa 825
Æthelweard, circa 850
Eadmund, 855–870

Beonna is only known to have issued a Sceat, with the legend partly in Runic lettering, Æthelberht Lul one type of Penny, the legend again partly Runic and Eadwald by two types, all these being of great rarity.

The Pennies of Æthelstan I fall into two classes, with and without busts. The former, struck about 827, are all extremely rare. The latter, struck after that year do contain a few types which are not of such a high degree of rarity.

The Pennies of Æthelweard and Eadmund are of one main class only, with numerous varieties, the majority of the former King's pieces being very rare while the majority of the types of the last East Anglian King are not of such rarity.

THE VIKING INVADERS

We come now to the coinages of the Viking Invaders, which will need a little patience. The story of these repeated invasions, lasting some 100 years, their effects on the various Anglo-Saxon kingdoms and on England as a whole is beyond the purpose of this work. Their effect on the coinage, resulting in such situations as quantities of Anglo-Saxon Pennies finding their way to Scandinavia, copies of Anglo-Saxon coins being made there, such copies finding their way back to England and similar matters, are also for students perhaps more advanced than our reader. They are of great interest and importance, but too lengthy and complex to be dealt with here. We are concerned only with the Viking Invaders known to have issued coins, whose leaders were as follows:

In Anglia
Æthelstan II Guthrum, 878–890/1
Oswald, dates unknown
'Halfdene' or 'Alfdene' of Denmark, circa 900

In Northumbria (York mint)
'Sievert-Siefred-Cnut' a group, circa 897
Earl Sihtric, dates unknown
'Raienalt', circa 910

Hiberno-Norse Kings of York
Sihtric, 921–926/7
Anlaf Guthfrithsson, 939–941
Anlaf Quaran Sihtricsson, 926/7, 940–943, 949–952
Sihtric II Sihtricsson, circa 941–943

Regnald II Guthfrithsson 941–943
Eric, 948, 952–954

The story of the coinage of the Viking Invaders, for the purposes of catalogue, starts with various imitations of the coins of Ælfred (whom we have not yet met), and of others, issued after A.D. 887. Both Pennies and Halfpennies appear in this series and all are extremely rare. They are followed by the Pennies of Æthelstan II Guthrum and by the single type of Penny and Halfpenny of the uncertain Danish King, 'Alfdene', again excessively rare pieces. Under the classification of St. Edmund appears a memorial coinage by Danish settlers, struck circa 890–905. The first type of Penny is not a rare piece, and contains the legend SC EADMUND REX with a letter A in the centre, while the reverse has the moneyer's name, which is sometimes followed by ME FEC (IT) (=made me) a cross pattée occupying the centre. The later coins in the issue are somewhat smaller than the earlier pieces. The legends are often blundered and the availability of the piece can in some measure be assumed from the fact that some sixty-nine moneyers' names appear. Here then is a piece which the collector has some chance of obtaining, as perhaps the sole representative of the coinage of the Viking invaders. A Halfpenny is also known, but it is a very rare piece. A very rare Penny of St. Martin of Lincoln was struck in about 917. Two further very rare pennies follow, possibly struck in East Anglia under Æthelred about 870.

Next come the Northumbria (York) series of the Sievert-Siefred-Cnut struck about 897, mostly very rare pieces, though some types are common. There is also a series of Halfpennies, again very rare coins. A small series of Pennies and Halfpennies from the Quentovic Mint, all very rare, precede a single Penny with the legend SITRIC COMES. This rare piece is attributed to Earl

Plate 9
1 William II, 1087–1100. A profile type from the Cambridge mint. The reverse has a cross pattée with an annulet in the centre over a cross fleury. **2** The cross voided type, struck at Guildford. The obverse resembles the two star type of William I. **3** The cross pattée and fleury type, struck, in this case, at Sandwich. **4** The cross fleury and piles type, this example from Shrewsbury. The piles are the little objects in the angles of the cross on the reverse. **5** Henry I, 1100–1135. The annulets type, so called from the small rings on either side of the bust. This Penny was struck at the Dover mint. **6** The profile-cross fleury type, this example struck at Bristol. Note the smaller size. **7** The PAX type. This example has no final S, and PAX is placed across the reverse. The coin was struck at Stamford. **8** The annulets and piles type, this example struck at Gloucester. The cross formation on the reverse is actually made up from four piles. **9** The voided cross and fleurs type, struck in London. **10** The pointed bust and stars type, this example from Wareham. Here a more ambitious three-quarter-facing portrait has been attempted, with a crown, indicated by three crosses (or perhaps fleurs). The whole obverse is a break with the long traditional 'bust in a circle' (or through circle) type. **11** The quartrefoil and stars type, with piles in the angles. This example struck at Hastings. **12** The larger profile type with cross and annulets on the reverse, this coin struck at Winchester. **13** The cross in quatrefoil type, struck at Winchester. Annulets in the angles of the cross. **14** The full-face cross fleury type, this example from Chichester. **15** The double inscription type. An unconventional type with a large profile bust taking up almost the whole of the obverse and with the legend in two concentric circles on the reverse. **16** The smaller profile-cross and annulets type, struck at Wallingford. Note the smaller size.

1

2

3

4

5

6

7

8

9

10

11

12

13

14

15

16

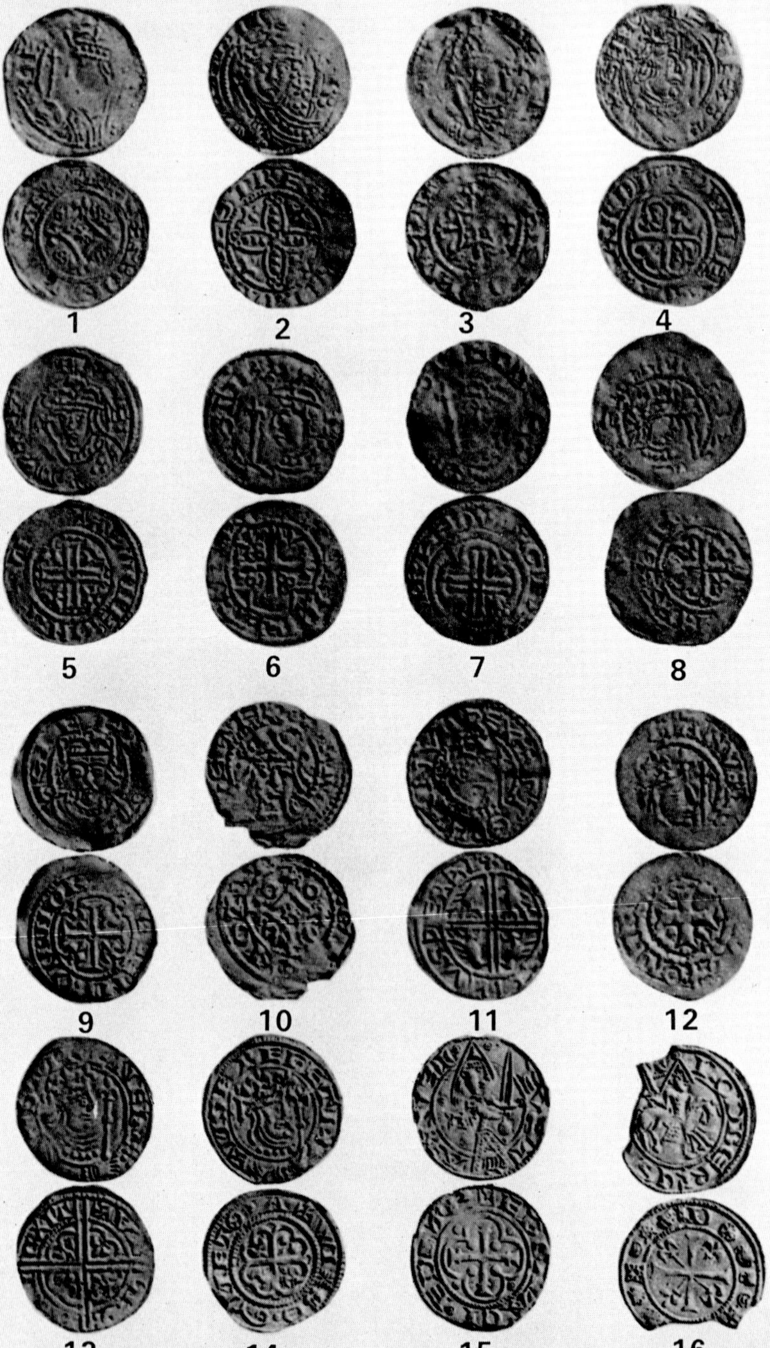
1
2
3
4
5
6
7
8
9
10
11
12
13
14
15
16

Sihtric, whose dates are unknown. Four types of Penny, all very rare appear under 'Raienalt', struck about 910, and conclude this section.

The Hiberno-Norse Kings of York series follows, consisting of the coins issued under Sihtric I, Anlaf Guthfrithsson, Anlaf Quaran-Sihtricsson and the remaining rulers given in the list. All their coins are very rare. The section concludes with the coinage of St. Peter of York (Circa 905–925), again all scarce or rare pieces.

WESSEX

The final coinage of the Anglo-Saxon kingdoms is that of Wessex, which, like Mercia is a large section. The Kings of Wessex were as follows:

Plate 10

1 Henry I, 1100–1135. Star in lozenge fleury type, this example struck at Northampton. Note the trefoils in the angles of the lozenge. **2** Pellets in quatrefoil type, from the Chester mint. An attempt at a bigger and more massive portrait. **3** Quadrilateral on cross type, struck at Bury. Again a large portrait, filling most of the obverse. **4** Stephen, 1135–1154. Watford type, so called from the place where found though this example was actually struck at Cardiff. A rugged portrait here, the reverse with a cross moline with a fleur in each angle. **5** The cross voided and mullets type, this specimen struck at Pevensy. Several cross voided types have been illustrated, this one has mullets in the angles: a star with a hole in the centre. **6** Profile, cross and piles type. This example struck at Castle Rising. In this design the piles are topped by three annulets: previously only a dot formed the apex. **7** The Awbridge type, so called from the find-spot. The reverse has a voided cross in a beaded quatrefoil. **8** This Penny of Stephen, found at Watford, is attributed to Queen Matilda and was struck at Ipswich. **9** The cross and fleurs type, this example struck at Norwich. The fleur-de-lis in the angles of the cross pattée are clearly seen. **10** The lozenge fleury and annulets type, this example possibly struck in Nottingham. Though not very well struck the fleurs at the points of the lozenge and the annulets are reasonably clear. The reading of the legend on a coin struck as is this needs considerable knowledge and experience: hence 'possibly Nottingham'. **11** Classified as the Midlands Group and struck at Derby. Note the birds in the angles of the voided cross. **12** Penny of the Eastern Group, struck at Lincoln. A thick cross fourchée on the reverse. **13** Struck on the Scottish border, possibly at Bamborough. Long cross voided on the reverse with fleurs in the angles. **14** The York Group, struck in that city. Note how the portrait is continued below the inner ring of beads to accommodate the arm and hand holding the sceptre. **15** Penny of the Baronial issues: this of Eustace Fitzjohn, struck at York and classified as the armed figure type. **16** Baronial issues, this of Robert de Stutville, struck at York. An early attempt to show an armed figure on horseback. As will be seen later the 'monarch-on-horseback' design was to be standard for a long period and was revived as lately as 1953.

Beorhtric, 786–802
Ecgberht, 802–839
Æthelwulf, 839–858
Æthelbald, 855–860, (for whom no coins are known)
Æthelberht, 858–865/6
Æthelred I, 865/6–871
Ælfred, 871–899
Edward the Elder, 899–924/5

The last two names here are familiar to all, Alfred the Great and his son Edward the Elder. Between them these two great Kings of Wessex did so much towards the unification of England into a kingdom, that after this period we shall be dealing with the coinages of the Kings of All England.

The two types of Penny issued by Beorhtric are extremely rare pieces. The coinages of Ecgberht are equally rare but more varied. They fall into various groups. From the Canterbury mint came the Pennies of Group I, struck about 826, Group II, struck about 825–830, and Group III, struck about 830–839. Group IV, struck about 835–839 come probably from the Rochester mint, London, the Rochester episcopal mint and the Winchester mint. No Halfpennies are known.

The coinage of Æthelwulf, again all Pennies, falls into three phases. Phase I, from about 839–843 contains portrait types, probably from the Rochester mint and non-portrait types probably from the Canterbury mint. A single type in this phase came from Winchester. Phase 2, from about 843–848 again contains portrait types, probably from the Canterbury mint and non-portrait types from Canterbury and Rochester. A further section of types with 'later' portraits may also come from Canterbury. The Pennies of Phase 3, struck from about 848/51–855 contain no portraits, and come from Canterbury, while the final Phase 4, struck about 855–859 are of the portrait type and almost all come from the Canterbury mint.

The five portraits of Æthelwulf (By courtesy of J. J. North)

Over the four phases five portraits appear, illustrated here by drawings taken from North. Most of the issues are rare or very rare.

The single type Penny attributed to 'Eanred' (whose name does not appear in the list of Kings) is a doubtful attribution, and represents one of the unsolved numismatic problems.

It was stated above that there are no known coins of Æthelbald, and North points out that those attributed to him in the British Museum Catalogue are nineteenth-century forgeries.

Two main types of Penny are known for Æthelberht, the first being only catalogued as scarce. Here again a large number of moneyers promise a fairly prolific coinage. There is also a third Penny tentatively attributed to this reign, known by a single rather badly struck specimen.

Two main types of Penny are known for Æthelred I, the first type is only catalogued as rare, some twenty-seven moneyers being employed in its production.

This brings us to Ælfred, in whose reign both Pennies and Halfpennies were struck. His coinage is somewhat complicated and is divided into First Coinage, about 871–875, Second Coinage, about 857–880, Third Coinage, about 880–885, and Fourth Coinage, about 887–899. These coinages are further subdivided into types, and except for the Pennies of the Fourth Coinage are mostly very rare pieces. The three types of Halfpenny are all very rare. Mints were in operation in various parts, including London, Canterbury, Exeter, Gloucester and Winchester. Coins from the Lincoln mint are classified as Danish imitations.

Finally the coins of Edward the Elder, all Pennies save for one very rare Halfpenny. The first type of Penny, which contains the title EADWEARD REX, with no portrait, a small cross pattée appearing in the centre of the flan is one which a collector may well acquire. Catalogued as scarce, there is the almost record number of some 115 moneyers' names known on the various pieces. Apart from London, mints were in operation in Bath, Canterbury and other places not so far traced. Brooke also gives a rare Penny from Winchester, but this has now been attributed to north-western mints.

KINGS OF ALL ENGLAND

No more than a very rapid review can be given of the coinages, mainly Pennies but with a few extremely rare Halfpennies here and there, of the first twelve Kings of All England. The period covered is some 140 years during which there are many types, groups and styles, large numbers of mints and moneyers and numerous problems.

First of all the Kings:

Æthelstan, 924–939
Eadmund, 939–946
Eadred, 946–955
Eadwig, 955–959
Eadgar, 959–975
Edward the Martyr, 975–978
Æthelred II, 978–1016
Cnut, 1016–1035
Harold I, joint King, 1035–1037, sole King, 1037–1040
Harthacnut, joint King, 1035–1037, sole King, 1040–1042
Edward the Confessor, 1042–1066
Harold II, 1066, January to October

The simplest way of indicating the large number of mints from which the coins of these last Anglo-Saxon Kings came is by the reproduction of North's map.

As will be seen the mints were eighty-seven in number, and the peak period when coins from eighty-four of them are known was from the reign of Æthelred II to Harold II (978–1066). At some of these mints, such as Berkeley or Crewkerne only one moneyer was at work, perhaps for only one reign, while in the larger mints, such as Lincoln and York, large numbers of moneyers struck coins during the various reigns. Over the period of eighty-eight years few moneyers seem to have worked for more than three reigns, though some did work during four. Nor did the moneyers necessarily work for consecutive Kings. At Lincoln, for example, the moneyer Wulfric struck coins during the reigns of Æthelred II, Cnut, Harold I, missed out Harthacnut, but worked again for Edward the Confessor. This could partly be explained by the fact that Harthacnut's coins are all very rare, though they come from some forty-nine of the probable seventy-seven mints in operation during the Cnut–Harold I–Harthacnut period, 1016–1042. It must also be remembered that Wulfric was a fairly common Anglo-Saxon name, so two different moneyers may have been involved.

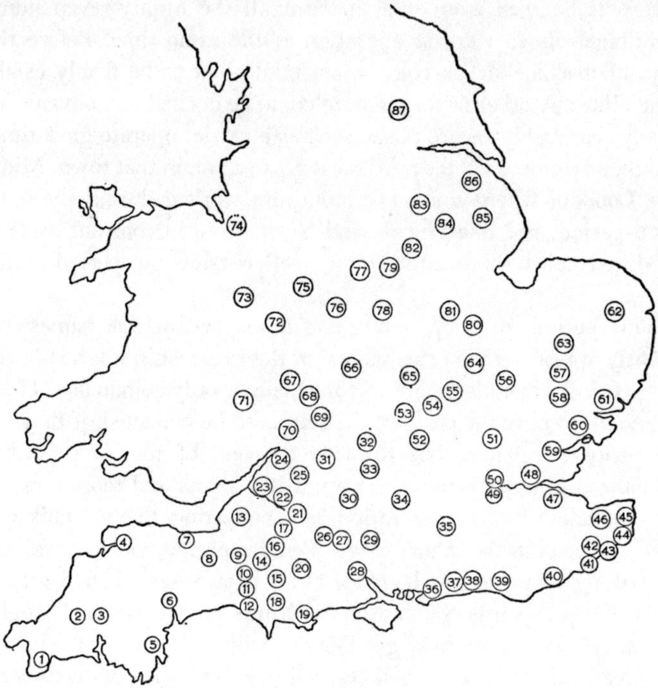

The Anglo-Saxon Mints, 973–1066 (By courtesy of J. J. North)

1 Castle Gotha
2 Launceston
3 Lydford
4 Barnstaple
5 Totnes
6 Exeter
7 Watchet
8 Taunton
9 Langport
10 Petherton
11 Crewkerne
12 Bridport
13 Axbridge
14 Ilchester
15 Milborne Port
16 Cadbury
17 Bruton
18 Dorchester
19 Wareham
20 Shaftesbury
21 Warminster
22 Bath
23 Bristol
24 Berkeley
25 Malmesbury
26 Wilton
27 Salisbury
28 Southampton
29 Winchester
30 Bedwyn
31 Cricklade
32 Oxford
33 Wallingford
34 Reading
35 Guildford
36 Chichester
37 Cissbury
38 Steyning
39 Lewes
40 Hastings
41 Romney
42 Lympne
43 Hythe
44 Dover
45 Sandwich
46 Canterbury
47 Rochester
48 Horndon
49 Southwark
50 London
51 Hertford
52 Aylesbury
53 Buckingham
54 Newport Pagnell
55 Bedford
56 Cambridge
57 Bury St. Edmunds
58 Sudbury
59 Maldon
60 Colchester
61 Ipswich
62 Norwich
63 Thetford
64 Huntingdon
65 Northampton
66 Warwick
67 Worcester
68 Pershore
69 Winchcombe
70 Gloucester
71 Hereford
72 Bridgnorth
73 Shrewsbury
74 Chester
75 Stafford
76 Tamworth
77 Derby
78 Leicester
79 Nottingham
80 Peterborough
81 Stamford
82 Newark
83 Torksey
84 Lincoln
85 Horncastle
86 Caistor
87 York

It will be seen from this that not all the eighty-seven mints mentioned above were in operation at the same time. Before the days of machine-struck coins when mints had to be firmly established like any other factory, a mint could be opened for convenience in any reasonably secure place, such as a castle, operate for a time, and then be closed till the need for it arose again in that town. Mints like London, where some 142 moneyers worked during the 978–1066 period, and like Lincoln and York, were in constant use and produced coins reign after reign, well outside the period stated above.

This period, of many mints and moneyers, whose names frequently appear on the coins, is one of the greatest in interest in the long period when the Penny was the main or only coin in use. There are now not only the coins of the reigns to be collected, if they are reasonably available, but towards the end of the Anglo-Saxon period as coinage becomes more prolific, mints and moneyers can also be taken into consideration as a collecting theme. This will reach its peak in the 'Short Cross' Pennies period, yet to come, but something of a start can be made at about this period. At last, and particularly towards the end of the Kings of All England Anglo-Saxon period, we begin to get Pennies with as low a rarity classification as Rare, Scarce or even Normal (neither scarce nor common). North publishes a number of most valuable tables at this point, giving the mints and moneyers of the more prolific coinage outputs in chart form. According to the reign and the varieties of Pennies issued these charts give such information as the reigns in which coins were being struck at which mint and by whom, the varieties which were being struck for each reign and at what mints and by what moneyers, and so forth, thus analysing a very complex period of Penny production and smoothing the path of the collector.

To go into any detail, even as brief as that which we have given so far, on the Pennies and Halfpennies of the Anglo-Saxon Kings of All England, would run this section into inordinate length. For example, during the period Æthelstan to Eadgar (924–975) 'coins of the succeeding Kings until the reform of Eadgar can be allocated to regions by their style of lettering and other criteria, in cases where they bear no mint signature. The differences of lettering are more noticeable on the "Two line" type although they also exist on the "Circumscription" type' (North). This is obviously a study in itself, with research still to be carried out and is not the sort of point on which to generalize in a book of this nature. It indicates the type of study and interest that goes into the collecting of these early Pennies, a series, as will be appreciated, in which collecting themes are numerous. The 'Two line' type is, of course, the type of coin having its legend in two lines, while with the 'Circumscription' type the legend runs round the coin in what most people consider a normal manner.

Very basically the Pennies form two main types, with and without portrait, though the subdivisions and varieties are almost endless. On this point Brooke says, 'Perhaps we should not be wrong in regarding the coinage from the reign of Edward the Elder to that of Æthelred II as undergoing experimental development in two directions, towards the introduction of the King's portrait as an essential part of the coin-type, and towards the establishment of a suitable variety of designs by means of which the King was able, at some date prior to the Norman Conquest, to enforce the payment of moneyers' fees; the payment was made obligatory on delivery of dies at such times as the type was changed. Each of the kings from Edward the Elder to Edgar struck a portrait coinage and a plain coinage, but in every reign the portrait coinage was considerably smaller than the other and, as we have seen, the composition of hoards suggests, or even demands, the conclusion that the two were issued at the same time. The kings seem at this period to be endeavouring to establish their effigy on the coin but at the same time to be not quite sure enough of their ground to abandon the traditional plain type; it is only at the end of Edgar's reign that the effigy wins the day, and from that time the coinage was never without it save in very exceptional issues . . .' To some extent part of these remarks can be applied retrospectively, as portrait and plain types among the Pennies had been struck since the coin's inception.

It must be remembered that the period of Kings of All England covers that of the long period of Danish raids which took place during the reign of Æthelred II from 980. There were raids on Hampshire, Thanet and Cheshire, to the final conquest of England by the Danes, culminating in the acceptance of Cnut as King. During this period vast sums were poured out in attempts to buy off the Danes, and it is at this period that the passing of English coins to Scandinavia, their being copied there, and copies getting back to England, referred to under the Viking Invaders, reaches its peak. During the 980–1016 period before Cnut became King on the death of Æthelred II and his son Eadmund Ironside, something like 149,000 pounds in gold and silver and tribute money were paid. As all know, it did not succeed in stopping the invasion, and when the Dane, Cnut, became King of England he treated it as a conquered province for some twelve months. Even then money still continued to flow out of the country, since Cnut dismissed his own (Danish) fleet with a payment of 10,500 pounds which he extracted from the citizens of London, and levied a danegeld of 72,000 pounds on the rest of England, thus bringing the total to the vast sum, in any age, of 231,500 pounds. Small wonder that so many mints were busy as Anglo-Saxon, now Danish conquered England, neared its end at the hands of a further conqueror, William I.

Plate 11

1 Penny of Henry of Blois, Bishop of Winchester. A further Baronial type struck during the reign of Stephen. **2** The Angavin party. Penny of the Empress Matilda, struck at Oxford. Note the slightly smaller flan. **3** The Angavin party. Penny of Henry of Anjou, struck at Hereford. **4** Classified among the uncertain baronial issues, this Penny was struck by Patrick, Earl of Salisbury at Salisbury. The last few illustrations underline the interest of the coins struck during civil war conditions. It brings to an end the issues of the troubled reign of Stephen, the last of the Norman kings. **The Plantagenet Kings. 5** Henry II, 1154–1189. The cross and crosslet type, this example struck at Newcastle. Note the little crosses, the crosslets, in the angles of the cross pattée. **6** Some examples of the prolific Short Cross coinage. Penny of Henry II struck at Wilton. Note the 'short cross' on the reverse, confined within the inner circle. **7** Richard I, 1189–1199. Short cross Penny, struck in London; reading HENRICVS. **8** John, 1199–1216. Short cross Penny struck in Norwich; still reading as for Henry II. **9** Henry III, 1216–1272. Short cross, struck in London. **10** Short cross. A Penny of John, struck at Rochester, and illustrated here to show how the design was built up from various irons, as explained in the text. On this clearly struck coin the 'bits and pieces' (the irons) which were used at this period to build up the design can be very simply broken down into their various parts. **11** Penny of the prolific Long Cross type: this of Henry III, struck in Gloucester. Note how the voided cross now reaches to the edge of the flan. **12** A further Long Cross example, struck at Bristol. **13** One more example, struck at Newcastle. **14** Edward I, 1272–1307. Struck at Bury. From 6 to 14 note how the 'building' of portraits (in particular) has resulted in many different aspects for the same king.

This concludes the series of illustrations tracing the history of the Penny so far. Something has been shown of the various classes into which the Penny has been put, reign by reign, by numismatists and the numerous terms which they use to describe the various parts of the design.

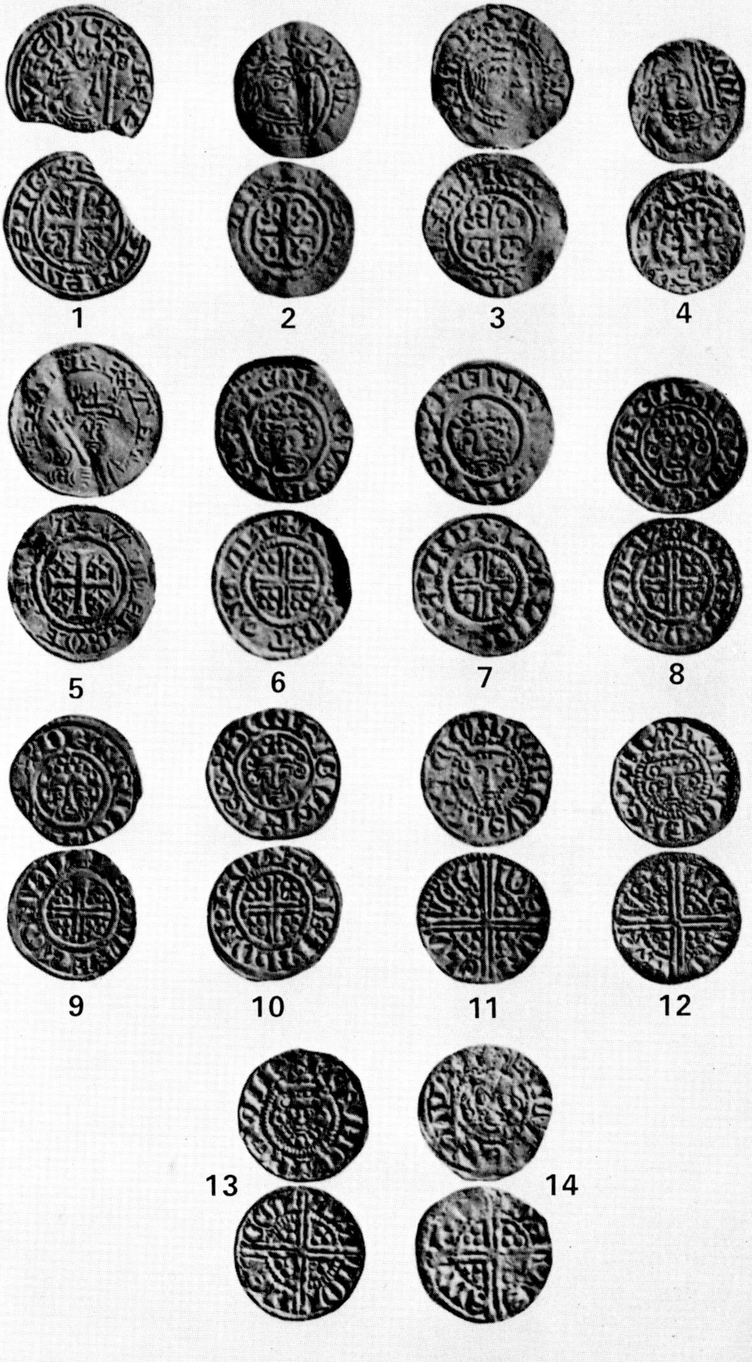
1
2
3
4
5
6
7
8
9
10
11
12
13
14

1

2

3

4

5

6

7

8

A few words on the lineage of the last Kings of this period may be of interest. Cnut had intended that England and Denmark should pass to his only legitimate son, Harthacnut, who was already ruling in Denmark. Threatened with invasion of that kingdom, and after much argument, a compromise was reached under which Wessex was given to Emma, Queen of Cnut and widow of the previous King, Æthelred II, to hold for Harthacnut while Harold, illegitimate son of Cnut and Ælfgifu of Northampton, became Regent of the rest of England. Harold died in March, 1040 and Harthacnut, invited to England, landed in June. Two years later to the month, Harthacnut died, age twenty-five. Edward, later called the Confessor, son of Æthelred II, who had been adopted by Harthacnut as a member of his household in 1041, was elected King by popular acclamation at London and crowned at Winchester in 1043.

Edward the Confessor died in January, 1066, and his brother-in-law was consecrated as Harold II. He reigned till the fateful 14th October, 1066 when his and England's future was decided at the battle of Senlac, frequently called the Battle of Hastings. After this battle the movements of William of Normandy soon made him master of the south-eastern counties; he was offered and accepted the kingdom at Berkhamsted, and was crowned William I at Westminster on Christmas Day, 1066.

THE NORMAN KINGS

This was a turning point in English history though not such a turning point in numismatic history as that of, say, 1662, when hammered coins were abandoned for ever and the 'new milled money' took their place. William I found the Penny long established in use and in production at many mints. This system he took over and North's map shows the seventy-six mints in operation during the period William I (1066) till Henry III (died 1272).

Plate 12 *The Later Hammered Coinage*
1 Edward I, 1272–1307. The first silver groat, struck in London, LONDONIA CIVI being the inner legend on the reverse. **2** Edward III, 1327–1377. The first gold Noble, value 6s. 8d., struck between 1344 and 1346. **3** The gold Quarter Noble of Edward III, of the Treaty period, 1361–1369. **4** Silver Half Groat (or Twopence), struck at Calais during the same period. **5** Silver Farthing (or quarter of a Penny), struck in London during the post-Treaty period, 1369–1377. **6** Richard II, 1377–1399. Gold Noble struck at Calais. **7** Gold Quarter Noble, of the same king. **8** Silver Penny of the same king, struck at York.

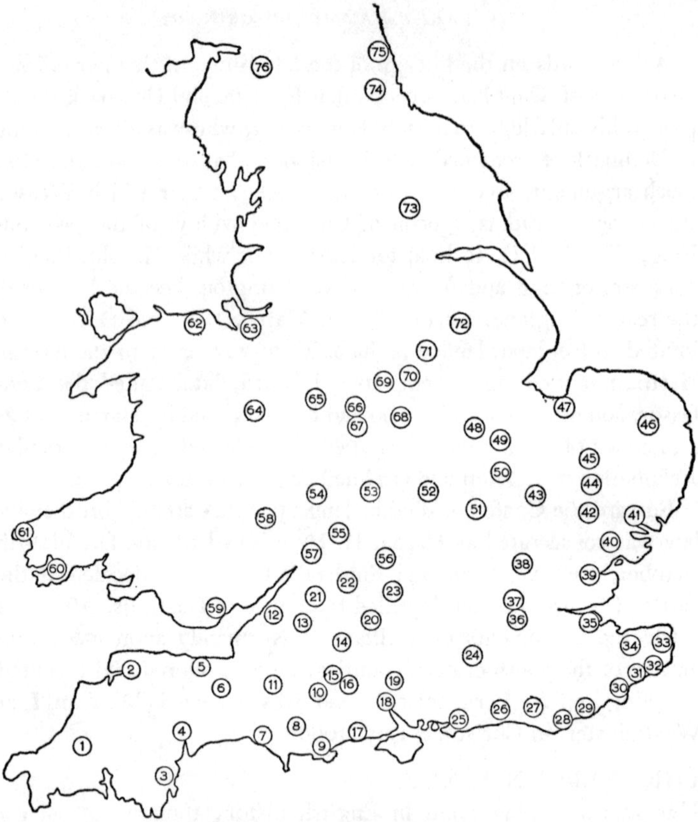

Map of the mints from William I to Henry III, excluding Stephen (By courtesy of J. J. North)

1 Launceston
2 Barnstaple
3 Totnes
4 Exeter
5 Watchet
6 Taunton
7 Bridport
8 Dorchester
9 Wareham
10 Shaftesbury
11 Ilchester
12 Bristol
13 Bath
14 Marlborough
15 Wilton
16 Salisbury
17 Christchurch
18 Southampton
19 Winchester
20 Bedwyn
21 Malmesbury
22 Cricklade
23 Wallingford
24 Guildford
25 Chichester
26 Steyning
27 Lewes
28 Pevensey
29 Hastings
30 Romney
31 Hythe
32 Dover
33 Sandwich
34 Canterbury
35 Rochester
36 Southwark
37 London
38 Hertford
39 Maldon
40 Colchester
41 Ipswich
42 Sudbury
43 Cambridge
44 Bury
45 Thetford
46 Norwich
47 Lynn
48 Stamford
49 Peterborough
50 Huntingdon
51 Bedford
52 Northampton
53 Warwick
54 Worcester
55 Winchcombe
56 Oxford
57 Gloucester
58 Hereford
59 Cardiff
60 Pembroke
61 St. Davids
62 Rhuddlan
63 Chester
64 Shrewsbury
65 Stafford
66 Lichfield
67 Tamworth
68 Leicester
69 Derby
70 Nottingham
71 Newark
72 Lincoln
73 York
74 Durham
75 Newcastle
76 Carlisle

This brings us to the consideration of the coinage, Pennies once more, of the Norman Kings of England who were:

William I, 1066–1087
William II, 1087–1100
Henry I, 1100–1135
Stephen, 1135–1154

The coinage of William I is summed up by North; 'When William of Normandy captured England, he found a currency of high standard, which compared favourably with the base feudal coinages of the French provinces. He continued, therefore, to strike pence of the same weight and fineness as his predecessors, and the profile of his first issue is very similar in style to that of Harold II. The most noticeable difference is that the majority of portraits on his coins are facing, whereas with the coins of Edward the Confessor the converse was the case. The variation, obtained by the addition of one or two sceptres, two stars, a sword, or a portico, to the obverse field, makes an interesting series of busts. The reverses show a number of geometrical designs usually with the cross as the central motif. On the last issue the popular word "PAXS" reappears as reverse type. The workmanship is good but tends to become coarser in the later issues. All types are scarce to rare, except the last, which is comparatively common, thanks to the Beaworth find (1833) which contained 6,439 specimens of this type.'

Of the system of money minting as a whole, Brooke says, 'Occasional references in Domesday, notices in the Pipe Rolls of the twelfth and thirteenth centuries, the *Dialogus de Scaccario* (*temp.* Henry II), together with information gleaned from the coins themselves, give us a fair picture of the system that obtained in the mints before and after the Conquest.

'The qualification for the possession of a mint was borough status, and to every mint (*moneta*) was attached an exchange (*cambium*); the function of the exchange was to purchase bullion for the mint and to issue coin from the mint to the public. As it was the only source through which the moneyer could circulate his coins, the exchange in the person of the warden (*custos cambii*) was a watch-dog set by the King over the moneyer; he checked the weight and standard of the coins and satisfied himself that they bore the true imprint. The mint had one or more moneyers, who were men of substance, (one in the reign of Henry III was the King's tailor, another the King's surgeon, another the King's goldsmith), personally responsible to the King, living rent-free and having the limited jurisdiction of *sac* and *soc*, and liable to a penalty of death or mutilation if convicted of forgery. The emoluments of the moneyer were obtained at the time of the Conquest neither by salary nor by commission (mintage); he made what profit he could after paying the necessary labour, buying dies from the graver, and paying at London, on receipt of his dies, the King's dues (usually 20s) when the type of the money was changed. Thus we learn from Domesday the explanation of the regular and frequent change of coin-types as a means of collecting the King's share of the profits, which was later taken in the form of seignorage.' Thus 'the system'. Let us take a glance at the sort of coins it produced.

The Pennies of William I fall into eight types, (i) Profile, rev., cross fleury, issued from 1066 till 1068, (ii) Bonnet, issued from 1068 till 1071 and based on the type of headgear shown as worn by the King in his facing portrait, (iii) is the Canopy type, issued from 1071 till 1074 and so designated on account of the pointed canopy, supported by two uprights which can be seen behind the facing bust of the King. Type (iv) is known as the Two Sceptres variety and was issued from 1074 till 1077, and refers to the fact that two sceptres are placed one on either side of the facing bust of William. Type (v) is designated the Two Stars, and refers to the appearance

Plate 13
1 Henry IV, 1399–1413. Gold Noble of the light coinage, struck in London. **2** Silver Groat, also struck in London. **3** Silver Penny from the York mint. **4** Henry V, 1413–1422. Gold half Noble. A particularly well-struck specimen of a very rare coin. Note the clarity of the mass of small detail. **5** Henry VI, 1422–1461 and 1470–1471. Silver Groat of the early Rosette-Mascle coinage, struck in London, the mint name appearing very clearly in the inner ring on the reverse. **6** Richard III, 1483–1485. Gold Angel. Note the initial mark to right of the angel's head, a sun and rose dimidiate (i.e. half of each joined together). Note also the R to left of the mast of the ship, the mast itself shown as a cross, and the shield of arms 'nailed to the mast'. **7** Silver Groat, struck at York, the inner legend on the reverse reading CIVITAS EBORACI. Note how the obverse design, in particular, is off-centre, also the initial mark, rose and sun dimidiate. **8** Henry VII, 1485–1509. Gold Sovereign of type IV, the first time this name, still in use, was given to a denomination in the English series. Note the regal conception of the king enthroned, with crown, sceptre and orb, the portcullis of the Tudors at his feet. Note also the shield of arms on the reverse, superimposed on a Tudor rose.

1

2

3

4

5

6

7

8

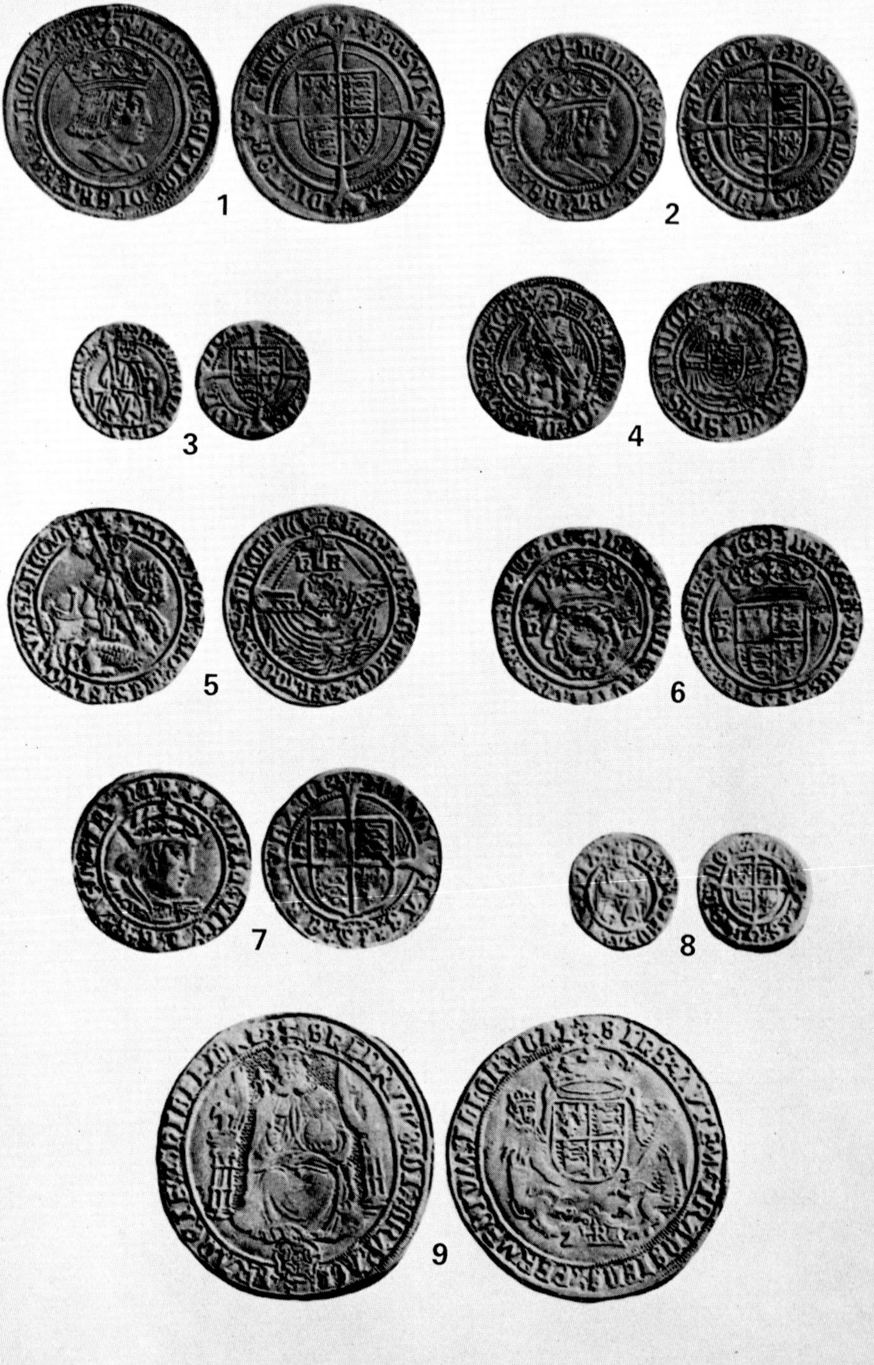
1
2
3
4
5
6
7
8
9

of a star on either side of the facing bust. It was issued between 1077 and 1080. Type (vi) is the Sword type. Here the facing bust of William I is enlarged to cut through the inner circle which has so far surrounded it to give the effect of a head-and-shoulders portrait. In his right hand the King holds a sword, apparently resting it slightly on his shoulder. The type was struck from 1080 till 1083. The next type, (vii) is the Profile, rev., Cross and Trefoils variety, and was struck from 1083 till 1086. Here we get one of the rare profile portraits of William I, which again breaks through the inner circle. A remarkably well defined left hand holds a sceptre with a fleur-de-lis by way of finial. The reverse has a cross pattée with an annulet in the centre, giving the appearance of a hole drilled through the cross at the junction, and in each angle is a voided trefoil, that is a trefoil or three-leaved sprig whose leaves are drawn in such a way as to appear to have an indentation, possibly the main stem of the leaf, in the centre. Final type (viii) is the Paxs, referring to the word PAXS, whose letters are placed in the angles of a cross pattée, each letter being contained within an annulet or circle. On the obverse of this type the King may be wearing any of three distinct types of crown as once more his head-and-shoulders bust breaks through the inner circle and faces us from his coin.

The reader now knows the significance of these periodic changes of type, and here sees them clearly and simply in operation.

The Pennies of William II carry on the system. They fall into

Plate 14

1 Henry VII, 1485–1509. Silver Testoon or Shilling, the first appearance of this denomination, and of a definite portrait rather than a representative face. **2** Silver Groat of the same type. **3** Silver Penny of the Sovereign type, struck in London. Compare with figure 8 on Plate 13. **4** Henry VIII, 1509–1547. Gold half Angel of the first coinage, 1509–1526. Note the portcullis initial mark on both sides, and the H by the mast. **5** Gold 'George' Noble of the second coinage, 1526–1544. Note the H K on either side of the mast. The 'angel' slaying the dragon has now become St. George. On the precedent that the monarch's name appears on the obverse of a coin, the ship side is the obverse of this piece. There are, however, a few deviations from this precedent, not necessarily among English coins. **6** Gold Crown of the same period, with H.A., crowned, on both sides. **7** Silver Groat, issued by Cardinal Wolsey at York. Note the Cardinal's hat below the shield on the reverse. **8** Silver Penny of the second type, struck in London. Note the 'Sovereign' type obverse. **9** Gold Sovereign of the third coinage, 1544–1547. Henry is shown as a much old man. The coin was struck in Southwark; note the initial mark S on both sides.

five types, the first being known as the Profile, the type being struck from 1087 till 1090. The second is the Cross in Quatrefoil type, struck from 1090 till 1093. This refers to the layout of the reverse, a cross pattée in a quatrefoil. The obverse has a facing bust which, in an example of the type struck at Salisbury makes William II look very like his father. Type (iii) is the cross voided variety, struck between 1093 and 1096. This refers to the reverse once again, a voided cross being an 'open' cross, a saltire with annulets at the ends occupies the X position. The obverse has a facing bust. Type (iv) is the Cross Pattée and Fleury type and was struck between 1096 and 1099. This type description refers again to the reverse, there being a fleur in the angles of the cross. Finally type (v) is the Cross Fleury and piles variety, struck between 1099 and 1100. The piles are formed of two curved lines united by a dot at the top but open at the bottom, not unlike the old type of wooden clothes peg. All types are rare, the last two being very rare.

Much the same pattern is followed by the Pennies of Henry I, but the dates of issues are not so closely known. The types are (i) Annulets, there being annulets by the side of the neck of the facing bust, (ii) Profile obverse with a Cross Fleury on the reverse, (iii) Pax type, the word appearing across the field on the reverse, (iv) Annulets and Piles, the reverse being composed of four annulets between four piles, the piles being set head to centre almost forming a type of cross, (v) Voided Cross and Fleurs, the reverse type, (vi) Pointing bust and Stars, the obverse, with the King pointing with his right hand, and with three stars in the field, (vii) Quatrefoil and Stars, (viii) Larger Profile on the obverse and Cross and Annulets on the reverse. Type (ix) is the Cross in Quatrefoil, reverse type, (x) the Full Face, obverse; Cross Fleury reverse, (xi) the Double Inscription type, the reverse having a double inscription between three beaded circles and type (xii) has a Smaller Profile obverse type and Cross and Annulets as the reverse design. It should be noted that type (xi) precedes type (x), giving a series with alternating and facing busts.

The types continue with (xiii) the Star in Lozenge Fleury reverse. This is a rather complicated design with, in the inner circle a square with slightly curved sides, its points terminating in fleurs and with a star in the centre, Trefoils composed of annulets are placed outside the square opposite each side. The last two types are (xiv) Pellets in Quatrefoil reverse type and (xv) Quadrilateral on Cross Fleury reverse. There is also a Halfpenny struck in this reign. Most of these pieces are rare to extremely rare coins except for types xiv and xv.

So far all has gone smoothly with the coins of the first Norman Kings, but with Stephen came anarchy, and with anarchy a complicated coinage. Perhaps a few words on the political situation might not be out of place, and may simplify the understanding of the coinage.

Stephen was born about 1094, the third son of Stephen, Count of Blois, and Adela, daughter of William the Conqueror. He was brought up at the court of his uncle Henry I, from whom he received in marriage Matilda or Maud of Boulogne, who was the niece of the Queen. He took the oath of fealty to his cousin, the Empress Maud, but as soon as Henry I died, Stephen caused himself to be proclaimed King. The dislike of Maud's husband, Geoffrey of Anjou, contributed in great measure to Stephen's success, and at first he was met with no opposition. But his misgovernment and his conduct towards the Church and the officials of the administration rapidly alienated his friends, and in 1138 the Empress invaded England in company with her half-brother Robert of Gloucester, an illegitimate son of Henry I, who held the strong fortress of Bristol, and whose power extended over both sides of the lower banks of the Severn. From 1138 to 1145 was a period of complete anarchy, sometimes one, sometimes the other party gaining the upper hand. Every lord of a castle acted as King in his own domain. The fearful effects of feudal government were for the first and last time fully exemplified in England. In 1145 Robert of Gloucester died and the Empress retired to Normandy, leaving Stephen master of England. But in 1152 her son Henry landed in England, and the war was renewed. In 1153 a treaty was made at Wallingford by which Stephen was to retain the crown during his lifetime, when it was to pass to Henry. In the next year Stephen died at Dover Priory on 25th October. (*Dictionary of English History*).

Thus the background. Because the coinage as a whole is not only complicated but practically all the pieces are very rare we will not spend too much time on it.

The substantive types were in some part established by finds of

Pennies at Watford, Awbridge, Linton and South Kyme, as well as other places. Matters were complicated by one result of the civil war by the failure to change the first type at the usual intervals; 'the system' failed to function.

As Brooke points out, 'The chief interest lies in the abnormal issues. The chronicles record an issue in 1149 by Henry of Anjou which came to be known as the Duke's money, and also the striking of coins by barons in their castles. This seems to imply a baronial coinage in the French feudal manner rather than a mere forgery of the current coin, and coins that survive show that the statement may be accepted in that sense. It does not rule out the possibility of irregular coinages bearing the King's name, which may account for the many coins of coarse and blundered work and for some that develop peculiar varieties of the normal types. They may, on the other hand, be the work of regular moneyers estranged from the unifying control of London.'

Not all the Pennies of this period are rough and badly struck. Later in his account Brooke points out, 'The York mint, isolated in the disordered state of the country during the civil war, rose to the occasion in designing attractive types and cutting dies of excellent draughtsmanship. Its coinage is not confined to issues bearing the King's name. There are coins struck in the name of Eustace, one of which, a fragment only, describes him as *Filius Iohannis* and thus

Plate 15

1 Henry VIII, 1509–1547. Silver Testoon of the third coinage, 1544–1547, struck in Southwark with the initial mark S. An example of the debased coinage, of such poor silver that the base metal showed through as the coin became worn. **2** Edward VI, 1547–1553. Gold Sovereign of the first coinage, still bearing the name of HENRIC 8. **3** Silver Groat, struck at Durham House, London. Durham House, one of the many palaces that once lined the Thames, stood just south of the Strand. The site is now in the Adelphi area where Durham House Street still remains. The coin is still in the name of Henry VIII, whose bust also appears. **4** Silver Groat of the first period of the second coinage of Edward VI, 1547–1549. The boy-king now has his own portrait and titles. **5** Gold Sovereign of the second period of the second coinage, 1549–1550. The young king is shown seated on an elaborately decorated throne with standing figures of angels on each arm. The reverse is of a similar design to that of the king's father, Henry VIII, but with E R clearly seen below the arms. **6** Gold Sovereign of the third period of the second coinage, 1550–1553. The king is now shown in full-length royal robes and is seated on an even more elaborate throne with a portcullis at his feet. Note the initial mark, the head of an ostrich, which dates the piece as struck in 1551.

1

2

3

4

5

6

1

2

3

4

5

6

identifies him with Eustace Fitzjohn who, after Henry's death, favoured the cause of the Empress and joined David at the Battle of the Standard.'

As will be seen, it is not difficult to become confused over the matter of names. We have already had two Matildas or Mauds; Matilda or Maud of Boulogne, niece of the Queen of Henry I and wife of Stephen, and the Empress Matilda or Maud, wife of Geoffrey of Anjou. We now have two Eustaces, Eustace Fitzjohn and Eustace, son of Stephen and his intended heir, who died before his father, in 1153. Thus, the finding of a coin bearing the name Eustace at this period offers a problem, but as Brooke points out, Eustace the King's son, was scarcely more than ten years of age when these coins were struck. In this period we also get coins assigned to Queen Matilda, and coins assigned to the Empress Matilda. All this is only mentioned to give some slight illustrations of the type of problem numismatists take delight in solving, and of showing how dangerous it is to jump to conclusions in numismatic research.

Perhaps the simplest way of giving some idea of the range of this very complex coinage consisting of pieces many of which the average collector will never see outside a museum, is to list the various sections given in North with the names of those who struck the coins under these sections, and to publish North's map of mints. All the coins are Pennies, and an explanatory comment will be given as necessary.

(1) The Substantive types. Finds made at Watford, Awbridge

Plate 16
1 Edward VI, 1547–1553. Gold Angel of the third period of the second coinage, 1550–1553. The initial mark, the head of an ostrich, again dates the piece as struck in 1551. **2** Base metal Penny, struck in London. **3** The first silver Crown in the English coinage, struck in 1551. The initial mark Y shows that it was struck at the Southwark mint. Though the gold Crown was to continue to be struck for about another 110 years, its silver equivalent was established in the above year, and has come down to us in an almost unbroken line to the cupro-nickel 'Churchill' Crown of 1965. **4** Mary, 1553–1554. Gold Sovereign, struck in 1553, with the date in Roman figures at the end of the obverse legend. The initial mark, a pomegranate, appears after the Queen's name, and is surrounded by four annulets. **5** Silver Groat of Mary, a fine portrait piece. **6** Philip and Mary, 1554–1558. Silver Shilling with facing busts. On only one other occasion, during the reign of William and Mary, 1689–1694 have two busts appeared on the obverse of English coins.

and elsewhere. Four main varieties, Watford, Cross voided and Mullets, Profile obverse Cross and Piles reverse, Awbridge type, struck about 1150–1158.

(2) Irregular Coins. North points out in respect of this series that 'during the anarchy many of the irregular coins were based on Type I of the regular coinage in which there are also a number of variations.'

I. Varieties of the First Type. Some nine in number some from uncertain mints, and from Canterbury, Oxford and possibly Exeter. Issues of Queen Matilda, circa 1417? Some five in number, from Ipswich, Sudbury and Bury St. Edmunds.

II. Local Variants. Of three main types, (i) Cross and Fleurs, (ii) Lozenge Fleury and Annulets, (iii) Lozenge and Fleurs. (i) from mints at Launceston (possibly), Northampton and Norwich, (ii) from, possibly Hereford or Huntingdon, Lincoln, Norwich and possibly Nottingham. (iii) from Leicester, a Midland Group from mints at Derby, Nottingham or Tutbury, Newark possible: an Eastern Group from mints at Lincoln and Thetford, possibly from Canterbury and Dudley.

III. Scottish Border issues, where the mints changed hands from time to time during the period. Struck by Stephen, two main varieties, one certainly the other possibly from Bamborough. Struck by David of Scotland (1124–1153), three main varieties, from one uncertain mint and from Roxburgh and Carlisle. Struck by Henry, Earl of Northumberland (1136–1152), three main varieties from Corbridge, Carlisle and Bamborough. Struck by the Bishop of Carlisle in the name of David, one type, from Carlisle. Struck by the Bishop of Durham in the name of Stephen, one type. One type from an uncertain mint.

IV. York issues. Five main varieties.

V. Struck from erased dies, i.e. defaced by the punching of a large or small cross into the die. Five main varieties, from mints at Bristol, Norwich, Thetford, Nottingham, Stamford and possibly Canterbury and York.

VI. Coins reading PERERIC. Of these Pennies North says, 'Equally uncertain is the meaning of the legend "PERERIC", which appears in the place of the King's name on certain coins of the first type. It is generally accepted that a meaningless legend

The mints of Stephen and the anarchy (By courtesy of J. J. North)

was deliberately used to strike an anonymous coinage. Evidence is in favour of these pence having been minted in 1135, before Stephen's claim to the throne had been accepted. However, they may date from 1141, during the King's captivity, when such a legend could have been used to conceal allegiance to either party. From Bristol, Canterbury, Lincoln, London, Stamford and Winchester.

VII. Baronial Issues. Struck by Eustace Fitzjohn at York, three main varieties. Struck by Robert de Stutville, two main varieties.

Struck by Henry of Blois, Bishop of Winchester, (brother of Stephen), one type.

VIII. The Angevin Party. Struck by the Empress Matilda. Two main varieties, from Bristol, Oxford, Wareham and possibly London. Struck by Henry of Anjou. Seven main varieties with three well-established sub-varieties from Hereford, Devizes, Gloucester, Malmsbury, London, Bristol, Sherborne and Ilchester or Wivelscombe.

IX. Uncertain Baronial Issues. Struck by Robert of Gloucester? one type. By William (of Gloucester? or de Mohun?). One type from Cirencester? Dorchester, Wareham and Wivelscombe? By Brian Fitzcount or Baldwin de Redvers, one type. By Patrick, Earl of Salisbury, one type. By Ranulf, Earl of Chester? one type. Finally a coin from a bishop, name unknown and two varieties that have so far defied all solution, but which have been assigned to Earl Reginald of Cornwall (Truro mint) but are probably East Anglian (? Thetford mint).

Thus something of the complex and rare coinages of the last of the Norman Kings. Here our Penny, still the only coin in general use, saw much service and many changes in the hands of many issuers. We can pass now to the Pennies of the Plantagenet Kings. Here there will be plenty of material for the collector, for we have before us the prolific issues known as the Long Cross and Short Cross coinages.

THE PLANTAGENET KINGS

Henry II, 1154–1189
Richard I, 1189–1199
John, 1199–1216
Henry III, 1216–1272

The coinage of the first three Plantagenets can be taken together, for reasons which will appear in a moment. One or two points need setting out first.

If any coins were issued before 1158 they were from the dies of Stephen. This over-run of the use of dies from one reign to the next is quite normal, and continues down to the present time. In 1158 a monetary reform took place. Obviously, after the chaos of the last reign something drastic had to be done. The reform was of such importance that contemporary records state that the new money was made the sole currency of the kingdom, the first time that this phrase is used. As Brooke points out, it 'means something more than the exclusion of foreign coin; it denotes the use of a single type of English money, and terminates the period in which types were changed at frequent intervals and the currency was therefore not of uniform design. The reform necessitated some new method of collecting the King's profits, which were previously paid when the type was changed; it probably modified to some extent the control under which the moneyer worked . . .' 'The system' commented on above was now altered.

The first coinage of Henry II is known as the Cross and Crosslets, or Tealby, type, and it was struck from 1158, the point of reform, till 1180. The designation Cross crosslets describes the normal reverse design, a cross pattée within the inner circle with a small cross pattée in each of the angles. The name Tealby became attached to the type by reason of a find of some 5,700 of these pieces at Tealby in Lincolnshire in 1807. It was a great misfortune to numismatists that 5,127 of these Pennies were melted down at the Tower Mint, so that the coins are now scarce. They were carelessly made, probably under pressure to produce an adequate number of the 'reformed' coins reasonably quickly. North considers them 'probably the ugliest in the whole of our coinage. A well-struck Penny with complete legend is of considerable rarity, and the few that exist are all from a northern mint.' In fact these Pennies were struck at thirty-two mints. This gives some idea of the numismatic destruction that can be caused by the ill-advised treatment of finds and hoards. The valuable evidence of some thirty-one mints was thoughtlessly cast into the melting pot.

The obverses of the Tealby coins are interesting. They show a facing bust, head and shoulders, of Henry II, crowned and robed, and holding a sceptre in his right hand. Six main differences of bust exist, while slight variations, often only to the drapery, make a total of nineteen varieties. They are illustrated here, as drawn by North. The various main types of bust represent different periods of issue, as though some vestiges of 'the system' still remained. Thus, of the six bust types under which the Tealby Pennies are catalogued, A was used from about 1158–1161, B from about

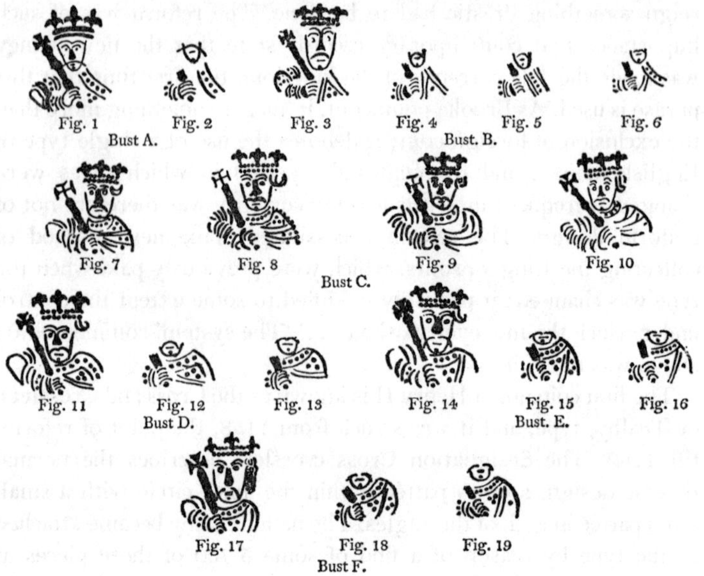

The six main differences of bust, Henry II (By courtesy of J. J. North)

1161–1166, C from 1161–1165, D from 1165–1168, E from 1168–1170 and F from 1170–1180.

In 1180 the Short-Cross coinage began to appear. It was designed by Philip Aimer, who was brought over from Tours for the purpose. Though this foreign goldsmith had been introduced because of the inefficiency of the English moneyers, 'the new design', says Brooke, 'does him little credit, an ill-modelled portrait is backed by a type which can only be recommended as being suitable for division into halves and quarters for small change.' Aimer was later dismissed under suspicion of fraud.

It is at this point that the Pennies of Henry II, Richard I and John, and the Short-Cross Pennies of Henry III come to be taken together. All the English pieces of these three Kings have the title HENRICVS REX, abbreviated in various ways. Considerable research, based upon the numerous varieties of the forms of lettering used succeeded into dividing this rather prolific coinage into eight classes. With two exceptions which occur in Class 8, none of the Short-Cross Pennies are classified as more than rare; scarce, normal or common being the rule.

Once divided into eight classes, further research and careful thought began to postulate acceptable dates during which the eight classes were struck. These are now usually accepted as follows. Class 1 was struck from about 1180–1189. All the pieces that can be fitted into this class therefore qualify as coins of Henry II. Class 2 has been dated from about 1189 to 1196 and Class 3 from about 1196 to about 1199, thus making such pieces the coinage of Richard I. Class 4 is dated from about 1199–1205 and Class 5 from about 1205–1218. These two classes are therefore the coinage of John. Class 6 is dated from about 1218–1223, Class 7 from 1223–1242 and Class 8 from about 1242–1247. This would bring all three classes into the Short-Cross coinage period of Henry III. There is a slight difference of opinion here in that two eminent authorities on the series, consider that Class 6 should be dated from about 1210–1218 and that Class 7 begins at 1218. As will be seen, this would lop off a little of the coinage usually ascribed to John.

Given a miscellaneous selection of Short-Cross Pennies a little study of the lettering types given in North, possibly reinforced by careful study of the descriptions given in Brooke and the selection can be broken down into its various classes (and a number of sub-classes which also exist), so that the collector has the satisfaction of dividing up his Short-Cross Pennies so far as humanly possible under the correct King when placing them in his cabinet.

There is far more interest and instruction in breaking down a lot of Short-Cross Pennies into their correct classes and reigns than might appear on the surface. A group of people engaged on such an exercise found that they had a most interesting afternoon at a Study Group held some years ago in Cambridge.

There is also another interest that attaches to the Short-Cross Pennies. From their design it is very easy to see how the letters and the various parts of the bust and of the whole device are made up from a series of punches. At the risk of loosing track of our main subject it is worth while saying a little about this here, since it affects not only the making of the dies of the Short-Cross Pennies but of many other coins as well.

At this period and for some time on either side of it, dies were not directly engraved. A series of punches, known as 'the irons' consisted in fact of small chisels, their points being in the form of parts of a curve, wedge-shaped units, dots, dashes, and so forth. Take as an example the fine specimen of a Penny of John, Class 5b, struck at Rochester mint. The effigy was probably constructed as follows. Three dots joined by minute lines, set like a pawnbroker's sign upside down formed the cross on a crown, itself composed of five dots. The curls of hair at the sides of the face are part circles with dots in them. The heavy eyebrows and nose were probably punched in from one 'iron' while the eyes are annulets, or pierced dots. The beard is made of straight lines, the chin of a dot and the mouth from two slightly curved 'irons'. The sceptre and hand could be all one 'iron' or could be built up from several. A further curved 'iron' made to join up with the inner circle from a sort of collar for the King. The lettering is similarly built up, piece by piece, sometimes a whole letter, sometimes a letter made from two or more 'irons'.

When all this had been punched into a piece of steel of requisite size and shape, an incuse master punch had been built up. This master punch could now be used as a die, since if struck on a flan of silver its incuse design would appear in relief on the silver flan, rather like turning a jelly out of a decorated mould. Careful study of a large number of Short-Cross Pennies could build up a catalogue of 'irons', a kind of die-maker's alphabet.

The Short-Cross Pennies were struck at some twenty mints, London and Canterbury employing by far the most moneyers. Here is yet another point of collector's interest in the humble series of poorly designed coins. The name of the mint and the name of the moneyer, both usually abbreviated, form the reverse legend. Here then is another possible collecting theme, moneyers and mints. North supplies his usual excellent table of mints in operation showing the coins of the various eight classes which came from such mints. Brooke, no less helpful, gives a list of the mints, with the

Plate 17

1 Elizabeth I, 1558–1603. Gold Sovereign, value 30/–, struck in fine gold, of the third issue, 1583–1603, with initial mark a scallop shell. The restoration of the coinage, debased by her father, Henry VIII, was finally accomplished during Elizabeth's reign. **2** Gold Pound Sovereign, with initial mark key. Note the detail of the portrait. **3** An unusual denomination in the English coinage, a silver Threefarthings, struck in 1561. Initial mark, pheon (arrow head) and date in Arabic figures above the shield on the reverse. **4** Silver Halfcrown with initial mark I=1601, though the same denomination was struck till 1603. **5** Gold Half Pound, struck by the mill and screw press, an early example of English mill coinage, the method of semi-mechanical production of coins in its experimental period.

1

2

3

4

5

1

2

3

4

5

6

names of the moneyers and the classes which each moneyer struck. Perhaps not so flexible as North's charts, but quite serviceable. It is sometimes said that the simplest things give the most pleasure. At the risk of over-emphasizing the Short-Cross Penny, it is at least simple, full of points of interest, and readily available in reasonable quantity at reasonable prices to the collector. To reach this point in numismatic history we have struggled through a lot of issues which, though of great interest were, more frequently than otherwise, so rare as to be beyond the reach of the majority of collectors. Thus, collectors who may come to regard the Penny as a collecting theme may give a sigh of relief when they see that the Short-Cross Penny is a type which has not only many facets of interest but is readily available.

So far as the coinage of the period is concerned, however, all was not well. 'So prevalent had clipping become towards the close of the Short-Cross issue', says Brooke, 'that in 1247 the treasurer was ordered to pay in the best money he had. The subject was considered by a Council at Oxford in 1247, but the Council's curious recommendation, that the standard, and not the form, of the coin should be changed, was set aside, and pennies of a new type were issued, which retained the weight of 22·5 grs. (grains) and silver 11 oz. 2 dwt. fine. Its type was determined by the desire to put an end to the abuse of clipping; the cross on the reverse was extended to the edges of the coin and pennies were declared illegal on which the four ends of the cross were not visible. For the first time the numeral was added to the King's title, *Henricus Rex Tercius*, later *Henricus Rex III*. The whole of the coinage at the royal mints for England, Ireland, and Wales was leased to the King's brother, the Earl of Cornwall, on the basis of an equal share in the profits.' Thus was born the Long-Cross Coinage of Henry III.

Apart from the length of the cross on the reverse these Pennies

Plate 18
1 Elizabeth I, 1558–1603. A pattern for a silver Shilling with initial mark key. **2** James I, 1603–1625. Gold half Sovereign of the first coinage, 1603–1604, with the first bust of the king and initial mark thistle. **3** Silver half Groat of the same coinage period. **4** Gold Rose-royal of the second coinage, 1604–1619. Initial mark a scallop shell. Throne with elaborately carved back and supports, the Tudor portcullis still at the Stuart king's feet. **5** Silver Shilling of the second coinage with the fourth type of bust. **6** Gold Laurel of the third coinage, 1619–1625, with James trying to look like a Roman emperor.

are very similar to the previous series. They were issued from 1247 till 1278 and have been classified into seven sections. Group I was issued from 1247–1248, Group II in 1248, Group III, with sub-groups *a* to *c* from 1248–1250, Group IV from 1250–1251, Group V, with sub-groups *a* to *g* are dated by Brooke by the sub-groups, *a*, *b*, 1251–1253, *c*, *d*, *e*, *f*, 1253–1258/60, sub-group *g*, 1258/60–1272, all dates being approximate. The two remaining groups, VI and VII, were struck after the accession of Edward I (1272–1307) between about 1272 and 1278, another instance of the over-run use of dies. Twenty mints were producing the coins, but after the main re-coinage rush was over these were reduced in about 1250 to four, London, Canterbury, Bury St. Edmunds and Durham.

Since, with the exception of Groups VI and VII the Long-Cross Pennies were all struck in the reign of Henry III there is not the interest of sorting them into different reigns. The mints and the moneyers remain, however, and with the help of Brooke or North a selection of these pieces can soon be classified. North's system is probably the most simple. The mints are listed and the classes struck at each mint is then given. For example, Bristol struck coins in groups 2–3a, 3b and 3c. Thus its entry reads BRISTOL (2–3c). This is followed by the names of the moneyers and the groups which they struck; thus for Bristol, Elis struck coins in groups 3a, 3b and 3c, so his entry reads Elis (3abc). With this mint table and a selection of Long-Cross Pennies, which again, apart from certain varieties, are not rare, the work of classification is simple and straightforward.

At this point it has been decided to leave the story of the Penny as a collecting theme. As will be seen, it continues to appear as a silver piece down to the present time. As a theme it is rapidly expanding. In time to come it will be available as a copper and then bronze, as well as a silver piece. The latter first continued on as a normal everyday coin and then became classified as part of the set of Maundy money, a circumstance which has kept it alive till now. With the coming decimal coinage a New Penny will be struck. This is as it should be. As was stated at the beginning of this section, a coin which has appeared continually for almost 1200 years should not lightly be cast aside. That it may look different and have a different relationship to the other coins in the range from that which it held in times past is of little moment. It has seen changes in size, weight, alloy, metal and design but it has survived them all. It should therefore pass on once again into our new coinage and help to serve us in whatever bleak or golden years may lie ahead.

Though we shall continue to tell its story, at this point we must leave it as our sole theme. English coinage is about to expand under Edward I (1272–1307), with new denominations added to the range. In seventy-one years gold will also appear in regular coinage, and the stage is set for general coinage expansion. We pass into the period of what might possibly be called the later hammered coinage, which will carry us from 1272 to 1662, three hundred years of great numismatic and collecting interest.

CHAPTER FOUR

The Later Hammered Coinage

It will not be possible to treat every and all denominations of the later hammered coinage of England in the detail which has been lavished on the Penny, otherwise a work of inordinate size would result. With the general expansion of the coinage now about to start many collecting themes will appear. So far as possible detail will be given, detail which may spark off collecting themes as well as telling something of this great period of our numismatic history, a period packed with interest and opportunity for the collector. We take up the story, therefore, with Edward I.

Edward I (1272–1307)
Son of Henry III

Though small expansion in the coinage has taken place, the series is not complicated with many coinage periods.

DENOMINATIONS

Silver: Groat, Penny, Halfpenny, Farthing.

From 1272–1278 the Penny, bearing the name of Henry III, and of the Long-Cross type, is still the sole denomination. The first type, Group VI in the Long-Cross classification system is a very rare piece while the second, Group VII is only scarce. A large number of the provincial mints had closed, and though Canterbury was still working these Pennies came only from London, Bury St. Edmunds and Durham.

In 1279 a new coinage was ordered. It resulted in the Groat, equal to four pence, the Penny, much as before but very slightly lighter in weight, a round Halfpenny and a similar Farthing, which

Plate 19

1 James I, 1603–1625. Silver Crown of the third coinage, 1619–1625, with initial mark lis and plumes over the shield on the reverse. **2** Copper Farthing of the same coinage period with initial mark stirrup on the obverse. **3** Charles I, 1625–1649. Gold Unite, value 20/–, the value figure appearing behind the head of the king. Struck at the Tower mint, London, with initial mark lis = 1625. **4** Silver Crown, with the same initial mark. **5** Silver Shilling, with initial mark tun (a barrel), used in the years 1636–1638.

1

2

3

4

5

1 2 3

4 5

6

appeared towards the end of the year 1280. These two coins brought to an end the Saxon and Norman practice of cutting Pennies into halves and quarters in order to obtain the small values.

The first Groat was a fine coin. It had the crowned facing bust of the King framed in a quatrefoil of well defined arches surrounded by the legend, EDWARDUS DI GRA REX ANGLE; Edward by the grace of God king of England. A small flower was placed in the spandrils of the quatrefoil and one on each side of the King's head. The reverse had a long cross, which it was ordained should reach to the edge of the coin, for the same reason as the long cross on the Pennies. In each angle were three pellets. The legend was placed in two circles, one within the other, and reads DNS HIBNE DUX AQUT——LONDINIA CIVI; thus continuing the King's titles as King of Ireland and Duke of Aquitaine. The second circle contained the name of the mint. The piece is described in this detail since broadly similar designs were to be used for a long period.

The piece became very rare, partly for a reason that is with us still: it was extensively used as an ornament. Pieces are found with solder marks and gilding on them, so the fashion of 'wearing' coins is not so new.

The Pennies of Edward I and II (1307–1327) are now normally taken together.* Since the King's name reads ED, EDW, EDWA

* But see page 82.

Plate 20
1 Charles I, 1625–1649. Gold Unite of the mill issue, struck by Nicholas Briot and having his initial mark, a flower and B on the obverse. **2** Silver Half-crown of the milled issue. The terms 'mill' and 'milled' are both used to describe mechanically produced coins. This piece also by Briot with initial mark anchor and B. Note the clarity of design and the neat workmanship of these two pieces. **3** Silver Halfcrown struck at York mint, with initial mark lion and EBOR below the horse. The shield is apparently being supported by a lion, whose claws appear to right and left and at the base. **4** Silver Shilling, struck at the Aberystwyth mint with Bushel's initial mark, an open book with ribband ties. **5** Silver Halfcrown struck either at Coombe Martin or Aberystwyth mint, the attribution being doubtful. **6** Silver Pound piece, struck at the Shrewsbury mint in 1642. Note the value, XX shillings, above an abbreviated form of the king's Declaration on the reverse. This and the previous piece show much evidence of hasty striking and the cracks and rough marks on the latter are common at this period. When a coin of this type is described as E.F., these facts have to be borne in mind. It is understood that the coin is E.F. for its type and period.

or EDWAR on the whole series it is not a simple matter to be sure to which of the two Edwards any one coin may be correctly assigned. Brooke was of the opinion that the Pennies reading EDWA or EDWAR could be assigned to Edward II. North tends to take the whole issue together, dividing it into fifteen classes. Pending the publication of his recent handbook* on the coinages of the first two Edwards it is simplest to follow Brooke's classification. The coins come from thirteen mints in the reign of Edward I and from five in the next reign.

As was seen in the story of the early Penny it had long been the custom for the Archbishops and Bishops of certain ancient towns, such as Canterbury, Durham and York, to receive privilege dies from which they were allowed to strike coins similar to those from the royal mints. To quote North, 'The re-organization of the coinage' (in 1279) 'brought about a change in the responsibility for the purity etc. of the coins, and the name of the moneyer, which had so long formed a part of the reverse inscription, disappears. There is one exception—that of Robertus de Hadeleie, who struck pence at the Abbot of St. Edmund, Bury privilege mint.

'The number of mints functioning was reduced to four or five normally, except in 1280–1281 when ten were striking, and 1300–1302 when the number was eleven.

'On the occasion of the re-coinage the question of the ecclesiastical privilege dies was examined. There were a most lucrative source of revenue to certain Bishoprics and abbeys, the main ones being those of the Archbishops of York and Canterbury, the Bishop of Durham and the Abbot of St. Edmund, Bury. Coins struck from privilege dies are usually distinguished by a special mark, such as the quatrefoil in the centre of the reverse of York pence, and the personal mark or crozier head used by the Bishops of Durham. The latter marks played a major part in the classification and dating of Edward I and II coins. Ecclesiastical marks appear on coins until the reign of Henry VIII, when Cardinal Wolsey exceeded his powers by placing them upon groats.'

Thus of the thirteen mints from which came the Pennies of Edward I, there were those at both Durham and York, while from Bury St. Edmunds came two of the classes of Penny (with five subclasses) on which the name of ROBERTUS DE HADELEIE

* Now published.

appears as moneyer and seven classes which read VILLA SCIED MUNDI.

As with the Short-Cross Pennies, the forms of lettering used have to be taken into account when classifying. So also do the initial crosses, usually placed at the start of the legend in the twelve o'clock position, the drapery at the King's throat and the various types of crown. There are also three distinct types of abbreviation marks, a wedge, a crescent and a comma. Finally the fleurs at the extremities of the King's crown, usually known as the side fleurs, are of two quite distinct types, all this having a bearing on the classification.

Given a selection of the Pennies of these two reigns one cannot divide them into classes without reference to the details given in North. So many minor varieties within the main classes exist that to republish them here would be simply to steal the work of others. The break between the Pennies of the two reigns comes with Class XI or late Class X and from then on till the final Class XV the coins are those of Edward II. With only one exception, coins in Class I, variety (b), none of the Pennies of the first two Edwards is rated higher than scarce, normal or common pieces being in the majority. The collector who is possibly following the Penny theme has here a further series in which he can indulge without great expense.

The Halfpence and Farthings of Edward I are similar to the pence and fall into seven and eight varieties respectively. They are mostly catalogued as scarce. Those of Edward II are of one main type only, the Halfpence being rare. North points out that they exist in several varieties. Both denominations are difficult to obtain in really fine condition.

Edward II (1307–1327)
Fourth son of Edward I

DENOMINATIONS

Silver: Penny, Halfpenny and Farthing.

During the periods 1296–1318 and 1333–1377, (Edward I, II and III), Pennies, Halfpennies and Farthings were issued from a mint at Berwick-on-Tweed. Like their ancient border town, which is referred to as a separate territory in certain Acts: as 'this Act covering England, Scotland and Berwick-on-Tweed': these coins do not fit into the same classes as those already dealt with. The Pennies are therefore catalogued in eight classes of their own. They are normal or scarce, save for those of Class VII and VIIIa, which are rare or very rare respectively. Once again the Halfpence and Farthings are the same type as the pence, and are scarce to very rare.

Edward III (1327–1377)
Son of Edward II

The coinage of Edward III is somewhat more complex than that of the two previous reigns, and falls into four groups.

DENOMINATIONS

First Coinage, 1327–1335
Silver: Penny, Halfpenny, Farthing.
Second Coinage, 1335–1343
Silver: Halfpenny, Farthing.
Third Coinage, 1343–1351
Gold: Florin, Half-florin, Quarter-florin, Noble, Half-noble, Quarter-noble.
Silver: Penny, Halfpenny, Farthing.
Fourth Coinage, pre-treaty period, 1351–1361
Gold: Noble, Half-noble, Quarter-noble.
Silver: Groat, Half-groat, Penny, Halfpenny, Farthing.
Fourth Coinage, treaty period, 1361–1369
Gold: Noble, Half-noble, Quarter-noble.
Silver: Groat, Half-groat, Penny, Halfpenny, Farthing.

Plate 21
1 Charles I, 1625–1649. Gold Triple Unite or three pound piece, struck at Oxford. The value, III pounds appears above the Declaration and ox below the date. This example of the series is struck on a small flan when compared with other strikings. **2** Silver half Pound, also struck at Oxford. X shillings on reverse. The king is seen riding over fallen standards and arms. **3** Gold Unite struck at Bristol in 1645 with BR in monogram as the initial mark. The reverse legend and the abbreviated Declaration appear on a continuous flowing ribband. **4** Silver Halfcrown with A below the horse and the date. Possibly struck on Lundy Island but more probably at Appledore in north Devon. Examples of what is known as double striking are evident on this piece. More than one blow was given by the hammer and the coin jumped out of position. This is seen in the break in the obverse legend at CAR OLVS and on the reverse at the end of the declaration. **5** Silver Halfcrown of the Truro mint, struck in 1642. Known as the 'galloping horse' type, the king is shown charging, trampling on arms thrown down by the retreating enemy. A remarkably well-struck and detailed piece, bearing in mind the Civil War conditions. The lion is back again, holding up the shield, below which the date appears.

III
RELIG·PROT
LEG·ANG
LIBER·PAR
1644

1

X
RELIG·PROT·LEG
ANG·LIBER·PAR
1642

2

3

4

5

1
2
3
4
5
6

Fourth Coinage, post-treaty period, 1369–1377
Gold: Noble, Half-noble.
Silver: Groat, Half-groat, Penny, Farthing.

Basic obv. legend: EDWAR D GRA ANGL Z FRANC DNZ HIB

It will be seen from the above that there are quite a lot of interesting points to be dealt with here. The reign was a long one and full of interesting events.

Till about 1343 things went along in much the same way as in the two previous reigns. The Pennies of the first coinage are so similar to those of Edward I and II that they can be classified as Class XVd under the classifications of that reign. Indeed, the Pennies of all three reigns used to be taken as a single numismatic unit. Later thinking, however, is in favour of the Pennies of Edward III being separated and placed in their correct reign. All the three coins of the First Coinage are rare or very rare.

The Halfpennies and Farthings of the Second Coinage are of a somewhat different design and are rarity normal save for the Halfpennies issued at Reading, which are rare.

Considerable changes now began to take place. As a result of an economic crisis in 1344 a new coinage was ordered, the denominations being given above under the Third Coinage period. It will be

Plate 22
1 Charles I, 1625–1649. Silver Crown from the Exter mint, struck in 1645. Initial mark castle on the obverse and Ex on the reverse. Date in the reverse legend. **2** Gold Unite of the Weymouth mint. No initial mark. The hidden lion is back once more holding up the shield. **3** Silver Halfcrown of the Worcester mint, 1646, probably struck at Hartlebury Castle, the fortified stronghold of the Bishop of Worcester. Note the tiny letters H C below the shield on the reverse. Initial marks, a pear on the obverse and three pears on the reverse, the arms of Worcester. No documentary evidence has so far been found proving that the piece was struck at Hartlebury, the attribution resting entirely on the two small letters. **4** Silver Halfcrown struck at Chester, initial mark three gerbs (wheatsheaves) CHST below the horse. **5** Silver Shilling struck during the siege of Carlisle, 1645. **6** Silver Halfcrown struck during the siege of Newark, 1645, the value XXX pence on the obverse. A contemporary newspaper (?) account has been seen wherein it is pointed out that people complained that these sharp-edged pieces cut holes in their pockets. The king, 'on being interviewed' promised that such an unfortunate shape should not again be used. He had taken refuge with the Scots army near Newark in 1646. The abbreviation OBS: on the reverse stands for 'obsessum', besieged.

noted that the first gold coin to be struck for general circulation was called the Florin, a name familiar enough today as a coin of 2s. value. The gold Florin of Edward III, however, had a value of 6s. Two Florentine goldsmiths, Kirkyn and Nicholyn, were brought over, appointed joint masters of the Mint and ordered to strike the new gold coinage. They produced the three pieces listed which at once attracted the name Florin. Hence the origin of the present name later applied to a silver coin. There is little chance of the collector seeing these pieces outside the larger museum collections. The gold piece was proclaimed in January, 1344, but lasted only till August of that year, when it was supplanted by the Noble, value 6s. 8d., and its half and quarter, all very rare pieces. This piece began a long line of coins similarly named. The design, with the King standing in a ship, was probably suggested by the naval supremacy won at Sluys in 1340. Similar designs continued to be used till the time of James I (1603–1626).

The Pennies, Halfpennies and Farthings of the Third Coinage fall into many varieties, and are generally similar in appearance to those of the Second Coinage. With certain exceptions they are not rare. The Pennies were struck at London, Canterbury, Durham, Reading and York, the mint names being on the reverse. The collector will have to cope with some eighteen varieties.

A little history is needed here to explain the three divisions of the Fourth Coinage. Edward II, the weakest of the Plantagenets, was forced to abdicate, and was probably secretly murdered in Berkeley Castle on 21st September, 1327. At his abdication his eldest son, then fifteen, was appointed guardian of the kingdom in October, 1326 and crowned as Edward III early in the next year. His regnal year one commences on 25th January, 1327. During the 1330s he was engaged in wars against the Scots, Scotland having been declared independent during the previous reign. Meantime difficulties with France had arisen, centred round the disputes between Philip of Valois and the Flemings, the Interruption to the Anglo–Flemish trade, (mainly the export of wool to the Flemish manufacturing towns: hence the ancient port of Boston, Lincolnshire, and the Woolsack in the House of Lords), and the aggression of Philip of Aquitaine. Edward declared war in 1337 but hostilities did not commence till July, 1338, when he crossed to Flanders, engaged in an alliance with the popular leaders who were opposed to their

Count, and concluded a league with the Emperor Louis V, who appointed Edward Vicar-General of the Empire. In 1339 Edward advanced into France, the French retreating before him. In 1340 he won the naval battle over the French at Sluys, already referred to. A nine months truce followed, during which Edward returned to England, to effect an administrative revolution. He did not return to France till 1342, but nothing effectual was done till 1346, when he again landed, this time at La Hogue in Normandy, with the intention of joining the Flemings. Edward found the French King, with a large army, between himself and Flanders. By a feint upon Paris, Edward managed to cross the Seine, crossed the river Somme at Abbeville, and won the Battle of Crecy on 6th August, 1346. He then blockaded Calais and took it after a siege of twelve months.

These activities had exhausted the English resources to such an extent that a truce was concluded and war did not begin again till 1355. An attack upon Calais effected nothing. and Edward had to return to repel a Scottish raid. Meantime his son, Edward the Black Prince won the victory of Poictiers and captured the French kingdom 19th September, 1356.

A further truce followed till 1359 when Edward again invaded France and laid waste Champagne. On 8th May, 1360, peace was made at Bretigny, the English obtaining Gascony and Guienne, with the countries of Saintonge, Perigord, Limoges and Cahors, besides Calais, and a sum of three million marks as ransom for the French King. The treaty of Bretigny was, however, broken and the war continued in Britanny and in the south. The French gradually recovered much of the lost territory so that at the end of Edward's reign little remained of his conquests but Calais and Bordeaux.

Against this background the Fourth Coinage of Edward III is divided into the three periods shown. Most of the gold pieces are rare except the nobles of the post-treaty period, which are catalogued as scarce. The rarity of the silver coins varies considerably according to period and type.

The King's titles are of interest. Claiming the throne of France he added REX FRANCIE, variously abbreviated, to the legend on his coins. This was replaced by the title of Duke of Aquitaine during the currency of treaty of Bretigny, but the French title re-appeared after the treaty had been broken. It then continues to appear among our monarchs' titles till the time of George III (1760–1820) 250 years after we had lost our last French possession.

The marriage of Henry II to Eleanor, Duchess of Aquitaine 1152) produced a coinage allied to our own, about which nothing more than a reference can be given here. It is known as the Anglo–Gallic series and comes into prominence during the wars with France when it was issued by Edward III and the Black Prince, the series continuing on into the reigns of Richard II and Henry IV, V and VI. The gold series of this period was the subject of a recent book, 'Anglo–Gallic Gold Coins', by Beresford-Jones. Some magnificent and now rare pieces, with colourful names like Pavilion, Leopard and Guiennois were struck at such mints as Bordeaux, Limoges, La Rochelle, and Rouen. Silver and billon coins were also struck and the series as a whole is a most fascinating study.

Richard II (1377–1399)

Son of Edward the Black Prince

The coinage of this reign is fairly simple and without the complexities of many classes.

DENOMINATIONS

Gold: Noble, Half-noble, Quarter-noble.

Silver: Groat, Half-groat, Penny, Halfpenny, Farthing.

Basic obv. legend: RICARD DEI GRA REX ANGL Z FRANC DNS HIB Z AQT.

Thus the same denominations and types were struck as in the previous reign. On some of the Nobles and Half-nobles a mark, such as a lion, an escallop (shell) or a crescent appear on the rudder of the ship. This system of privy marks, used to distinguish the various issues, was continued and developed during the next two reigns, Henry IV and V. Initial marks, sometimes also used as mint marks, take their place in the reign of Edward IV (1461–1483) and these continued in use until the end of the reign of Charles I (1625–1649).

The Nobles and Half-nobles, which were struck at London and Calais mints, the latter's pieces having a flag at the stern of the ship, are classified into four main types on the basis of the lettering used on them. These four types of lettering are, firstly lettering similar to that on the coins of Edward III and so referred to; Type I, straight sided; Type II, with fishtails or bifurcations at the ends of the letters and Type III, a small, irregular lettering which is mixed in with other types.

Of the Nobles of London there are five main varieties with all four types of lettering, while of Calais there are four types, again with all four lettering styles. The same applies to the four types of Half-noble from each of the same two mints. Of the Quarter-noble there are three types. The French title is usually omitted, there being hardly enough room to crowd it on to so small a coin. All the gold pieces are from scarce to very rare.

In the silver range the Groats and Half-groats were struck in London only and are scarce to extremely rare. The six main types of Penny came from the London, Durham and York mints. Some coins struck from locally made dies at the latter mint, with legends often blundered, are common. The other varieties are from normal to very rare. The two types of Halfpenny, struck in London only, are common, while the Farthing, of three types, was struck only in London and is rare, the third type being extremely rare. Richard II was the last of the Plantagenet Kings, the throne now passing to the House of Lancaster.

Henry IV (1399–1413)
Son of John of Gaunt

Though the reign of Henry IV was short there were two coinages:

DENOMINATIONS

Heavy coinage
Gold: Noble, Half-noble, Quarter-noble.
Silver: Half-groat, Penny, Halfpenny, Farthing.

Light coinage.
Gold: Noble, Half-noble, Quarter-noble.
Silver: Groat, Half-groat, Penny, Halfpenny, Farthing.

Basic obv. legend: HENRIC DI GRA REX ANGL Z FRANC DNS HIB Z AQ

The two types of coinage, heavy and light, resulted from another economic crisis. We have no monopoly of such crises in our time, they occur again and again as we shall see. In almost every case they have an effect on the coinage. This particular crisis was caused partly by the export of English coin and the import of large quantities of base foreign currencies. During the first thirteen years of the reign only small quantities of either gold or silver coins were struck. As a result all the heavy coinage is rare.

To offset the financial crisis the weights of the coins were reduced. The Noble fell from 120 to 108 grains and the Penny from eighteen to fifteen grains. Though the output was large, specimens of the light coinage are rare. In the absence of the numeral IV after the King's name it is possible that some of the coins normally classified under Henry V, where the numeral is also missing, belong to his predecessor. This is one of the numismatic problems of the period.

The Heavy Coinage series was struck from 1399–1412. The two types of Nobles and Half- and Quarter-nobles (early and late styles) came from the mints of London and Calais. The Nobles and Halves from Calais have the usual flag at the stern of the ship. In the silver range the Half-groats were of one type only, struck in London. There were three types of Penny from London and two from York. The two types of Halfpenny and the single type of Farthing come from London alone.

The brief Light Coinage was struck from 1412–1413. The three gold denominations come from London only and are of one type each. In the silver range the two types of Groat and Half-groat were from London only. There were two types of Penny from London, one from York and one from Durham. The two types of Halfpenny and the single type of Farthing come from London alone.

Henry V (1413–1422)
Eldest son of Henry IV

A further short reign, with a compact coinage, but of many classes.

DENOMINATIONS

Gold: Noble, Half-noble, Quarter-noble.
Silver: Groat, Half-groat, Penny Halfpenny, Farthing.

Basic obv. legend: HENRIC DI GRA REX ANGL Z FRANC DNS HYB

The coinage was the same weight as the light series of the previous reign, and its dies were frequently used. To distinguish them a privy mark, mullet (star), a broken annulet (circle), or a trefoil were stamped in the field of the coin. These marks classify the coins into their various types or varieties. Three busts were used, the first usually being known as the 'emaciated' bust. The second can be identified by the sidelocks of hair added to the King's face, while the third bust is of altogether neater workmanship, probably engraved by Bartholomew Goldbeter, Master of the Mint in 1422. This issue has no privy marks in the field but the altered bust permits reasonably easy identification.

Once again the lettering plays a part in the classification of the types, there being three main classes. The differences, though marked, are not so clearly defined as was the case with the lettering of Richard II.

The coinage as a whole is divided into seven classes or varieties, A to G. Nobles exist of all seven classes, Half-nobles and Quarter-nobles in five. In the silver range Groats fall into four of the classes and Half-groats into five. Pennies exist in all seven classes and were struck at London, York and Durham. Not all the classes exist for each mint. The Halfpenny, struck only in London, falls into five classes, and the Farthing, of London only, is of only one type. The gold pieces are all scarce to extremely rare but with a few exceptions the silver coins are scarce, normal or common.

Henry VI (1422–1461 *and October*, 1470–*April*, 1471)
Son of Henry V

Though the simple list of denominations might lead one to think that the coinage was reasonably uncomplicated, in fact it falls into many classes. The second short reign of Henry VI raises a question and complicates the coinage. The Wars of the Roses are almost upon us, and we will deal with the historic side of the picture as concisely as we can.

DENOMINATIONS

Gold: Noble, Half-noble, Quarter-noble.
Silver: Groat, Half-groat, Penny, Halfpenny, Farthing.

Basic obv. legend: HENRIC DI GRA REX ANGL Z FRANC DNS HYB

A series of privy or distinguishing marks which appear on the coinage of Henry VI have facilitated its division into eleven classes. We illustrate them here, from the drawings published by North.

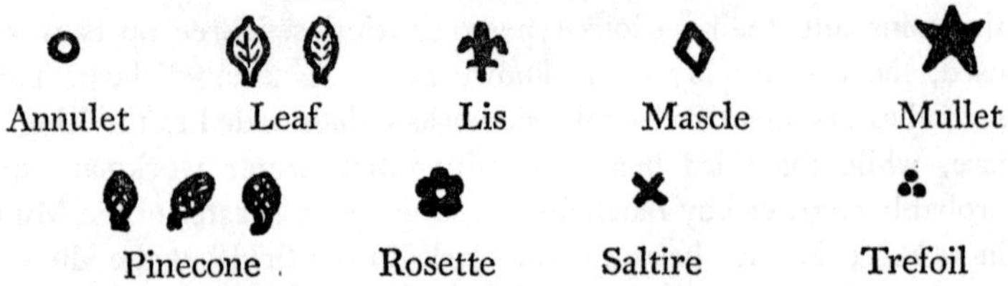

The privy or distinguishing marks on the coinage of Henry VI (By courtesy of J. J. North)

These distinguishing marks are found either in the field of the coin or in the guise of stops in the legend. The eleven classes into which the coins evolve upon study of these marks are as follows:

Annulet, 1422–1427
Rosette-Mascle, 1427–1430
Pinecone-Mascle, 1430–1434
Leaf-Mascle, 1434–1435
Leaf-Trefoil, 1435–1438
Trefoil, 1438–1443
Trefoil-Pellet (the Pellet is a 'dot'), 1443–1445
Leaf-Pellet, 1445–1454
Unmarked, 1445–1454
Cross-Pellet, 1454–1460
Lis-Pellet, 1454–1460

Under these classifications the following coins were issued.

ANNULET

Gold: Nobles from London, Calais, with the usual flag at the stern of the ship, and York, with a lis at the stern.
Half-noble from London, Calais (flag) and York (lis).
Quarter-noble from the same mints.
Rarity: rare to normal.

Plate 23
1 Charles I, 1625–1649. Silver Shilling struck at Pontefract while under siege. Note the cannon pointing out of the right hand tower of the castle. On some pieces a hand holding a sword appears in the same position. **2** Commonwealth and Cromwell, 1649–1660. Gold Unite of the Commonwealth. **3** Milled silver Crown of Cromwell dated 1658, the year of his death. The piece is usually considered to be a pattern. **4** Charles II, 1660–1685. Hammered gold Unite of the first issue, initial mark crown. **5** Hammered silver Sixpence of the third issue, same initial mark. Hammered coinage was struck during this reign from 1660 till 1662, after which this method of coin production in England ceased.

CR

1

THE COMMONWEALTH OF ENGLAND
GOD WITH US
XX

2

PAX QVAERITVR BELLO

3

FLOREBUNT CONCORDIA REGNA
C R

4

VI

5

1

2

3

4

5

6

7

8

9

10

Silver: Groat, from London, (two varieties) Calais, also two varieties or types, and York.
Half-groat, from London, Calais and York.
Penny, from London, Calais and York.
Halfpenny from London, Calais and York
Farthing, from London and Calais.
Rarity: extremely rare to common.

ROSETTE-MASCLE

Gold: Nobles from London and Calais (flag).
Half-noble from London and Calais (flag).
Quarter-noble from London and Calais.
Rarity: very rare.

Silver: Groat from London and Calais.
Half-groat from London and Calais.
Penny from London, Calais, York and Durham.
Halfpenny from London and Calais.
Farthing from London and Calais.
Rarity: rare to common, Farthing, very rare.

PINECONE-MASCLE

Gold: Nobles from London only.
Half-noble from London only.
Quarter-noble from London only.
Rarity: extremely or very rare.

Silver: Groat from London and Calais.
Half-groat from London and Calais.
Penny from London, Calais, York (two varieties) and Durham.
Halfpenny from London and Calais.
Farthing from London and Calais.
Rarity: rare to normal: Calais Farthing very rare.

Plate 24 Milled Coinage. phase one, 1662–1816. *Gold Five Guineas*
1–6 Charles II, 1660–1685. The five obverse types and the single reverse type. 1, 2 and 3 have the same head but 2 has an elephant and 3 an elephant and castle. The same applies to 4 and 5. **7–10** James II, 1685–1688. The busts are the same but one obverse has an elephant and castle below. The difference between the reverses is simply that the sceptres are placed in the wrong order, a small point only to be seen through a glass.

LEAF-MASCLE

Gold: Noble from London only.
Quarter-noble from London only.
Rarity: extremely rare.

Silver: Groat from London and Calais
Half-groat from London and Calais.
Penny from London and Calais.
Halfpenny from London and Calais.
Rarity: rare to normal.

LEAF-TREFOIL

Gold: Noble from London only.
Quarter-noble from London only.
Rarity: extremely rare.

Silver: Groat from London and Calais (two classes).
Half-groat from London only (two classes).
Penny from London and Durham
Halfpenny from London and Calais.
Farthing from London only.
Rarity: extremely rare to normal.

TREFOIL

Gold: Noble from London only.
Rarity: extremely rare.

Silver: Groat from London and Calais (three classes).
Halfpenny from London only.
Rarity: rare to normal.

TREFOIL-PELLET

Silver: Groat from London only.
Rarity: normal.

LEAF-PELLET

Gold: Noble from London only.
Rarity: extremely rare.

Silver: Groat from London only (four classes).
Half-groat from London only (two classes).
Penny from London, York and Durham.
Halfpenny from London only.
Farthing from London only.
Rarity: scarce to normal. Farthing very rare.

UNMARKED

Silver: Groat from London only.
Half-groat from London only.
Rarity: scarce.

CROSS-PELLETT

Silver: Groat from London only (three classes).
Half-groat from London only.
Penny from London, York and Durham
Halfpenny from London only (two classes).
Farthing from London only.
Rarity: rare to normal, Farthing very rare.

LIS-PELLET

Silver: Groat from London only.
Rarity: scarce.

A note of interest here is that the York royal mint comes into operation in 1423–1424. Not only does it produce Groats and Half-groats for the first time since the reign of Edward III but gold is struck there for the first time. The Nobles, halves and quarters will be noted under the annulet coinage.

The coinage of the second short reign of Henry VI, from October 1470 till April 1471 is a small one, the range being as follows:

DENOMINATIONS

Gold: Angel, Half-angel.
Silver: Groat, Half-groat, Penny, Halfpenny.

Basic obv. legend: HENRIC DI GRA REX ANGL Z FRANC.

These denominations and the types of the coins are similar to those of Edward IV and six initial marks, Cross pattée, Restoration cross, Short cross fitchée, that is with the bottom arm slightly pointed, Trefoil, with and without a stem, Rose and Lis are used at the start of the legend. The Angels and Half-angels come from London and Bristol, the latter, as with those of Edward IV having a letter B in the waves below the ship. In the silver range groats were struck in London, York, with E (Eboracum) on the King's breast, and Bristol with a B in the same position. Half-groats and Pennies were struck at London and York, the Half-groat having an E as before and the Penny a G and a key by the bust. For the latter mint the Halfpenny was struck at London and Bristol. The gold coins in this short series are from rare to extremely rare and the silver rare or scarce except for the extremely rare York Half-groat.

Thus the coinage of the last of the Lancastrian Kings. The House of York now takes over the English throne and something of this story will be told in a moment.

Edward IV
First reign 1461–1470, second reign 1471–1483
Son of Richard, Duke of York

DENOMINATIONS

First reign
Gold: Noble, Ryal, Half-ryal, Quarter-ryal, Angel.
Silver: Groat, Half-groat, Penny, Halfpenny, Farthing.

Basic obv. legend: EDWARD DI GRA REX ANGL Z FRANC DNS HIBERNIE.

DENOMINATIONS

Second reign.
Gold: Angel, Half-angel.
Silver: Groat, Half-groat, Penny, Halfpenny.

Basic obv. legend: EDWARD DI GRA REX ANGL Z FRANC.

Before starting on the coinage something of the historic scene must be set, thus explaining the two reigns and two coinages of Henry VI and Edward IV.

The dynastic civil war, usually known as the Wars of the Roses, had started with the Battle of St. Albans, 22nd May, 1455, six years before the end of the first reign of Henry VI. The basic cause of the war was the rival claims of the Houses of York and Lancaster to the throne of England: further detail need not concern us here,

Plate 25 Gold. Five Guineas
1–3 William and Mary, 1689–1694. Obverse plain and with elephant and castle. One reverse type only. **4–7** William III, 1694–1702. First bust without and with elephant and castle, second bust usually called the 'fine work' type on account of the greater clarity of detail. The reverse design resumes the four crowned shields of arms.

GVLIELMVS · ET · MARIA · DEI · GRATIA

1

GVLIELMVS · ET · MARIA · DEI · GRATIA

2

3

GVLIELMVS III DEI GRA

4

GVLIELMVS III DEI GRA

5

GVLIELMVS III DEI GRA

6

7

ANNA DEI GRATIA
VIGO

1

ANNA·DEI·GRATIA·

2

ANNA·DEI·GRATIA

3

ANNA·DEI·GRATIA·

4

5

6

7

8

the whole matter was most involved. The name given to the war is said to have been derived from the fact that the Yorkists adopted the white rose as their badge and the Lancastrians the red rose. Legend has it that these roses were plucked by antagonists in the garden of Middle Temple, London, where such roses bloom still.

Before Edward IV was proclaimed King the Wars of the Roses had continued with the Battle of Blore Heath, 23rd September, 1459, the Battle of Northampton, 10th July, 1460, the Battle of Wakefield, 30th December, 1460, the Battle of Mortimer's Cross, 2nd February, 1461, the Second Battle of St. Albans, 17th February, 1461, a skirmish at Ferry Bridge in March 1461 and the Battle of Towton, 29th March, 1461. In some of the battles Edward took part, as will be seen.

Edward, born in September 1442, was the son of Richard, Duke of York, and Cicely Neville, sister of Richard, Earl of Salisbury. The Neville's were one of the powerful families of the time, and appear frequently in the story of the Wars.

When the Duke of York advanced his claim to the throne of England in 1460, young Edward, then Earl of March, was sent to gather troops on the Welsh borders. While thus engaged he heard of his father's defeat and death at Wakefield in December. Hastening northward, he was pursued by the Earl of Pembroke, turned on him and inflicted a crushing defeat at the Battle of Mortimer's Cross, near Wigmore. Meantime the advance of Queen Margaret's lawless northern troops, Margaret was the Queen of Henry VI, excited the fears of the citizens of London. Edward therefore marched to London and was hailed as King on 4th March, 1461. He was then joined by his cousin, Richard, Earl of Warwick and together they hastened northwards, met the Lancastrian army at Towton and inflicted on it a heavy defeat. He then returned to London and was crowned on 29th June, 1461. When Parliament met in November it recognized Edward IV as succeeding to the rights of Richard II, and attainted Henry VI of high treason.

Plate 26 Gold. Five Guineas
1 Queen Anne, 1702–1714. The rare piece struck from gold captured at the battle of Vigo Bay. **2** Similar bust but without VIGO. **3** Third type obverse with larger lettering. **4** Fourth type with new broader bust. **5** First reverse type, before the Act of Union with Scotland. **6** Second reverse type after the Union and incorporating the Scottish arms. **7** Third reverse type with broader shields. **8** Fourth reverse type, similar to the second but with larger lettering.

With foreign help, Queen Margaret was still holding out in the north, but the victories at the Battle of Hedgeley Moor, 25th April, 1464, and at Hexham, together with the capture of Henry VI in 1465, appeared to make Edward IV secure on the throne.

Edward, however, now imperilled his own position by secretly marrying the Lady Elizabeth Grey, the widowed daughter of a Lancastrian baron. This marriage displeased both the Earl of Warwick and the powerful Nevilles, who had planned a Burgundian or French marriage alliance as a way of securing the throne from foreign attacks in aid of the Lancastrians. A tug-of-war now took place. The Nevilles tried to keep Edward dependent on themselves while he, as a counterpoise, advanced his wife's relations to positions of power. Meantime the breach between Edward and Warwick rapidly widened, and in 1467 ended in open rupture between them over a proposed continental alliance, Warwick prefering France and Edward, Burgundy.

This ended Edward's popularity for the time being. There was a rising of discontented peasantry in the north under 'Robin of Redesdale'; the Duke of Clarence, Edward's brother, allied himself with Warwick, and both joined with the discontented Commons in pressing for reforms. This caught Edward unprepared and he was made prisoner by Archbishop Neville till Warwick, seeing that a division between the Yorkists meant success for the Lancastrians, brought about a pacification and Edward was released.

Apart from putting down a rising in Lincolnshire with great promptitude and sternness, Edward still seemed to be unprepared for the situation. Warwick and Clarence, as he well knew, were plotting against him, and had fled to France and joined with Queen Margaret. When Warwick landed in England in September 1470, Edward was quite unprepared to meet him and, being deserted on all sides fled to Flanders on 29th September. The Lancastrian King Henry VI was released from captivity on 3rd October and re-crowned on 13th October, 1470. Hence Henry's second coinage.

Edward now set about gathering troops and on 14th March, 1471, landed in England, declaring that he had only come to claim his ancestral possession, the Duchy of York. However, his popularity revived and he was soon again proclaimed King. He marched on Coventry, where Warwick was stationed. The Duke of Clarence now deserted Warwick and joined his brother and together they hastened back to London, hotly pursued by Warwick. The clash came on 14th April, 1471, when the armies met and the second Battle of Barnet was fought. A monument now marks the spot, on the A1000, a mile north of Barnet church. Warwick was killed in the crushing defeat of his forces and Edward now turned his attention to Queen Margaret, who had landed at Weymouth. Edward overtook her forces at Tewkesbury, where he defeated them at the Battle of that name on 4th May, 1471. Already proclaimed King, and with Henry VI in the Tower, Edward returned in triumph to London on 21st May and on the same night Henry VI was put to death. Hence Edward's second coinage.

One more battle in the Wars of the Roses still had to be fought, that of Bosworth, 22nd April, 1485, but this does not concern us yet, as it took place in the reign of Richard III.

We can now return to the coinages of the two reigns of Edward IV. As might be expected it is one of considerable interest.

Messrs. Blunt and Whitton carried out a very comprehensive research into the coinage of the two reigns of Edward IV and published their work in the *British Numismatic Journal*, No. XXV. For the whole period they divided the coinage into twenty-two types, dating each type as follows:

For the first reign:

I–IV 1461–1464
V (gold) March 1465–July 1465
V (silver) August 1464–July 1465
VI July 1465–July 1466
VII July 1466–July 1467
VIII July 1467–July 1468
IX 1469–March
X March 1469–1470
XI Mid 1470–3rd October, 1470.

For the second reign:

XII April–Autumn 1471
XIII Autumn 1471–23rd February, 1472
XIV 22nd February, 1473–Mid 1473
XV, XVI, XVII Mid 1473–3rd February, 1477–Early 1480
XXI Early 1480–12 February, 1483
XXII 12th February, 1483–April 1483

Eight initial marks were used during the first reign and fifteen in the second. The coinage of the first reign subdivides into Heavy Coinage, 1461–1464/5; when the gold Noble weighed 108 grains and the Penny fifteen grains; and the Light Coinage where the gold Ryal weighed 120 grains and the Penny twelve grains. In the coinage reform of 1411 the ratio between gold and silver had been fixed at one hundred to nine. This ratio Edward IV retained and this had the effect of raising the currency value of the Noble from its traditional 6s. 8d. to 8s. 4d. Since 6s. 8d. had for long been the standard fee for certain professional services—indeed it so remained well into the twentieth century, in the 1930s a solicitor charged 6s. 8d. for writing a letter and 3s. 4d. for a telephone call—the Angel weighing eighty grains as against the Noble's 120 grains, automatically became worth 6s. 8d.

The purpose of the reform of 1464 was to attract bullion to the mint at a price at which the Tower mint could compete with mints abroad. The plan succeeded and over two years the Tower mint coined 12,000 lbs. of gold and 55,000 lbs. of silver. The royal mints at Canterbury and York were once more brought into operation and mints were opened at Bristol, Coventry and Norwich. The mint at Calais, however, does not seem to have been in use. The episcopal mints of Canterbury, York and Durham were also active.

As to the actual coins themselves, in the Heavy Coinage period, Nobles of two varieties were struck at London only. Both varieties are extremely rare. No other gold coins were struck during this period. In the silver range Groats of five varieties were struck in London only, all catalogued as scarce. Half-groats of four varieties, again from London only, are rare to very rare pieces. Pennies came from London, Durham and York, and Halfpennies and Farthings from London only. The date types or classes naturally ran from I to IV. The Farthing is extremely rare, the Halfpennies rare and the Pennies normal to very rare according to mint and variety.

In the Light Coinage period in the gold range, Ryals were struck

Plate 27 *Gold. Five Guineas*
1–2 George I, 1714–1727. One type only. **3–7** George II, 1727–1760. 3 is obverse type one, with young head. 4 is the same head with E.I.C. below; metal from the East India Company. 5 is the old head, obverse type three with LIMA below the bust. 6 is a similar head, obverse type four but without the word Lima. 7 is the reverse common to all types.

1

2

GEORGIVS·II·DEI·GRATIA

3

GEORGIVS·II·DEI·GRATIA
E·I·C

4

GEORGIVS·II·DEI·GRATIA
LIMA

5

GEORGIVS·II·DEI·GRATIA

6

7

1

2

3

4

5

6

7

8

9

10

in London, rarity normal, at Bristol, with a B in the waves below the ship, rare, in Coventry (C in waves) and Norwich (N), both very rare pieces and in York (E), rare. Half-ryals came from London, scarce, Bristol, rare, Coventry and Norwich, very rare and York, rare, the provincials with their usual mint mark letters. Quarter-ryals of two varieties, extremely rare and scarce respectively, were struck in London only and the Angel, an extremely rare piece, in London. In the type-date classes these pieces cover the periods V to IX. Due to the combination of initial marks used, already the varieties are beginning to proliferate so that one gets *a*'s, *b*'s and so forth attaching to the main type-dates. Incidentally, the reason for the rarity of the Coventry and Norwich pieces is that these mints only worked from July to September 1465.

In the silver range the Groats of the London mint exist in eighteen varieties and cover the type-dates from V to XI, the last of the first reign types. Light Groats were struck from the dies that had been used for the heavy coinage, resulting in the design 'running off' the flan of the coin, since the light Groats were slightly smaller in size. The designs of both, however, are similar. The London Groats are common, those of Bristol normal, those of Coventry scarce and those of Norwich and York normal. The provincial coins carry their usual mint marks, and occur from V up to type-date XI.

The Half-groats came from the same mints, Coventry and Norwich being very rare, Bristol rare and the London pieces scarce. Canterbury Royal and Canterbury episcopal mints now come into the picture, producing Half-groats of normal rarity. The use of many combinations of the initial marks produced a large number of Half-groat varieties, the type-date periods being from V to X.

The Pennies are complicated by the varieties produced by the York episcopal mint. London, scarce, and Bristol, rare, struck Pennies, the former in type-dates from V to X and the latter VII and VIII, with the name of the mint appearing. The issuers of the

Plate 28 *Gold. Two Guineas*
1–5 Charles II, 1660–1685. 1, pointed truncation; 2, the same but with elephant; 3, rounded truncation; 4, the same but with elephant and castle; 5, common reverse type. **6–7** James II, 1685–1688. One type only. **8–10** William and Mary, 1689–1694. 8, first obverse with elephant below busts; 9, the same with no elephant. 10, common reverse type.

York episcopal Pennies can be determined by reference to the privy marks which occur on either the obverse and/or the reverse. During the Sede Vacante period which, according to the type-date classes produced was from 1464–1465/6, there are quatrefoils by the bust. The pieces by Archbishop Neville all have a quatrefoil in the centre of the reverse, while some have a G and a key, a quatrefoil or a trefoil by the bust, or no mark, according to the type-date classes, which range from VI to X, with the addition of two local types. All these York episcopal pieces are of normal rarity. Canterbury Royal mint produced Pennies also, type-date VII, very rare, as did Canterbury episcopal mint, type-dates VI–VII, scarce. In Durham Bishop Lawrence Booth produced Pennies in type-date classes V to VIII, with his privy marks by the bust. These consist of B and D, a quatrefoil and B, D and a quatrefoil, quatrefoils, trefoils or lis by the bust.

Halfpennies were struck by London, normal, Bristol, rare, York Royal, scarce, Canterbury Royal, scarce and Canterbury episcopal, rare, mints, in type-dates V to VIII.

As may be remembered, the coinage of the second reign of Edward IV starts with type-date XII. In the gold range Angels were struck in London from XII to XXII and are of normal rarity. Bristol, with its usual B also struck some Angels, period XIV, which are extremely rare. Half-angels were struck in London only, type-dates XII, extremely rare, XIV/XII, also extremely rare and XIV–XXII scarce.

In the silver range Groats were struck in London, XII–XXII, catalogued as common, at Bristol, XII and XIV, normal, and at York Royal XII, normal. Half-groats came from London, XII–XXII, normal rarity, from Bristol, XII, very rare, from York Royal, XII, very rare and from Canterbury Royal XVIII, XX and XXI, normal.

The Pennies are again complicated by the issues of the York episcopal and Durham issues. London-struck Pennies in type-dates from XII to XXII, normal rarity, and Bristol for the period XII, extremely rare. The York episcopal issues were by Archbishop George Neville, and Archbishops Lawrence Booth and Thomas Rotherham with three Sede Vacante issues. Neville marked his issues with the quatrefoil, the G and key, or G and rose, Booth with a B and key privy mark, and Rotherham with a T and key

The first Sede Vacante period firstly had the G and key, then no privy mark, followed by E and rose, the second such period had the G and key, and the third Booth's B and key, all these privy marks being by the bust. The type-date periods covered were from XII to XXI.

The Canterbury Royal mint Pennies occur with and without a C on the breast of the King and are rare. At Durham Bishop Booth issued Pennies in type-date classes XII to XV before going to York as Archbishop, together with three issues from local dies which carried no privy mark on the obverse but had D in the centre of the reverse as did the Booth issues from XIII to XV. The D on the reverse appears on the one Sede Vacante issue, which was from local dies, while the last two issues from Durham for the reign, those of Bishop William Dudley, had on the obverse a V to right of the bust and a D and V respectively. Both had the D in the centre of the reverse, the dies in both cases being of local workmanship. All issues are normal as regards rarity.

Finally Halfpennies were struck in London, XII to XXII, normal rarity, at Canterbury Royal, XVII, XIX and XXI periods, very rare, and at Durham, with the D on the reverse, extremely rare.

That in its briefest form represents the coinage of a complex series, issued during a complicated period in our history. It is a difficult coinage on which to give any concise guide, but one of very great interest to those who are prepared to take a little time and trouble to study it.

Edward V (9th April–25th June, 1483)
Eldest son of Edward IV

This short reign had an equally small coinage, some issues being in doubt and all extremely rare.

DENOMINATIONS

Gold: Angel, Half-angel.
Silver: Groat, Half-groat(?), Penny(?).

Basic obv. legend: EDWARD DI GRA REX ANGL Z FRANC.

Two initial marks in use, a boar's head on the obverse and a sun and rose dimidiate on the reverse.

With this reign goes the story of the Princes in the Tower. Briefly the facts are that Edward, born in November 1470, created Prince of Wales in 1471 and Earl of Pembroke in 1479, was sent to

Ludlow in 1482 under the guardianship of his uncle, Earl Rivers. He was at Ludlow when his father, Edward IV, died in 1483, and almost at once he set out for London. Travelling across country in a general south-easterly direction he reached Stoney Stratford on what is now the A5, part of Watling Street and then probably the only main road out of London in a north-westerly direction, on 29th April, 1483. Here he was met by the Duke of Gloucester who had already arrested Lord Rivers and Lord Grey. Edward continued on to London with Gloucester, and arrived on 4th May. Meantime the Council had apparently already recognized Richard as Protector, the new King being only thirteen. The coronation was fixed for 22nd June. Richard, the 'protector'(!) was the son of Richard, Duke of York, whom we have seen killed at the Battle of Wakefield, and brother of Edward IV and George, Duke of Clarence, all of whom we have met.

Richard promptly had Edward V lodged in the Tower while Edward's mother, hearing of the arrest of Rivers and Grey, sought sanctuary at Westminster. Rivers and Grey had been sent to Pontefract, where they were beheaded about 13th June. Soon after Richard compelled the Queen to deliver up the young Duke of York, and sent him to join his brother Edward in the Tower. It is at this point, about 21st June, that Edward V's deposition seems to have been decided upon. On 22nd June a certain Dr. Shaw, brother of the then Lord Mayor of London, insisted in a sermon which he delivered that both Edward V and the Duke of York were illegitimate sons of Edward IV. The result of this was that on 25th June a deputation of nobles and citizens of London waited on Richard and offered him the crown. This he accepted and his reign began the next day. Meanwhile the two young Princes remained shut in the Tower, where they were certainly put to death at some time between June and October by their uncle Richard's order. The mystery surrounding the whole affair has led many to doubt whether the murder actually took place. The historian, Gairdner, carried out a thorough investigation of all the circumstances and sums up the evidence as follows.

'Some time after Richard had set out on his progress (August, 1483), he sent a messenger named John Green to Sir Robert Brackenbury, the Constable of the Tower, commanding him to put his young nephews to death. This order Brackenbury would not obey, and Green returned to his master at Warwick. Richard was greatly mortified, but sent one Sir James Tyrell to London, with a warrant to Brackenbury to deliver up to him for one night all the keys of the Tower. Tyrell thus took the place into his keeping, and engaged the services of Miles Forest, one of those who kept the Prince's chamber, and John Dighton, his own groom, to carry out the wishes of the tyrant. These men entered the chamber when the two unfortunate lads were asleep, and smothered them under pillows; then having called Sir James to see the bodies, buried them at the foot of a staircase.' The details of the murder were obtained from a confession made by Sir James Tyrell in 1502, when he was imprisoned in the Tower on a charge of treason, and there is no reason for doubting its substantial accuracy; in addition to which, the story was corroborated by a discovery made in the reign of Charles II when, under the staircase leading to the chapel in the White Tower, the skeletons of two young lads, whose apparent ages agreed with those of the unfortunate Princes, were found buried.

Perhaps the collector may think we are spending his time on recounting such facets of the history of England. So many incorrect accounts of events such as this gain credence, that it is worth the reading time to spend a moment absorbing the true facts. The collector may well be a visitor to the Tower of London, long the seat of the principal mint of England and Britain. On such a visit he will be standing on the very stones where such events happened, for happen they did. Though he may be surrounded by boisterous schoolchildren, romping and eating ice cream, within the Tower of London so much history has been written, so many 'deaths' have occurred, that one can but wonder that the very stones do not still run with blood. A tourists' visiting point now, but the Tower must surely be the bloodiest fortress of all the fortresses and castles which the visitor will see in Britain.

During the short months when Edward V was by title King of England a coinage was struck. It has been listed above and was struck in London only, at that very Tower in which the unfortunate lad, a simple pawn in the power-game then proceeding, was to meet his death. Little he saw of London, or of his kingdom.

It is hardly necessary to state that all five denominations, two of them problematical, are extremely rare.

Richard III (1483–1485)
Son of Richard, Duke of York and brother of Edward IV

A further short reign, producing a small coinage. The Wars of the Roses were still not quite over. Richard III was to die, fighting desperately at the last battle of the Roses, the Battle of Bosworth, 22nd August, 1485. As his epitaph an unbiased chronicler says, 'Unscrupulous, cruel, and violent as Richard was, he was, however, probably no worse than contemporary princes and statesmen; no worse, certainly, than his brother or his successor.'

DENOMINATIONS

Gold: Angel, Half-angel.
Silver: Groat, Half-groat, Penny, Halfpenny.

Basic obv. legend: RICARD DI GRA REX ANGL Z FRANC.

Though the coinage of the reign is basically simple the initial marks are complicated. In essence three only were used but of the first, sun and rose dimidiate, three varieties exist. Of the second, a boar's head, two varieties were used while the third, a lis, was used only by the Durham episcopal mint.

In the gold range three main varieties of the Angel were struck. Basically they have the letter R and a rose on either side of the ship's mast, and a cross above a shield, on the reverse. The legend on the first variety still reads EDWARD, but had an R over an E on the reverse in the position stated. The second variety reads RICARD in the main obverse legend, but the R is still sometimes over an E or over a rose on the reverse. The third variety reads RICARD or RICAD in the main legend, but all three varieties exist with various combinations of the first two initial marks above listed. The first and third varieties are extremely rare and the second rare. The Half-Angel is simple, only one type or variety being struck. It has an R and a rose beside the ship's mast and only one type of boar's head from the possible two was used as the initial mark. Both the gold denominations were struck in London only.

In the silver range Groats were struck in London, two varieties, both scarce and with a complexity of initial marks 1 and 2. York also struck Groats, which are rare. Half-groats were struck in London only, in two varieties, both very rare. Pennies were struck in London, very rare, York, with a quatrefoil in the centre of the reverse design, rare, two varieties, and at Durham, rare, with a D in the centre of the reverse. The very rare Halfpenny of the reign was struck in London only.

Richard III was the last of the Kings of the House of York. Perhaps the Wars of the Roses, like so many other wars, had been in vain. Our next King, Henry VII, was of the House of Tudor.

Henry VII (1485–1509)
Son of Edmund Tudor, Earl of Richmond

Until this time we have been dealing with coins on which the King's head or bust had been presented full face over a very long period. We now come to a period when the portrait of the King began to take on the semblance of a true portrait, and something of this will be said as our story proceeds.

DENOMINATIONS

Gold: Sovereign, Ryal, Angel, Half-angel.
Silver: with facing bust: Groat, Half-groat, Penny, Halfpenny, Farthing.
In profile: Testoon, Groat, Half-groat.

Basic obv. legend: HENRICUS DEI GRACIA REX ANGLIE ET FRANC DNS IBAR.

The initial marks used during this reign take on an increased interest. It is now possible to assign dates during which the marks were in use. Coins are not yet dated in arabic figures, though this practice is not now so far ahead. By kind permission of Mr. North the mint marks of this and some future reigns are illustrated, from his drawings. Thus, when a coin bearing any of these marks comes into the hands of the collector he can assign it to its correct period.

As mentioned above a considerable change in coin design is about to take place. For some 150 years, as has been seen, the types had varied little. The change made during this reign marks the Renaissance in the design of our coins and the end of medieval art. The change is somewhat tentative. The first issues continued in the medieval style. The Sovereign is of four types, all extremely rare. The types can be dated by the initial marks, Cross Fitchée on reverse, Cinquefoil, Dragon and Lis on obverse with Dragon on reverse respectively. There is one type only of the Ryal, struck about 1489–1490, extremely rare. There are five classes of Angel,

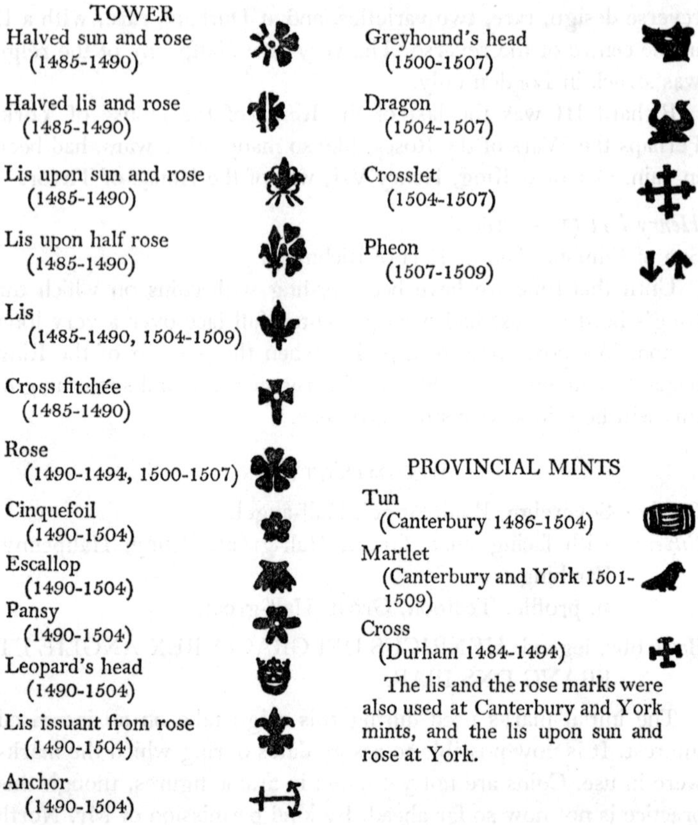

The initial marks on the coinage of Henry VII (By courtesy of J. J. North)

all rare or scarce, with a complex series of initial mark combinations. The Half-angel is of four classes or varieties, again with an interesting series of initial marks. All these gold pieces were issued in London only.

The first series of silver continued with the facing bust. The

Plate 29 Gold. Two Guineas

1 William III, 1649–1702. 1701, struck in this year only and of the 'fine work' type obverse (see the Five Guineas). **2** Queen Anne, 1702–1714. One type only with post-Union reverse. **3** George I, 1714–1727. One type only. **4–8** George II, 1727–1760. Three obverse types, young, intermediate and old head. Two reverse types, the first used only in 1734.

GVLIELMVS DEI GRA

1

ANNA DEI GRATIA

2

3

4

GEORGIUS II DEI GRATIA

5

GEORGIVS II DEI GRATIA

6

7

8

1

2

3

4

5

6

7

8

9

10

11

12

13

14

15

Groats were issued in London only and are scarce or normal in their four varieties. Half-groats were struck in London, three varieties, the first very rare, and in Canterbury by Archbishop Morton, whose initial M appears in the centre of the reverse. An issue is also attributed to the King and Archbishop jointly with no M. Half-groats were also struck at York and are not rare. The feature of interest in the Groats and halves is in the six types of crown on the King's head.

The Pennies are of two distinct types. The first is similar to previous types and was struck at London, Canterbury, York and Durham, and is rare to normal according to variety, of which there are six. The second type shows the King enthroned in place of the usual bust. For the period a die of this design was no small achievement. The reverse foreshadowed the type of reverse to be used in the second, profile, coinage, being the royal arms superimposed on a cross pattée. These pieces came from London, York and Durham in eight varieties, all but one being of normal rarity. Finally, Half-pennies were struck at London, Canterbury and York, are of the old type of design and are normal to rare. As with the groats, various types of crown were used. Last in the series was a Farthing from London only, a very rare piece.

With the profile issue of silver coins of Henry VII we come, as was stated above, to a turning point in the design of our coinage. It is not only a profile view but a portrait of the King that now begins to appear, together with the numeral after the King's name.

The profile portrait of the ruler was not adopted instantly as the standard type. As we shall see, the full face was used again. But the profile now introduced laid the foundation of the custom of showing the monarch thus. It was finally to become the standard type with the introduction of milled coinage in 1662. Before that, as will be seen, many fine profile portraits came and went

Plate 30 *Gold. Guineas*
1–10 Charles II, 1660–1685. The nine obverse types. 1, pointed truncation; 2, similar with elephant; 3, pointed truncation, second type; 4, similar with elephant; 5, pointed truncation, third type, more steeply sloping; 6, similar with elephant; 7, rounded truncation; 8, similar with elephant and castle; 9, similar with elephant only. 10, common reverse type. **11–15** James II, 1685–1688. The four obverse types. 11, first bust; 12, similar with elephant and castle; 13, second bust, thinner with more prominent nostrils; 14, similar with elephant and castle. 15, common reverse type.

on our coins. A word on the designer who started the profile-portrait issues is not, therefore, out of place at this point.

He was Alexandre de Bruchsella, and was probably Flemish. His name is variously spelled, Bruchella, Brugsaal and other variations. The denomination which illustrates the artistry which he brought to the subject is the Testoon or Shilling. This itself was a new denomination, of medium size when compared with the then Sovereign and Ryal, being fractionally larger than the present day Florin. This gave the artist a reasonably large area in which to present the portrait. Three varieties of Testoon appeared, the first probably a trial issue. Unfortunately all three varieties are now extremely rare. The somewhat smaller Groat, however, contained a similar profile portrait. Five varieties were struck, four classified as tentative and one as regular issues. The fifth variety is, fortunately for the collector, of normal rarity. The profile Testoon and Groat were struck in London only. There were two varieties of Half-groats from London, two from Canterbury and three from York, three of the five varieties from these two mints being of normal rarity.

Says H. G. Stride, in a Paper before the National Numismatic Congress in 1965, 'When real portraiture was introduced on the coins by Bruschella's portrait of Henry VII a punch was engraved by an artist-engraver, a craftsman of rare talents. The fact that his retirement from the mint at the beginning of Henry VIII's reign compelled the use for sixteen years of Bruschella's portrait of Henry VII on Henry VIII's coins is an indication of the difficulty experienced in finding a suitable artist-engraver.' In fact, a new high standard having been set, artistic talent now had to measure up to it. We shall see something of the re-use of Henry VII's portrait on the coins of the next reign in a moment.

Henry VIII (1509–1547)
Son of Henry VII

From now until the end of the hammered coinage series the coinage classifications and the denominations within these classifications tend to multiply.

DENOMINATIONS

First coinage (1509–1526)
Gold: Sovereign, Angel, Half-angel.
Silver: Groat, Half-groat, Penny, Halfpenny, Farthing.

TOWER

Pheon
(1509-26; 1541-42)

Castle
(1509-26)

Castle with H
(1509-26)

Portcullis crowned
(1509-26)

Rose
(1526-29)

Lis
(1529-32;1538-41;1544-47)

Arrow
(1532-42)

Sunburst
(1537-37)

Annulet and pellet
(1544-47)

DURHAM

Spur rowel
(1523-26)

Star radiant
(1526-44)

Crescent
(1526-29)

Trefoil
(1526-29)

Lis (1509-26)—See above.

CANTERBURY

Martlet
(1509-26)

Pomegranate
(1509-26)

Cross fitchée
(1509-26)

Cross patonce
(1526-32)

T (1526-32)

Warham's (uncertain) mark
(1526-32)

Catherine wheel
(1533-44)

Rose (1509-26). See above

Lis (1509-26). See above.

YORK

Martlet (1509-14). See above.

Star (1514-26). See above.

Pansy
(1514-26)

Escallop
(1514-26)

Voided cross
(1514-30)

Acorn
(1526-30)

Key
(1530-44)

BRISTOL

W.S. (1546-47)

SOUTHWARK

Lombardic E (1544-47)

Roman E (1544-47)

S (1544-47)

The initial marks on the coinage of Henry VIII (By courtesy of J. J. North)

Second coinage (1526–1544)

Gold: Sovereign, Angel, Half-angel, George Noble, Half George Noble, Crown of the Rose, Crown of the Double Rose, Halfcrown.

Silver: Groat, Half-groat, Penny, Halfpenny, Farthing.

Third coinage (1544–1547)

Gold: Sovereign, Half-sovereign, Angel, Half-angel, Quarter-angel, Crown, Halfcrown.

Silver: Testoon, Groat, Half-groat, Penny, Halfpenny.

Basic obv. legend: (Groats) First and second coinage, HENRIC VIII DI GRA REX AGL Z FRA

From 1542 onwards, HENRIC VIII (sometimes 8) DI GRA AGL FRA Z HIB REX

Again initial marks play an important dating role in this very complex coinage, and are once more reproduced from North's drawings.

It has already been stated that the English hammered coinage will not fit nicely and snugly into a convenient classification system. The list of denominations given above helps to lend colour to this point. So far an attempt has been made to give as much guidance as possible on the hammered issues. Detail has been sparse, leaving much work to be done by further reading. Even so detail will have to be cut back even further, at any rate for the coinage of this reign, if this book is ever to fit between two covers, for we still have some 400 years ahead of us. We must, therefore, try to cover the ground a little more rapidly.

The events of this historic reign brought with them a financial crisis, and sowed the seed of an even worse monetary crisis to

Plate 31 *Gold. Guineas*

1–4 William and Mary, 1689–1694. Three obverse types. 1, conjoined busts; 2, similar with elephant and castle; 3, similar with elephant only. 4, Common reverse type. **5–12** William III, 1694–1702. Five obverse types. 5, first bust; 6, similar with elephant and castle; 7, second bust; 8, similar with elephant and castle. 9, third bust, 'fine work' type. (See the Five Guineas.) Three reverse types. 10, normal figures and date; 11, larger date figures and lettering; 12, narrower crowns above shields, scroll-type harp. **13–19** Queen Anne, 1702–1714. Five obverse types. 13, first type; 14, similar with VIGO below bust; 15, similar with elephant and castle; 16, new bust; 17, similar with elephant and castle. Two reverse types, pre-Union and post-Union.

1

2

3

4

5

6

7

8

9

10

11

12

13

14

15

16

17

18

19

1

2

3

4

5

6

7

8

9

10[1]

11[2]

12[3]

13[4]

14[5]

15[6]

16[7]

17[8]

come. As mentioned above, the early coinage of Henry VIII was similar to that of his father, and the profile issues continued to bear the portrait of Henry VII, but with Henry VIII's titles.

By 1526 it became necessary to re-organize the coinage once more, and this task was entrusted to Cardinal Wolsey, then at the height of his power and of his influence on Henry VIII. The step had become necessary to prevent the considerable importation of French and Flemish gold coins, which were driving English gold coins out of circulation. With no gold coins in our hands today this may take a little assimilating. No 'foreign' coins circulate in Britain today but the position has passed to one of 'paper work', where the American Dollar is set against the British Pound, which strengthens or weakens in its value according to the trust put in either currency by the international bankers. A further fact is that in most countries of the world, certainly in Britain and the United States, the coins in day-to-day use have no value whatsoever, but are simply token pieces of base metal. They do not, therefore, have to be valued as coins one against another. Very roughly the present situation boils down to how much gold each leading nation has, often in bar metal, with which to back its coinage, should the coinage, theoretically, ever have to be backed. So, gold goes in and out of the Bank of England, in and out of Fort Knox, in and out of the Bank of France and of the Russian treasury. All else is done 'on paper', with no coinage of any intrinsic value being in circulation.

Wolsey, however, was faced with the problem of equating coins with each other. He tackled the matter primarily by re-valuing English gold coins at the rate of twenty-two shillings to the

Plate 32 Gold. Guineas
1–9 George I, 1714–1727. Seven obverse types. 1, first bust, tie with two ends, PR EL (Prince Elector) in the reverse legend; 2, second bust with lock of hair on shoulder and curl round truncation; 3, third bust in lower relief and no curl round truncation; 4, fourth bust, one end of tie in a loop; 5, fifth bust, similar but with elephant and castle; 6, sixth bust, smaller and older head, no loop to tie; 7, seventh bust, similar with elephant and castle. Two reverse types. 8, the first with PR EL in legend used only with obverse 1 in 1714; 9, used for all other dates. **10–17** George II, 1727–1760. Eight of the eleven obverse types. 10 (1), young head with small lettering; 11 (2), similar with larger lettering; 12 (3), second young head, narrower; 13 (4), similar with E.I.C.; 14 (5), similar head, no E.I.C., larger lettering; 15 (6), similar with E.I.C.; 16 (7), intermediate head with small lettering; 17 (8), similar with E.I.C. (continued on Plate 33).

Sovereign and then by issuing a new coin, the gold Crown of the Rose, which was the same weight and standard as its imported French rival, the Ecu au Soleil. This brought the gold in the Crown of the Rose down to twenty-three carat, whence it became known as 'crown gold'. The next step was to adjust the entire gold coinage by striking the larger gold pieces in standard gold, twenty-three carat three-and-a-half grains, and again revaluing the Sovereign at 22s. 6d. At this point the very rare pieces the George Noble and the Half George Noble, of which the British Museum's specimen is now probably unique, were struck. The Crown of the Rose, an extremely rare piece now, did not survive for long, and was replaced by the Crown of the Double Rose, valued at five shillings, and thus originating the present nominal value of our cupro-nickel Crown, five shillings.

At this point Wolsey took one step too far. No doubt feeling secure in his temporal power, and in his standing with his King, he allowed to be issued from his privilege ecclesiastical mint at York coins on which he placed his cardinal's hat as episcopal mark, as well as his initials on the reverse. All might have been well, had he confined such marks to his Pennies. The fact that he placed similar privy marks on Groats, was, it is said, too much for Henry VIII. This assumption of the royal prerogative the King would not stomach, and these privy marks would have figured in the charges brought against Wolsey, had he lived to stand trial. That he did not every schoolboy knows.

But the real picture is probably somewhat larger than that. Readers of Alexandre Dumas's historical romances will know that, though the author may have treated true history somewhat roughly, his picture of the power of the church over the monarchy is often clear enough, in the persons of such Cardinals as Mazarin and Richeleau. Of such an encroachment on his royal powers Henry VIII would have none. Apart from the fact that he obviously regarded himself as an absolute monarch, what in these less regal times would have earned him the unenviable title of Dictator, he needed money. He also wanted to divorce his Queen, Katherine, partly because he needed a male heir to succeed him.

Henry VIII, unable to obtain the Pope's agreement to his divorce from Katherine, finally, through the Parliament of 1534, separated the Church of England from the Papal headship and instituted it as a national Church under the headship of the King. The title 'Defender of the Faith', bestowed on Henry some years previously, now took on a new meaning. There was soon no limit to the royal power, nor to the subservience of Parliament. The monasteries were suppressed in 1536 and 1539, yielding considerable treasure. Henry had dissipated the large fortune left to him by his father, and he soon disposed of the monastic money. By 1542 he was again on his 'beam ends' for money. Now the coinage itself had to be debased. A similar situation was not to arise again till the aftermath of World War I, 1920, and again after World War II, which has reduced our coinage to nothing more than tokens.

The slight debasement of the coinage which Wolsey had carried out in 1526 gave the clue. Debasement had yielded revenue then, it would do so now. During the next four years the fineness of the gold coinage came down from twenty-three to twenty carats, while the silver coinage was debased to an even greater extent. On such coins as the Testoon, where Henry is shown full face: a particularly Holbeinish portrait, the heavily debased silver soon wore thin. With such pieces the collector will frequently find a copperish glint, giving rise to a nick-name for the King at that period, 'old copper-nose'.

The effect of this debasement was to put Wolsey's coinage policy almost into reverse. *He* had to combat the intrusion of foreign gold coins; now English gold coins began to pour out of the country. Oman's comment is worth quoting.

'The immediate consequence of issuing a coinage in which too little silver exchanged for a gold sovereign or angel was, of course, that gold began to pour out of England on a much greater scale than before. The government stormed at secret exporters—but no government can ever be so Argus-eyed as to defeat the merchants' well-laid plans for getting the commodity out of the country. Silver began to be the main thing in currency within the realm.'

Quite apart from the money which Henry himself squandered, he was 'beginning to be cumbered by much debt arising from a new war with France.' (Oman). To make matters worse, 'silver was at the moment a falling commodity, and all over Europe it was worth much less than ten times its weight in gold. . . . The fact was that the influence of silver from America was just beginning to be felt—Cortes and Pizarro had been at work since Henry came to the throne.' (Oman).

Against such a chaotic financial background England, magnificent in its Field of the Cloth of Gold, in its fine new palaces, such as St. James's and Hampton Court, staggered on the verge of bankruptcy. Henry married and re-married, hopeful, like Napoleon, of generating a male heir to succeed him. In the event he left but a child to occupy his throne, and daughters to succeed his son, in whose reign England was to rise to new heights, the reign of Elizabeth I. Against this background the coins, given above, break down into varieties now listed, in which the initial marks play so important a part.

As well as the initial marks listed certain personal initials appear on some denominations, such as H K=Henry and Katherine of Aragon; H A=Henry and Anne Boleyn, H I=Henry and Jane Seymour, and the initials of the Archbishops and Bishops striking coins at their privelege ecclesiastical mints. Here we get such initials as T D=Thomas (Ruthall) at Durham, E L=Edward Lee of York, and the controversial T W=Thomas Wolsey, Cardinal magnificent in a magnificent personality age.

We can, therefore, only set down the denominations in slightly more detail than that given above and show at least where the various denominations were struck. It is hoped that even this sparse treatment may spur the advanced collector to the consultation of the real erudite works. Thus, briefly, the collector will find the denominations struck at the following mints:

First coinage (1509–1526)

Gold: Sovereign, from London, extremely rare.
Angel, from London, rarity, normal.
Half-angel, from London, scarce.

Plate 33 Gold. Guineas
1–3 George II, 1727–1760. The remaining three of the eleven obverse types. 1 (9), similar to obverse eight but with larger lettering; 2 (10), similar with LIMA below bust; 3 (11), final type with old head and large lettering. **4–8** The five reverse types used for the Guineas of George II. 4 (1), large shield; 5 (2), smaller shield; 6 (3), the shield is more square; 7 (4), similar with slightly larger lettering; 8 (5), similar with large lettering. **9–14** George III, 1760–1820. The six obverse types. 9 (1), first bust; 10 (2), second bust; 11 (3), third bust; 12 (4), fourth bust; 13 (5), fifth bust; 14 (6), sixth bust, the 'Military Guinea'. **15–18** The four reverse types of George III Guineas. 15 (1) with curved figure 1 in the date; 16 (2), similar, but with a Roman figure 1; 17 (3), the well-known 'Spade' reverse type; 18 (4), the 'Garter' type, used only with obverse 6, the 'Military Guinea'.

1

2

3

4 [1]

5 [2]

6 [3]

7 [4]

8 [5]

9 [1]

10 [2]

11 [3]

12 [4]

13 [5]

14 [6]

15 [1]

16 [2]

17 [3]

18 [4]

1

2

3

4

5

6

7

8

9

10

11

12

13

14

15

16

17

18

19

Silver: Groat, from London, portrait of Henry VII, titles of Henry VIII. Rarity, normal.
Half-groat, from London, rarity normal.
From Canterbury by Archbishop Warham, normal.
From York, by Archbishop Bainbridge, normal.
Penny, from London, normal.
From Canterbury, by Archbishop Warham, normal.
From Durham, by Bishop Ruthall, rare.
Halfpenny, from London, normal.
From Canterbury, by Archbishop Warham, rare.
Farthing, from London, extremely rare.

Second coinage (1526–1544)

Gold: Sovereign, from London, very rare.
Angel, from London, very rare.
Half-angel, from London, extremely rare.
George Noble, from London, very rare.
Half George Noble, from London, extremely rare.
Crown of the Rose, from London, extremely rare.
Crown of the Double Rose, from London, rare to very rare according to initial mark and personal initials.
Halfcrown, from London, very rare to rare, according to initial mark and personal initials.

Silver: Groat, from London, omitting the Irish title, common.
With the Irish title, extremely rare.
From York, by Thomas Wolsey, normal. (This was the

Plate 34 Gold. Half Guineas
1–4 Charles II, 1660–1685. Three obverse types. 1, pointed truncation; 2, rounded truncation; 3, similar with elephant and castle. 4, common reverse type. **5–7** James II, 1685–1688. Two obverse types. 5, type one, plain; 6, type two with elephant and castle. 7, common reverse type. **8–11** William and Mary, 1689–1694. Three obverse types. In the second (9) the busts are somewhat broader and fuller than in the first type (8); the third type (10) is similar with the elephant and castle: the castle practically crowded off: added. 11 is the common reverse type. **12–15** William III, 1694–1702. The only difference between the two obverse types, 12 and 13, is that the second has the addition of the elephant and castle. 14 is reverse type one and the second reverse type (15) has a larger harp. **16–19** Queen Anne, 1702–1714. The obverse types. 16 and 17 are similar but the second has VIGO added below the bust. Two reverse types, 18, pre-Union; 19, post-Union.

coin that would cause one of the indictments against Wolsey, as above).

Half-groat, from London, omitting the Irish title, scarce.
With the Irish title extremely rare.
From Canterbury, by Archbishop Warham, common, or normal without his personal initials.
By Archbishop Thomas Cranmer, normal.
From York, by Archbishop Thomas Wolsey, normal.
By Archbishop Edward Lee, common.

Penny, from London, normal.
From Canterbury, by Archbishop Warham, rare.
By Archbishop Cranmer, rare.
From Durham, by Bishop Thomas Wolsey, common with his initials, normal without.
By Bishop Cuthbert Tunstall with his personal initials, C.D., common.
From York, by Archbishop Edward Lee, very rare.

Halfpenny, from London, normal.
From Canterbury, by Archbishop Warham, rare.
By Archbishop Cranmer, rare.
From York, by Archbishop Thomas Wolsey, rare.
By Archbishop Edward Lee, rare.

Farthing, from London, two varieties, extremely rare.

Third coinage (1544–1547)

Gold: Sovereign, from London, two varieties, extremely rare and very rare.
From Southwark, (a branch of the London mint at the Tower), very rare.
From Bristol, very rare.

Half-sovereign, from the Tower, London, scarce.
From Southwark, scarce.
From Bristol, very rare.

Angel, from London, scarce.

Half-angel, from London, rare.

Quarter-angel, from London, two varieties, rare.

Crown, from London, Tower mint, scarce.
From Southwark, scarce.
From Bristol, normal.

Halfcrown, from London, Tower, rare.
From Southwark, rare. (Two types).
From Bristol, rare.

Silver: Testoon (with the facing, 'old coppernose' bust).
From London, Tower mint, rare.
From Southwark, rare.
From Bristol, rare.

Groat, (similar bust) from London, Tower mint, normal.
From Bristol, normal.
From Canterbury, normal.
From York, normal.

Half-groat, from London, Tower mint, scarce.
From Southwark, scarce.
From Bristol, normal.
From Canterbury, normal.
From York, normal.

Penny, from London, Tower mint, normal.
From Southwark, normal.
From Bristol, normal.
From Canterbury, normal.
From York, normal.

Halfpenny, from London, Tower mint, normal.
From Bristol, rare.
From Canterbury, scarce.
From York, scarce.

It cannot be too strongly emphasized that the above list is only intended to show the collector what coins were struck, the mints from which each denomination came, and the rarity of each. The above list is subdivided many times by the all-important initial marks, personal initials of those who caused the various coins to be struck, and similar considerations. In this book we can but give a rough guide. Further reading, both in history and numismatics must be undertaken by those interested in the complexities of the English hammered coinage. Here we can but guide and suggest.

Edward VI (1547–1553)

Son of Henry VIII and Jane Seymour

A boy King, with but six years to reign, whose administrators had to face the financial chaos left by Henry VIII.

DENOMINATIONS

In the name of Henry VIII.

Gold: Sovereign, Half-sovereign, Crown, Halfcrown.
Silver: Groat, Half-groat, Penny, Halfpenny.

In the name of Edward VI

First period (April 1547–January 1549)

Gold: Half-sovereign, Crown, Halfcrown.
Silver: Shilling, Groat, Half-groat, Penny, Halfpenny.

Second period (January1549–April 1550)

Gold: Sovereign, Half-sovereign, Quarter-sovereign, Half-quarter-sovereign.

Silver: Shilling.

Third period (1550–1553)

Gold: Sovereign of thirty shillings, Sovereign of twenty shillings, Half-sovereign, Crown, Halfcrown, Angel, Half-angel.
Silver: Crown, Halfcrown, Shilling, Sixpence, Threepence, Penny, Halfpenny, Farthing.

Basic obv. legend: EDWARD VI D G ANGLIE FRANCIE Z HIBERNIE REX.

Once more a grave financial crisis faced England. Indeed it had done so for some years during the preceding reign. Now the government decided that the coinage must and should be restored to its former fineness and that the base metal coinage of Henry VIII should be eliminated as soon as possible.

More easily said than done. The country's finances were in so disastrous a state that till 1549 the old base issues had to be continued. Until April 1547 Edward VI's coinage still carried the titles and portrait of Henry VIII. In one of the series of gold Half-sovereigns the face of the enthroned King had been touched up to give it a youthful appearance, but Henry's name remained. A number of coins bearing Edward's name did begin to be struck, and on the silver his profile portrait began to appear. The Testoon or Shilling of this period is interesting, since it was not only struck in considerable numbers, but for the first time in our history it bore its date. This was the very beginning of the elimination of mint or privy marks used in some instances to indicate the date or period of years during which a coin of any particular denomination was struck.

By 1549 it was at last possible to make a start with the restoration of the coinage to a metal standard which had some relationship with the stated exchange value of the coin itself. Gold was now struck in twenty-two carat metal, but silver still had to wait to be uprated. A good deal of juggling took place with the silver pieces, with Shillings struck which were of at least two weights and fineness. In fact these Shillings were the guinea-pig, since they provided the revenue to meet the cost of the final uprating of the coinage. Their metal content even came down still further and in 1551 their value was reduced to ninepence and later to sixpence. Even though we are now close upon the Third Period coinage listed above, these very base pieces continued to circulate at their reduced value till 1560, ten years into period three. Their value was further written down to fourpence halfpenny or twopence farthing, according to the amount of debasement in the silver. They had to be countermarked with the head of a greyhound or a portcullis to signify their new low values and this countermarking in itself is a point of interest to the collector.

But at last, during the Third Period coinage (1550–1553), improvements in standard began to be possible. It had been a hard uphill fight to restore English coinage and the fight was still on. Today, with money in our hands that is worth nothing by such standards one can but marvel that our ancestors actually 'brought it off' and gave England a worthy coinage. It is more than doubtful that we could do the same thing today. What would it cost us now to put silver and gold back into everyday circulation?

With the introduction of Edward VI's Third Period coinage in 1550 an event took place that was to be of the greatest importance to collectors. Till now the Crown had been, as we have seen, a gold coin. While gold Crowns were still to be struck for some time to come, in 1551 there was put into circulation a handsome silver Crown of five shillings exchange value. Here was born the ancestor of the 'Churchill Crown', and of all the silver crowns which we shall meet as our story unfolds. As the Lingford and Whetmore collection catalogues prove, the silver Crown of Britain is a collector's piece: a fine portrait coin on which many collectors have specialized. Its size, though unpopular now as a circulating coin for this reason, gives the artist and engraver a scope for his art, for good portraiture and for the production of a really fine coin: one that gives the collector great satisfaction.

The first silver Crowns of 1551, bearing in mind that the dies were engraved by hand and the coins were similarly struck, were magnificent pieces. They 'went into production' to use the modern phrase, and, presumably, into general circulation. With all our modern mechanical aids to coin production we cannot now produce so fine a coin for general circulation as was produced by hand methods in 1551. Our modern mechanization can produce in pattern and proof coins finer work than could be done by hand in 1551, but not for the production model. If the collector doubts this, let him compare the production model of the 1551 Crown with the production model of the 1951 or 1953 Crown. All are illustrated in this book. The latter is probably the better comparison, since both show a horse and rider. In 1551, Edward VI, sharp and clear on his horse. In 1953, Elizabeth II on her horse, the outlines dulled and fogged.

To go with the new silver Crown a Halfcrown was struck, similar in design, and a Sixpence and Threepence were struck for the first time. Thus we now see the origins of a number of coins familiar to us all in the silver, later cupro-nickel and nickel-brass series. Initial marks still played their important part by dating the various issues, and a mint opened at Durham House, Strand, London, functioned briefly during 1548–1549, never to be re-opened.

The issues listed above came from the following mints:

In the name of Henry VIII.

Gold: Sovereign, from the Tower, very rare.
From Bristol, very rare.
Half-sovereign, from the Tower, rare.
From Southwark, rare.
Crown, from the Tower, scarce.
From Southwark, very rare.
Halfcrown, from the Tower, scarce.
From Southwark, rare.

Silver: Groat, from the Tower, normal.
From Southwark, normal.
From Durham House, rare.

From Bristol, scarce.
From Canterbury, normal.
From York, normal.
Half-groat, from the Tower, normal.
From Southwark, normal.
From Durham House, very rare.
From Bristol, rare.
From Canterbury, normal.
From York, normal.
Penny, from the Tower, normal.
From Southwark, extremely rare.
From Durham House, very rare.
From Bristol, normal.
From Canterbury, normal.
Halfpenny, from the Tower, scarce.
From Canterbury, scarce.
From York, scarce.

Coinage in the name of Edward VI.
First period (April 1547–January 1549)
Gold: Half-sovereign, from the Tower, very rare.
From Southwark, rare.
Crown, from the Tower, extremely rare.
Halfcrown, from the Tower, extremely rare.
Silver: Shilling, from Durham House, rare.
Groat, from the Tower, rare.
From Southwark, rare.
Half-groat, from the Tower, rare.
From Southwark, rare.
From Canterbury, rare.
Penny, from Southwark, rare.
From Bristol, rare.
Halfpenny, from the Tower, very rare.
From Bristol, very rare.

Second period (January 1549–April 1550)
Gold: Sovereign, with uncrowned bust, from the Tower, very rare.
Half-sovereign, from the Tower, two types, extremely rare and rare.

From Durham House, two types, both extremely rare.
With crowned bust from the Tower, rare.
From Durham House, extremely rare.
Quarter-sovereign, two types, from the Tower, very rare.
Half-quarter-sovereign, two types, from the Tower, very rare.

Silver: Shilling, from the Tower, three types, scarce or rare.
From Bristol, rare.
From Canterbury, scarce.
From Durham House, four types, rare.
The above with dates in Roman figures.

Third period (1550–1553)

Gold: Sovereign of thirty shillings, from the Tower, extremely rare.
Sovereign of twenty shillings, from the Tower, very rare.
Half-sovereign, from the Tower, rare.
Crown, from the Tower, very rare.
Halfcrown, from the Tower, very rare.
Angel, from the Tower, extremely rare.
Half-angel, from the Tower, extremely rare.

Silver: *Crown, from the Tower and Southwark, scarce.
(fine) *Halfcrown, from the Tower and Southwark, scarce.

Plate 35 Gold, Half, Quarter and Third Guineas
1–3 George I, 1714–1727. There are three obverse types, but only two are illustrated. The first (1) has the tie with two ends and a lock of hair on the shoulder. The second (not illustrated) is similar, with elephant and castle added: so rare that no example is available for illustration. The third type (2) has the tie with two ends but there is no lock of hair on the shoulder and the king is older; the whole bust is smaller. 3 is the common reverse type. **4–8** George II, 1727–1760. The five obverse types. Type one (4), young head; type two (5), similar with E.I.C. added; type three (6) intermediate head; type four (7) similar with LIMA added; type five (8) old head with letter larger. **9–10** The two reverse types. The first (9), normal, the second (10), similar but with lettering larger, the crown and shield fuller. **11–17** George III, 1760–1820. The seven obverse types. 11, first bust; 12, second bust; 13, third bust, considered to be of inferior workmanship; 14, fourth bust, similar but of better workmanship; 15, fifth bust; 16, sixth bust, very similar but rounder and broader; 17, seventh bust. **18–21** The four reverse types. Type one (18), curved figure 1 in date; type two (19), Roman figure I in date; type three (20), 'Spade' type, type four (21), 'Garter' type. **22** George I Quarter Guinea. **23** George III Quarter Guinea. **24–27** George III Third Guineas.

1 2 3

4 5 6 7 8

9 10

11 12 13 14

15 16 17

18 19 20 21

22 23

24 25 26 27

CAROLVS II DEI GRA

1

CAROLVS II DEI GRATIA

2

3

CAROLVS · II · DEI · GRATIA

4

1662

5

6

7

8

9

Shilling, from the Tower and Southwark, common.
Sixpence, from the Tower and Southwark, normal.
From York, scarce.
Threepence, from the Tower, normal.
From York, scarce.
Penny, from the Tower, extremely rare.
* First instances of dates in Arabic figures.

Silver: (base) Shilling, from the Tower, scarce.
Penny, from the Tower, normal.
From York, normal.
Halfpenny, from the Tower, extremely rare.
Farthing, from the Tower, extremely rare.

Once more initial marks play the key role in dating the various pieces.

When the silver Crowns and Halfcrowns began to be struck in the third period the initial mark Y, which had been in use at the Tower till 1551, was transferred to the Southwark mint where E had formerly been in use. Southwark mint is still commemorated by Mint Street.

It is worthy of note that in this reign there appeared pattern pieces in the English series. A pattern has come to be known as a coin struck to a design which is not afterwards used. In modern times it is also synonymous with a highly polished, brilliant striking, quite unblemished and of the highest quality workmanship. Proof pieces are of similar appearance, but from a design accepted for issue. Such pieces become more frequent in the milled series. We shall not have much to say about them since they form a subject in themselves and are usually, as with these patterns of Edward VI, of very considerable rarity.

Mary (1553–1554)
Daughter of Henry VIII and Katherine of Aragon

Plate 36 Silver. Crowns
1–4 Charles II, 1660–1685. The four obverse types. The main difference between 1 and 2 is the rose below the bust. There are considerable differences in the portraits of 3 and 4. **5–6** The two reverse types. The first was used in 1662 only; apparently it failed to please. The main obvious difference between the two types is in the first and third shields of arms. Some pieces in 1662 have the date in Arabic figures as part of the edge legend. **7–9** James II, 1685–1688. Two obverse busts and one reverse type only.

TOWER

Lis (1547-48, 1550-51) 

Arrow (1547-49) 

K (1547-49)

Grapple (1549) 

Pheon (1549) 

Trefoil (1549) 

Six (1549-50) 

Swan (1549-50) 

Rose (1549-51) 

Y (1549-51)

Lion (1550-51) 

Martlet (1550-51) 

Ostrich head (1551) 

Tun (1551-53) 

Escallop (1551-53) 

SOUTHWARK

E (1547-49)

DURHAM HOUSE

Bow (1548-49) 

BRISTOL

W.S. (1547-49)

T.C. (1549)

CANTERBURY

t (1549-50)

T (1549-50)

Rose (1549). See above.

Lis (1549). See above.

YORK

Lis (1547-48). See above.

Pierced mullet (1552-53) 

The initial marks on the coinage of Edward VI (By courtesy of J. J. North)

DENOMINATIONS

Gold: Sovereign, Ryal, Angel, Half-angel.
Silver: Groat, Half-groat, Penny.
Basic obv. legend: MARIA D G ANG FRA Z HIB REGINA

Mary was born in 1516. During her childhood there seems to have been a perpetual political question as to what should be done about Mary. Various alliances were suggested. By the time she was two years old a treaty had been concluded for her marriage with the Dauphin, Francis. When this treaty was broken off it was arranged that she should marry Charles V, and there was also the project of marrying her to Francis I of France. By this time Mary was eleven years old. She was very carefully educated and proved to be an accomplished child. When Anne Boleyn captured the fancy of Henry VIII, and after their marriage in 1533 when Anne became Queen, Mary was very roughly treated. By an Act of 1534 she was declared illegitimate, and forced to sign a document to this effect. Two years later, apparently to make certain of the matter, she was again declared illegitimate. The background to all this was Wolsey's unsuccessful attempt to obtain Henry's divorce from Katherine of Aragon; Wolsey's fall from power; Henry's private marriage with Anne in 1533, confirmed by Archbishop Cranmer who had carried out the ceremony in January; and Anne's coronation in June.

However, by an Act of 1544 the succession to the throne was secured on Mary. By this time her mother had died, and Anne Boleyn, after giving birth to Elizabeth (later Elizabeth I) in September 1533, and to a second child, which was dead at birth, in 1536, had been committed to the Tower on charges of treason and adultery and there beheaded in May of that year. By the time of the Act of 1544, Henry had married Jane Seymour, who had given birth to Edward, (later Edward VI), and Henry had contracted his fourth marriage with Anne of Cleeves.

On the death of Henry VIII, Edward, as the sole male child, became King and when he died in 1553, Mary laid claim to the crown. Meantime the Duke of Northumberland had conceived the idea of aggrandizing his own family by obtaining the crown for Lady Jane Grey, the daughter of the Marquis of Dorset, and marrying her to his, Northumberland's, son, Lord Guilford Dudley. Northumberland therefore induced Edward VI, a sick child with the shadow of death upon him, to alter the succession in favour of Jane Grey and against Mary. Though Lady Jane Grey was proclaimed Queen in London on 9th July, 1533, she obtained no support, while Mary, travelling towards London soon found herself at the head of a large band of supporters. Northumberland's supporters meanwhile deserted him, his scheme fell, and he proclaimed Mary Queen at Cambridge on 20th July. She was declared legitimate once more and was crowned in October 1553.

All the coins listed above, with the exception of the Angel, which is rare, and the Groat, which in some varieties is of normal rarity, are very rare pieces, the Sovereign and Ryal being dated in Roman figures. Additional to these pieces was a base silver Penny, the existence of which is now regarded as doubtful.

Philip and Mary (1554–1558)

DENOMINATIONS

Gold: Angel, Half-angel.

Silver: Shilling, Sixpence, Groat, Half-groat, Penny. (Fine to base).

Basic obv. legend: PHILIP Z MARIA D G REX Z REGINA

The question of what to do about Mary resolved itself in January 1554. She concluded a marriage treaty with Philip of Spain, and married him in July, to the complete disappointment of her subjects.

What had started as a reign which had opened well now became a disaster. Though nominally King, Philip remained in England little more than a year. Disgusted with his wife, with the country and with its Parliamentary constitution, he returned to Spain in September 1555 and did not return. In the next month his father, Charles V, abdicated the crown of Spain in Philip's favour, thus

Plate 37 *Silver*. *Crowns*

1–2 William and Mary, 1689–1694. One type only. Note the odd position of the date, which led to trouble in 1692. **3–9** William III, 1694–1702. Four obverse types, the third (5) was only used once in 1696 and this extremely rare piece with the 'fine work' portrait may be a pattern. The portrait is quite different from the 'fine work' type Five Guineas. The three reverse types are usually classified by the type of harp, i.e. first type (7) early harp; second type (8), ordinary or more normal harp; third type (9), late harp, used on Crowns at the end of the series.

GVLIELMVS ET MARIA DEI GRATIA

1

2

GVLIELMVS III DEI GRA

3

GVLIELMVS III DEI GRA

4

GVLIELMVS III DEI GRA

5

GVLIELMVS III DEI GRA

6

7

8

9

1

2

3

4

5

6

7

8

bringing to that throne the mortal enemy of Elizabeth I and setting in train the wars with Spain and the Spanish Armada.

However, Philip remained in England long enough to hurry on the Catholic reaction and to start what became known as the 'Spanish terror'. Of the Smithfield martyrs and the many others who lost their lives in this wave of persecution nothing need be said here. In the midst of it Philip persuaded Mary to declare war on France. In spite of one brilliant victory at St. Quentin, the campaign was a complete disaster and cost us our last French possession, Calais.

It is said of Mary that, once the terror had been started she probably knew less than half of what was going on. She was already ill, and in any case was by no means of a cruel and harsh disposition, being honestly anxious for the welfare of her country and for the good of the Church. But for the Spanish marriage the reign might have been very different. She died in 1558, aged only forty-two, a sad figure in our history.

The only two gold coins struck during the reign, the Angel and Half-angel are both very rare pieces. The Shillings are of three main types, the last very rare, the first two scarce. With the Sixpences they are remarkable in being the only English coins on which the busts of both the King and Queen appear, face to face. The only other instance of a King and Queen appearing together on our coinage is during the reign of William and Mary (1689–1694). Here the busts appear side by side, and William and Mary were Joint Monarchs.

The main varieties of Philip and Mary's Shillings, within the three main types are that they are found (*a*) without date or mark of value, (*b*) with mark of value, XII, on reverse, but with no date, (*c*) dated 1554 or 1555 above the busts and with mark of value on reverse and (*d*) dated 1555 below the busts, with mark of value on the reverse. On some pieces the Spanish titles, which came with Philip, are omitted. Of the Sixpences the first variety has the full

Plate 38 *Silver. Crowns*
1–5 Queen Anne, 1702–1714. All three portraits are slightly different, the first had the word VIGO below in 1703 only. Pre-Union and post-Union reverse types, the latter with plumes or roses and plumes in the angles. **6–8** George I, 1714–1727. One obverse and two reverse types. Altered dates, 1716 to 1718 and 1718 to 1720 exist. SSC in 1723 only.

English and Spanish titles, was issued in 1554 but is undated, (scarce), the second has the English titles only and is dated 1555 or 1557 above the busts, (scarce), while the third has the English titles only and the date, 1554 or 1557, below the bust, (extremely rare). The mark of value is, of course, VI. The Groats, whose rarity is normal, have a very charming portrait bust of Mary, facing left.

Elizabeth I, (1558–1603)
Daughter of Henry VIII and Anne Boleyn

DENOMINATIONS

Hammered issues, first coinage (1558–1561)

Gold: Sovereign of thirty shillings, Angel, Half-angel, Quarter-angel, Half-pound, Crown, Halfcrown.

Silver: Shilling, Groat, Half-groat, Penny. Some countermarked Testoons of Edward VI also circulated.

Hammered issues, second coinage (1561–1582)

Gold: Angel, Half-angel, Quarter-angel, Half-pound, Crown, Halfcrown.

Silver: Sixpence, Threepence, Half-groat, Threehalfpence, Penny, Three-farthings.

Hammered issues, third coinage (1583–1603)

Gold: Sovereign of thirty shillings, Ryal Angel, Half-angel, Quarter-angel, Pound, Half-pound, Crown, Halfcrown.

Silver: Crown, Halfcrown, Shilling, Sixpence, Half-groat, Penny, Halfpenny.

Milled issues.

Gold: Half-pound, Crown, Halfcrown.

Silver: Shilling, Sixpence, Groat, Threepence, Half-groat, Three-farthings.

Basic obv. legend: ELIZABETH D G ANG FRA ET HIB REGINA.

A large number of initial marks play their usual important part for the collector in dating the various coins.

By the time Elizabeth I ascended the throne of England she had already learned much of what political intrigue can try to accomplish. A quotation from the *Dictionary of English History* will give some idea of the troubled waters through which she had to steer her

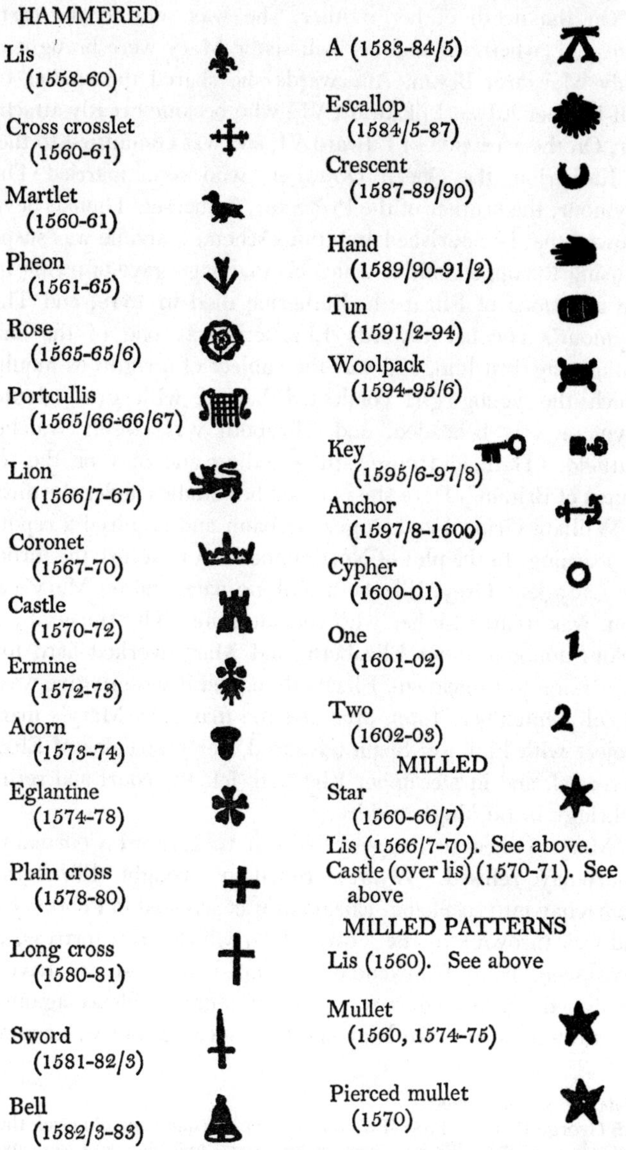

The initial marks on the coinage of Elizabeth I (By courtesy of J. J. North)

early life, and give a clue to her personality as Queen of England.

'On the death of her mother, she was sent to the castle of Hunsdon, where she and her half-sister Mary were brought up by Lady Margaret Bryan. Afterwards she shared the studies of her half-brother Edward [Edward VI] who became greatly attached to her. On the accession of Edward VI, she was committed to the care of Katherine, the Queen Dowager, who soon married Thomas Seymour, the brother of the Protector, Somerset. Thomas Seymour showed that he nourished ambitious schemes, and he was suspected of using the opportunities which his marriage gave of trying to win the affections of Elizabeth. Katherine died in 1548, and Thomas Seymour's conduct towards Elizabeth was one of the charges brought against him, and was the subject of a rigorous inquiry, in which the young girl conducted herself with great dexterity. Seymour was beheaded, and Elizabeth was closely watched at Hatfield. [Hatfield House, still standing and now on the tourist routes of Britain.] Here she pursued her studies under the direction of William Grindal and Roger Ascham, and acquired a reputation for learning. In the plot of Northumberland to secure the throne for the Lady Jane Grey, Elizabeth took no part, and on Mary's accession, was treated by her with consideration. The Imperial ambassadors doubted about Elizabeth, and Mary worked hard for her conversion to Romanism. Elizabeth judged it wise to give way, and on 9th September, 1553, attended the mass. As Mary's marriage project with Philip of Spain advanced, her suspicions of Elizabeth increased, and in December Elizabeth left the court and retired to Ashridge in Buckinghamshire.

'Mary wished to marry Elizabeth to Edward Courtenay, but Courtenay refused. Wyatt's rebellion brought Elizabeth and Courtenay into suspicion. Elizabeth was arrested in February 1554, and was thrown into the Tower. [To which grim fortress, as we have seen, many "unwanted" in our history so far have been consigned.] Every effort was made to obtain evidence against her, but without success. In May she was released, but was committed

Plate 39 Silver. Crowns

1–5 George II, 1727–1760. Two obverse types, young and old head, the latter with LIMA in 1746. Three reverse types, roses and plumes, roses, and plain in the angles. There were no Crowns of George III in the Milled Coinage, phase one.

1

2

3

4

5

CAROLVS II DEI GRATIA

1

CAROLVS·II· DEI·GRATIA

2

CAROLVS·II· DEI·GRATIA

3

CAROLVS·II· DEI·GRATIA

4

CAROLVS·II· DEI·GRATIA

5

IACOBVS·II· DEI·GRATIA

6

IACOBVS·II· DEI·GRATIA

7

16 85

8

to the care of Sir Henry Bedingfield, and was sent to Woodstock. Philip of Spain, on his arrival in England, showed more consideration towards Elizabeth. He wished to marry her in such a way as to promote his own political plans. First a marriage with the Duke of Savoy was proposed, and in April 1555, Elizabeth was summoned to Hampton Court, whence, at the end of the year, she went to Hatfield. It needed all her cleverness to escape the marriage with the Duke of Savoy, which would have sent her away from England. When this was abandoned, there came a proposal for Eric of Sweden, son of Gustavus Vasa, which was also refused.

'Elizabeth in her early days found herself surrounded by snares. She learned to trust no one, to act circumspectly, to assume an ambiguous attitude which did not commit her to anything definite, and to be prepared for any emergency. . . . When Elizabeth succeeded to the crown, on 17th November, 1558, she had already gained a large experience of the world and the difficulties which beset her. She never forgot that her position must be maintained by herself alone, and that her interests were not those of any particular party or system. She never laid aside her skill in balancing herself between opposing parties and husbanded her resources so as to profit by their mistakes.'

With all this experience behind her, Elizabeth came to the throne at the age of twenty-five, to find the concluding moves in the restoration of the coinage still to be faced. Some base silver remained in circulation in 1558, and by 1560 the Testoons or Shillings of Edward VI still in use were countermarked and further reduced in value to Fourpence halfpenny and to Twopence farthing, all the base silver money left being finally cleared away by 1561. The considerable variety of denominations, nine gold and eleven silver, issued during this long reign will have been noted from the list of denominations above. With the exception of the Sovereign of thirty shillings, the Ryal, Angel and its subdivisions, which were struck in fine gold, the remainder of the denominations except the Halfpenny have the profile portrait of the Queen on the obverse and

Plate 40 *Silver. Halfcrowns*
1–5 Charles II, 1660–1685. Five obverse types, all with differing portrait and detail. Only one reverse type was used and was similar to the second reverse type of the Crown, Plate 36, no. 6. **6–8** James II, 1685–1688. Two obverse and one reverse type only.

the royal arms on the reverse. To avoid confusion among the silver denominations of a shilling or less a rose was placed behind the Queen's head on alternate denominations. Thus a small lesson has to be learned by heart by the collector of these pieces, thus:

Shilling, no rose, no date.
Sixpence, with rose, dated in arabic figures.
Groat, no rose, no date.
Threepence, with rose, dated.
Half-groat, no rose, no date.
Three halfpence, with rose, dated.
Penny, no rose, no date.
Three farthings, with rose, dated.
Halfpenny, no rose, no date.

None of the coins listed at the head of this section came from any mint other than the Tower. Indeed the long history of the established provincial mints and the ecclesiastical privilege mints was over. When we come across provincial mints again they are temporary, and called into being by such events as civil wars, (Charles I), re-coinage, (William III), coinages struck by subcontractors to the Royal Mint, (Soho and the other various Birmingham mints), exhibitions, (Festival of Britain, 1951) or international war, (branch mint set up in the country during World War II against the possibility of the Royal Mint being demolished by enemy action).

Those collectors who might have been stimulated to take an interest in the Penny will note that it is still a silver piece, and in this reign is classified as of normal rarity. The Halfpenny is remarkable in having no legend, and the Three halfpence and Three farthing pieces, struck for some twenty years are unique to this one reign. The milled Three halfpence which the collector may encounter in later times is a colonial piece and was not intended for circulation in Britain. Collectors of the silver Crown will observe its reappearance at the very end of the reign, when it was struck in 1601 and 1602. Dates in Arabic figures appeared on some denominations, as stated above. They were to appear and disappear in the reigns still to come till they appeared permanently on the milled series of coins. The Elizabeth I Crowns were only dated with the last figure of the date, 1 and 2 respectively, these figures being placed in the position associated with many of the mint, initial or privy marks; at twelve o'clock.

For some time experimental work had been going on in Europe with primitive machinery for producing coins. Since the coins produced promised well, being more regular in shape than hammered coins it was felt that a forward step was being made against coin clipping. A former workman in the Paris mint was brought over to England and machinery was set up from which was produced our first milled coinage in about 1560. The workers at the mint opposed the new methods, fearing unemployment, and the experiment came to an end after the striking of the milled coins listed above. One hundred years were to elapse before milled coins were finally to supersede the long series of hammered coins of England.

As in the reign of Edward VI a small number of pattern pieces were struck in the reign of Elizabeth I. They are all of extreme rarity and not likely to come the way of the collector, but they should be set down, just for the record.

Elizabeth I was the last of the Tudor monarchs, and with her death the Stuarts ascended the throne of England, in the person of James I.

Before we consider his coinage a word should be said about him. James I was the son of Mary, Queen of Scotland: usually known as Mary, Queen of Scots: and Henry Darnley. His mother had already been married to Francis II of France. Thus his mother had already been Queen of France for a short period before her sickly and, it is said, impotent husband died. On his death Mary returned to Scotland and married her cousin, Henry Darnley, which marriage she soon regretted. After Mary had conceived a child, later to become James VI of Scotland and James I of England, Darnley was killed in a house at Kirk o' Field, which was demolished by explosives while he was within. It has never been proved that Mary was a party to Darnley's death. Suspicion fell on her, and falls on her still, although there is no clear evidence. We cannot go into Scottish history here. It can only be said that after a colourful career Mary, Queen of Scots, who had been declared Queen of England by the French and Spanish courts, became the prisoner of Elizabeth I of England.

Elizabeth regarded Mary as a threat to her own sovereignty, and finally caused her to be beheaded in the castle of Fotheringay on 8th February, 1587. This event made her son James, in name at least, King of Scotland, as James VI. Visitors to Scotland who are conducted round such national shrines as Edinburgh Castle, in which James was born while the castle was almost under seige, will hear him referred to as James the sixth and first. On the death of Elizabeth I, James VI of Scotland set out for England, where he was proclaimed King in March 1603, and crowned in Westminster Abbey on 25th July. Thus while the political union of the two kingdoms had to wait till the reign of Queen Anne (1702–1714), James VI and I united the kingdoms by being King of both. This fact is referred to in the legends on his English coinage.

Tempting as it is to trace the complex history of the sovereigns of England and Scotland at this period, each with a background of murder, marriage and divorce, death on the block, and political intrigue, we must reluctantly confine ourselves to the considerations of the coinage of James I.

James I (1603–1625)

Son of Mary, Queen of Scots and Henry Stuart Darnley

DENOMINATIONS

First coinage (1603–1604)

Gold: Sovereign, Half-sovereign, Crown, Halfcrown.

Second coinage (1604–1619)

Gold: Rose-ryal, Spur-ryal, Angel, Half-angel, Unit, Double-crown, Britain Crown, Thistle Crown, Halfcrown.

Third coinage (1619–1625)

Gold: Rose-ryal, Spur-ryal, Angel, Laurel, Half-laurel, Quarter-laurel.

For all three periods above.

Silver: Crown, Halfcrown, Shilling, Sixpence, Half-groat, Penny, Halfpenny.

Copper: Farthing.

Basic obv. legend: IACOBUS D G ANG SCO FRAN ET HIBER REX on the first coinage.

IACOBUS D G MAG BRIT FRAN ET HIB REX on the second and third coinages.

Initial marks again play an important part and were as follows:

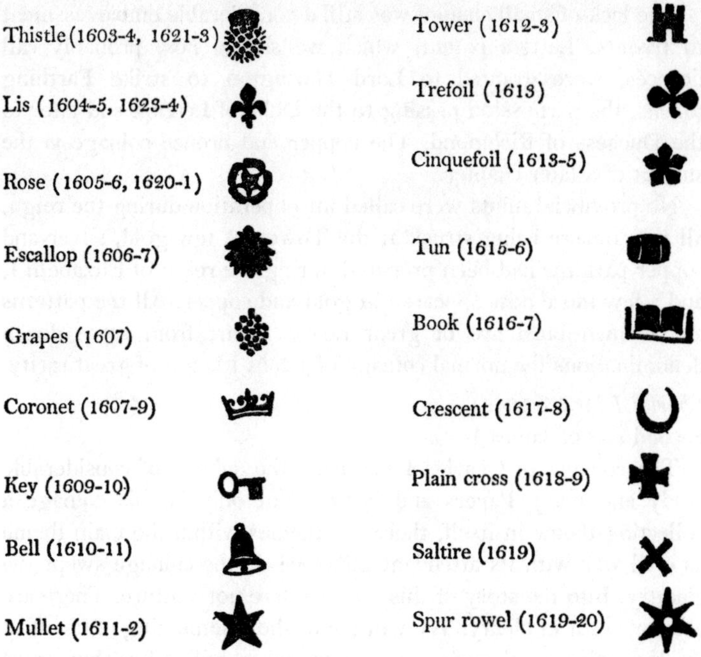

The initial marks on the coinage of James I (By courtesy of J. J. North)

Once more in this reign we get a large number of denominations. Since James was King of both Scotland and England the royal shield of arms was altered. The arms of the Scottish kingdom now appeared in the second quarter while on the first coinage SCO is added to the legend.

In the third coinage a piece which quickly became known as a Laurel was struck. On this piece, value twenty shillings, James appeared in profile with a laurel wreath, Roman style, on his head.

The Half and Quarter-laurel had a similar bust.

The practice of showing the value of a coin on the coin itself, usually in Roman figures, now began to become more firmly established. We referred above to the tentative start of this practice, but it now became more usual. Silver which was mined in Wales began to be indicated as to its source by plumes of feathers, usually above the shield of arms. This practice also continued for several reigns to come, well into the milled period of our coinage, the form of metal-source indicator varying.

The lack of small change was still a considerable embarrassment to traders. Letters patent, which we should now probably call licences, were granted to Lord Harington to strike Farthing tokens, the permission passing to the Duke of Lennox and later to the Duchess of Richmond. The copper and bronze coinage is the subject of a later chapter.

No provincial mints were called into operation during the reign, all the coinage being struck at the Tower. A few gold, silver and copper patterns had been prepared during the reign of Elizabeth I, and a few more now appeared in gold and copper. All the patterns so far mentioned are of great rarity. Apart from some dozen denominations the normal coinage of James I is not of great rarity.

Charles I (1625–1649)
Second son of James I

The coinage of Charles I has been the subject of considerable study and many Papers and books. Not only is this coinage a collecting theme in itself, there are themes within the main theme as civil war with its attendant influence on the coinage swept the country. Into the story of this war we dare not venture. There are accounts of it in plenty. We will try to show something of its effect on the coinage, though here again space will allow but scant treatment.

It was stated earlier in this section on hammered coinage that no nice orderly arrangement of presentation, reign by reign, would be possible. Even such loose rules of presentation as we have tried to follow must now largely be abandoned in the complex series with which we now have to deal. Things started smoothly enough, and the usual list of denominations and initial marks can be given.
From the Tower mint.

DENOMINATIONS

Gold: Angel, Unite, Double-crown, Britain Crown.
Silver: Crown, Halfcrown, Shilling, Sixpence, Half-groat, Penny, Halfpenny.
Copper: Farthing tokens.

Basic obv. legend: CAROLUS D G MAG BRI FR ET HIB REX

It should be explained that the denomination, Unite, a gold pound piece of this and the previous reign, refers to the uniting of the kingdoms of England and Scotland. A little confusion

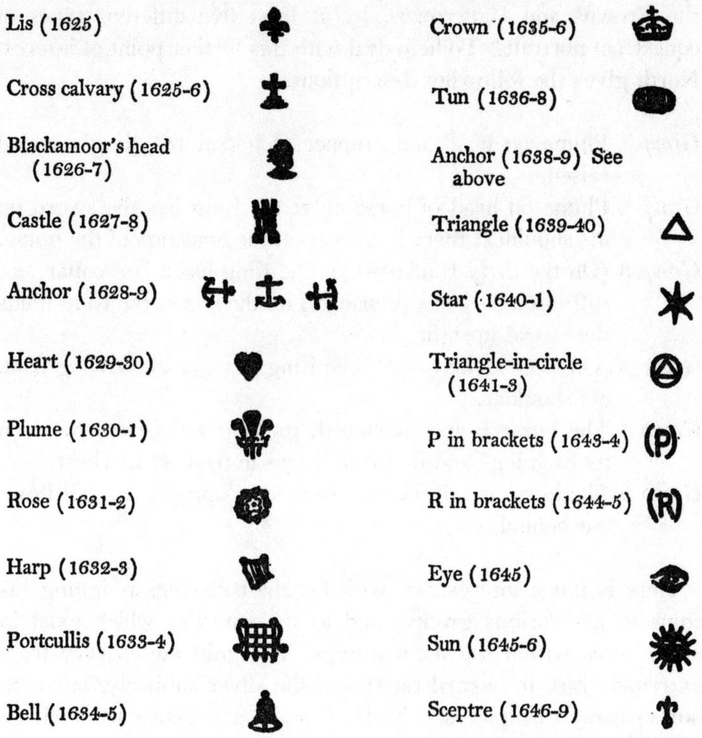

The initial marks on the coinage of Charles I (By courtesy of J. J. North)

sometimes arises, since as a pound piece it is also a unit of coinage. The Britain crown also mentioned in both reigns, was a gold piece originally of five shillings, but raised to 5s. 6d. in 1611. Though it circulated till about 1661 it was only struck in the reigns of James and Charles I.

Though it might be thought that the Tower coinage would be simple and straightforward, it is complicated by many variations of the bust and the shield of arms. Some seven busts exist, and these and the various types of shield are used to divide the coinage into various issues, while the initial marks help to date those pieces; the majority in the case of the Tower issues; which do not contain the date in Arabic figures.

The various bust varieties appear on the gold and smaller silver pieces. Matters are further complicated on the larger silver coins, the Crowns and Halfcrowns, by at least five different types of equestrian portraits. To help deal with this further point of interest North gives the following descriptions.

Group 1 Plume on head and crupper of horse: the King's sword raised.
Group 2 Plume on head of horse only: the King has the sword on his shoulder: there is a cross on the housings of the horse.
Group 3 (On the early Halfcrowns) The King has a lace collar vice ruff: no caparisons (housings) on the horse: the King holds the sword upright.
Group 3 (On later Halfcrowns) The King has a cloak flowing from his shoulder.
Group 4 The horse is foreshortened, its long tail passes between its back legs and its mane shows in front of its chest.
Group 5 The horse is tall with its head very upright. Its tail flows out behind.

Here is much interesting work for the collector, assigning his coins to the various groups, and to the varieties which exist in many cases within the main groups. The gold pieces vary from extremely rare to normal rarity and the silver similarly, but with not so many rare pieces. The Half-groats and Pence start with a type on which there is no bust. This is confined to the first type only, the remainder of the issue having busts as grouped into the seven divisions already referred to. The Halfpennies have, like the first type of Half-groats and Pence, a rose in place of a bust. With the

Plate 41 *Silver. Halfcrowns*
1–5 William and Mary, 1689–1694. The two obverse types are quite distinct. The first might almost be called the 'long neck' type. Of the three reverse types the first (3) was used in 1689 only, the second (4) in 1689 and 1690; note the difference in the shield of arms; and the third (5) was similar to the reverse of the Crown and caused the same trouble over the date figures. **6–8** William III, 1694–1702. There was really only one obverse type in general use, the first type (6), but some pieces struck in 1696 had a variety of the first obverse (7). The second type (8) was only used once in 1696 on an extremely rare piece, an example of which is in the British Museum. The first type (6) appears with the various provincial mint letters added: B C E N Y and y. **9–12** Four reverse types. Type one (9) small shields; type two (10) larger shields with early type harp; type three (11) still larger and squarer shields; type four (12) similar, with plumes in the angles.

1

2

3

4

5

6

7

8

9

10

11

12

1

2

3

4

5

6

7

8

9

10

11

12

13

Halfpence the type does not change, there being a rose on both sides, and there is no initial mark or legend. Collectors who may still be following the Penny will find the series interesting and with no great rarities among the various groups.

Copper Farthing tokens, still issued under licence, continue into this reign.

Apart from the normal Tower issues there also appeared a series of pieces usually classified as Nicholas Briot's coinage. Here again much study has been given to the series and a great deal written about it. The shortest adequate account is given by North: 'Perhaps the most notable event during this period of peace was the employment at the mint in 1625 of Nicholas Briot, who was formerly with the Paris mint. Once again the mill was introduced into England, and some examples exist of coins being struck by it from current dies. However, it is more customary to find Briot's own dies used to strike coins by machinery. He was a great artist and, besides his beautiful patterns and proofs, he engraved dies for the majority of the York coins. His influence can also be seen in the busts and equestrian figures on some Tower coins, as well as on a number struck at the provincial mints of York, Oxford, Truro and Weymouth.'

Here we see a little of the shape of things to come: the opening of provincial mints during the Civil War period. In fact Briot, who died about 1646, had quite an adventurous career in coinage. As well as his post at the Tower and his work at other mints, he held the position, for a time, of Master of the Mint in Scotland.

So far as the English coinage is concerned before the Civil War started, Briot's work at the Tower falls into three periods. These are:

First milled issue (1631–1632)

Plate 42 *Silver. Halfcrowns*
1–3 Queen Anne, 1702–1714. Three obverse types, all slightly different. The first is with and without VIGO added in 1703. **4–5** The reverse types. Pre-Union, either plain, with plumes or with roses and plumes. Post-Union either plain, with plumes or with roses and plumes. **6–8** George I, 1714–1727. One obverse type. Two reverse types the second with SSC used in 1723 only. **9–13** George II, 1727–1760. Two obverse types, young and old head, the latter with LIMA added in 1745 and 1746. Three reverse types, roses and plumes, roses and plain. There were no halfcrowns of George III in the Milled Coinage, phase one.

DENOMINATIONS

Gold: Unite, Double-crown, Crown.
Silver: Crown, Halfcrown, Shilling, Sixpence, Half-groat, Penny.

Initial marks, an anemone and letter B, or a daisy and letter B. The gold pieces are from extremely rare to rare.

Second milled issue (1638–1639)

DENOMINATIONS

Silver: Halfcrown, Shilling, Sixpence.

Initial mark, an anchor, usually with letter B. The Halfcrowns are rare, the Shillings and Sixpences scarce.

Hammered issue (1638–1639)

DENOMINATIONS

Silver: Halfcrown, Shilling.

Initial marks, an anchor and a triangle over an anchor. Both denominations are very rare.

We now come to the provincial mints, the first of which was opened before the Civil War. Thomas Bushell, an engineer-speculator at this time, convinced the government that he could drain the silver mines of Wales, thus probably being able to work to a greater depth, and that the silver extracted from them should be coined at a mint to be set up at Aberystwyth. He obtained the necessary permission, and the mint was opened in 1638, striking coins from dies prepared in London, a number of mint workers being seconded to the new mint to assist. The larger denominations have a Welsh plume on both sides, and the privy mark, a book, was that of Bushell. In 1642, the year of the start of the Civil War, Aberystwyth mint was closed and moved over to Shrewsbury. Its issues were:

ABERYSTWYTH MINT (1638–1642)

Gold: Unite. (Now attributed to Chester mint.)
Silver: Halfcrown, Shilling, Sixpence, Groat, Threepence, Half-groat, Penny, Halfpenny.

Initial marks, gold, a plume, silver, a book.

The gold Unite is extremely rare and the silver issues vary from very rare to common.

When the Aberystwyth mint moved to Shrewsbury the following denominations were struck.

SHREWSBURY MINT (1642)

Gold: Triple unite.

Silver: Pound, Half-pound, Crown, Halfcrown, Shilling.

Initial or mint mark, plume, with and without a band to hold the triple feathers together.

All the denominations are from extremely rare to rare.

The Triple unite or three pound piece is of great interest and has been, with others of the same denomination from Oxford, the purpose of a separate study. It was the gold coin of the highest exchange value in the hammered series, an obvious attempt, brought about by war, to provide a high value by minimum effort. We shall see this happen again with the silver Pound piece, the largest silver coin ever struck in the English series.

Once the Civil War had started mints appeared and disappeared as occasion demanded. They all worked for the royalist cause since London was lost at the outset, the Tower mint remained in Cromwellian hands. It continued to strike coins bearing the King's effigy. This was necessary if the coins were to gain ready acceptance. Till Charles was defeated, (still questionable when the Civil War started), he was still King. Not even Cromwell dared to usurp the King's position on the coinage till Charles was dead.

The remaining provincial mints are:

YORK MINT (1642–1644)

Silver: Halfcrown, Shilling, Sixpence, Threepence.

Initial mark, a lion.

Rarity, rare to normal.

ABERYSTWYTH (1646 or Coombe Martin mint 1647–1648)

Silver: Halfcrown, Shilling, Sixpence, Groat, Threepence, Half-groat, Penny.

Initial mark, a crown.

Rarity, extremely rare to rare.

The possible Coombe Martin mint has never been supported by documentary evidence. It remains one of those interesting numismatic and historical puzzles. Thus the above pieces are questionable as to their ancestry. It is thought that they were probably struck at Aberystwyth during the period when it was re-opened. Since hammered coins need no installation of machinery for their production a mint could be set up almost on demand.

OXFORD MINT (1642–1646)

Gold: Triple unite, Unite, Half-unite.

Silver: Pound, Half-pound, Crown, Halfcrown, Shilling, Sixpence, Groat, Threepence, Half-groat, Penny.

Mint or initial mark, plumes with band.

Rarity, extremely rare to scarce.

Since Oxford became the headquarters of the King and his supporters the issues from this mint are of the greatest interest and are of great variety. The King 'borrowed' the college plate, silverware being then the more usual table-ware among the upper classes. Many of the coins which come from this mint are probably made from such silver, thus giving them an added interest. Many of the coins carry the abbreviations OXON, or OX, and the varieties of design are numerous. Much as one would like to enlarge on them, space will not permit.

BRISTOL MINT (1643–1645)

Gold: Unite, Half-unite.

Silver: Halfcrown, Shilling, Sixpence, Groat, Threepence, Half-groat, Penny.

Mint marks: BR in monogram, a shape that could be an acorn or a pear or even a heart, a small plume, of the smaller Shrewsbury type.

Rarity: Gold extremely rare, rare to scarce except the Half-groat and Penny which are very rare and extremely rare respectively.

TRURO MINT (1642–1643)

Gold: Unite.

Silver: Half-pound, Crown, Halfcrown, Shilling.

Plate 43 Silver. Shillings
1–6 Charles II, 1660–1685. Five obverse types, all slightly different, the first used only in 1663. One reverse type only. **7–8** James II, 1685–1688. One type only. **9–10** William and Mary, 1689–1694. One type only.

1

2

3

4

5

6

7

8

9

10

1

2

3

4

5

6

7

8

9

10

11

12

13

14

15

Initial marks: A rose, a bugle.

Rarity: Gold extremely rare, silver, extremely rare to scarce.

TRURO or EXETER MINT

Silver: Halfcrown.

Initial marks: A rose.

Rarity: Extremely rare to rare.

EXETER MINT (1643–1646)

Silver: Crown, Halfcrown, Shilling, Sixpence, Groat, Threepence, Half-groat, Penny.

Initial marks: Ex, a rose, a castle.

Rarity: Extremely rare to scarce.

WEYMOUTH MINT (1643–1644)

Gold: Unite.

Silver: Halfcrown.

Mint marks: A castle, helmet, a shape that may be a leopard's head, a lion, two lions, a lis, a rose and a star. Some marks occur in the legend rather than in the usual mint mark position.

Rarity: Gold, extremely rare. Silver, very rare to rare.

SANDSFOOT CASTLE MINT (1644. Near Weymouth).

Gold: Unite.

Silver: Halfcrown.

Plate 44 Silver. Shillings

1–9 William III, 1694–1702. Seven obverse types. The second was used only once in 1696 on an extremely rare piece noted by B. A. Seaby and known as the 'hair across breast' variety. The first, third and fourth types occur with the provincial mint letters in 1696 and 1697. The fifth is known as the 'flaming hair' type and was only used briefly in 1698 and 1699, the type being rare. The sixth is known as the 'high hair' type and was used in 1699, 1700 and 1701. The seventh type has a small plume below the bust and was used in 1700 only on an extremely rare piece. There is really only one reverse type but with many minor variations. The second type (9) has the arms of Ireland and Scotland transposed and occurs on a very rare 1697 piece from the Chester temporary mint. Another with the arms of France and Ireland transposed is known from the York mint in the same year and is extremely rare. A further piece with obverse 3 from Chester with arms in the wrong order is believed to exist. The reverse can have plumes in the angles from 1698 onwards and roses are known in 1699. Lions vary in size and many minor varieties exist.

10–15 Queen Anne, 1702–1714. Four obverse types, VIGO being added to the first in 1702 and the second in 1703. The two main reverse types are pre-Union and post-Union and both can have plumes or roses and plumes added in the angles.

Initial marks: Boar's head, helmet, lis and a rose which occurs in the legend.

Rarity: Gold, extremely rare. Silver, extremely rare to rare.

WEYMOUTH or SANDSFOOT CASTLE MINT

Silver: Shilling, Sixpence, Groat, Threepence, Half-groat.

Initial marks: A bird, boar's head, a cannonball and four lis, castle, cross and four annulets, a helmet, lion, lis, a shape possibly pear, rose, a scroll (like a large flattened X).

Rarity: Extremely rare to rare, mainly very rare.

WORCESTER MINT (1646)

Silver: Halfcrown.

Initial marks: A pear on obverse: three pears on reverse. The letters H C appear on the reverse below the shield of arms.

Rarity: Very rare.

CHESTER MINT (1644)

Gold: see Aberystwyth, p. 142.

Silver: Halfcrown, Threepence.

Initial marks: Cinquefoil, plume, a gerb (wheatsheaf) on its side, three gerbs upright.

Rarity: Very rare to rare, mainly rare.

UNCERTAIN MINTS

(*a*) an extremely rare Halfcrown, mint mark two inter-linked Cs.

(*b*) 'Lundy Island', 1645–1646.

Silver: Halfcrown, Shilling, Sixpence, Groat, Threepence, Half-groat.

Mint marks: A, or A on its side, B.

Rarity: Extremely rare to scarce, mainly very rare.

A few words should be said about the doubtful mints. Worcester has never been established by documentary evidence. The initials H C point to the coins having been struck at Hartlebury Castle, the palace of the Bishop of Worcester, and a moated minor stronghold at this period. It stands still,* and is located a few miles outside Kidderminster, and might thus be remote enough from Worcester city to be used as a mint. It could base its claim as the Worcester mint on its official standing as the Bishop's residence.

* Part of it is the Worcester County Museum.

Lundy Island also has never been authenticated as a mint. Certainly Thomas Bushell, mentioned above, was in the island, and there were some plans for making it a stronghold for the King. There is no documentary evidence that coins were ever struck on the island, and present opinion favours Appledore (A mint mark), and Barnstaple or Bideford (B mint mark). As shown, one type of Halfcrown may have been struck at either Exeter or Truro. Activities at Weymouth and Sandsfoot Castle, nearby, overlap. Certainly it would be better strategy to establish a mint in a castle rather than in a town when the former was available, even at some distance from the actual town itself, c.f. Hartlebury Castle. The Halfcrown from the Uncertain mint (*a*) has been attributed, with no evidence, to Coventry or Corfe Castle, Dorset. We shall probably never know its true origin. All such problems add spice to the interest of collecting.

Finally in this series we come to the Siege pieces, struck in towns and/or castles which, while under siege ran out of money and were forced to produce coins of their own, usually from domestic plate. In a few cases the hallmark or parts of the original design still remain on the pieces. They were struck in a variety of denominations and in a number of shapes, as will be seen. Of all the places besieged Scarborough produced the most fantastic series of denominations, and a word will be said about them in a moment. Taking the besieged towns or castles in alphabetical order the picture is as follows.

CARLISLE. Besieged from October 1644 till June 1645. Coins struck in May 1645.

DENOMINATIONS

Silver: Three Shillings, circular.
Shilling, circular or octagonal.

Rarity: Extremely rare and very rare.

COLCHESTER. Besieged from June till August 1648.

DENOMINATIONS

Gold: Ten shillings, circular.

Rarity: Extremely rare.

NEWARK. Besieged several times, finally surrendered on 6th May, 1646.

DENOMINATIONS

Silver: Halfcrown, Shilling, Ninepence, Sixpence, all diamond shaped.

Rarity: Rare or scarce. Of all the siege pieces these are probably the least rare. The modern town of Newark-on-Trent takes pride in its collection of its siege pieces, though many of the collection were stolen in recent times. The town has also a fine exhibit of Charles I gold coins from a local find, arranged, for presentation as part of the Civic Plate, by the writer of this book.

PONTEFRACT. Besieged June 1648 to March 1649.

DENOMINATIONS

Gold: Unite, of octagonal shape.

Silver: Two shillings, of diamond shape.
Shilling, shaped diamond, round or octagonal.

Rarity: Gold, extremely rare, silver, the Two Shillings extremely rare, the Shilling, rare.

A point of interest here is that the silver coins show the castle gateway. From the window of the right-hand tower protrudes a hand, brandishing a sword, in defiance. On some pieces this is replaced by a cannon: both postulating defiance to the Cromwellian army.

SCARBOROUGH. Besieged from July 1644 till July 1645.

DENOMINATIONS

Silver: Five Shillings and Eightpence: Five Shillings: Three Shillings and Fourpence: Three Shillings: Two Shillings and Tenpence: Two Shillings and Sixpence: Two Shillings and Fourpence: Two Shillings and Twopence: Two Shillings: One Shilling and Ninepence: One Shilling and

Plate 45 Silver. Shillings
1–6 George I, 1714–1727. Two obverse types, the difference being that the second has a looped tie. It can occur with and without W.C.C. added. Of the four reverse types the third (5) is only used in 1723 and can occur on a very rare piece with the arms of France at the top. The second type (4) was used only in 1720 and 1721 while the fourth (6) is only used from 1723 till 1726 in conjunction with obverse two with the letters W.C.C. **7–12** George II, 1727–1760. Two obverse types, young and old head, with LIMA added to the latter in 1745 and 1746. Four reverse types; plumes; roses and plumes; plain; roses only.

1

2

3

4

5

6

7

8

9

10

11

12

GEORGIVS · III DEI · GRATIA ·

1

GEORGIVS · III · DEI · GRATIA ·

2

GEOR:III D:G: BRITT:REX F:D:
1816

3

4

1787

5

1787

6

7

Sixpence: One Shilling and Fourpence: One Shilling and Threepence: One Shilling and Twopence: One Shilling and One Penny: One Shilling: Elevenpence: Tenpence: Eightpence: Sevenpence: Sixpence: Fourpence.

Rarity: All extremely rare.

The explanation of this bewildering series of denominations is that the value of the coins was decided by the intrinsic value of the silver from which they were made. In fact this is coinage production method in reverse. Instead of a predetermined weight of silver being struck into a Penny or a Shilling, when a coin had been struck its value was set by its silver value, thus giving rise to this long list of unusual denominations.

A number of gold and silver pattern pieces were struck, in spite of the Civil War, and are of the greatest rarity. Copper Farthing patterns were also struck, all very rare or rare coins. Aberystwyth and Oxford mints also produced some silver or gold and silver patterns, respectively, all extremely rare pieces.

Thus, very briefly, the coinage of a period of the greatest interest: a coinage that has been a collecting theme for many collectors. One would have wished to give more detail, had space permitted, but the collector is assured that there are many works of reference available for his use. A collecting theme the coinage of Charles I is probably the most interesting and stimulating of all the possible themes in English coinage. A theme which collectors of like mind get together to discuss, one which is the subject of Papers before the learned Societies and on which much interesting research work still has to be carried out.

THE COMMONWEALTH OF ENGLAND (1649–1660)

DENOMINATIONS

Gold: Unite, Double-crown, Crown.

Plate 46 Silver. Shillings

1–7 George III, 1760–1820. Three obverse types, the first only used with the first reverse type (4) to produce the 'Northumberland' Shilling of 1763. The third obverse type properly belongs to the section 'Milled Coinage phase two'. Three reverse types, the first explained above. The difference between the second (5) and third (6) is that in the former there are a number of tiny hearts round the animal in the second canton of the arms of the Electorate (9 o'clock position). These are omitted in the third reverse. The fourth reverse (7) only occurs with the third obverse and belongs to the next milled coinage phase.

Silver: Crown, Halfcrown, Shillings, Sixpence, Half-groat, Penny, Halfpenny.

Legends

Obv.: THE COMMONWEALTH OF ENGLAND.

Rev.: GOD WITH US followed by the date in Arabic figures.

Initial marks: A radiant sun, 1649–1657. an upright anchor, 1658–1660.

Rarity: Very rare to normal.

From the point of view of design a dull, colourless coinage. The sequence of the legends soon gave rise to the jibe that Cromwell had placed England (and himself) first: on the obverse: and God second: on the reverse.

The coins of the Commonwealth period were still produced by the hammering method, though this was now well on its way to oblivion.

Under the Commonwealth which, it soon appeared, was to take the shape of a military dictatorship, the country remained restless. It is said that Cromwell was offered the crown of England, which he refused. The Council of Officers, for reasons which we cannot detail here, decided to make a single person head of the government. Cromwell was accordingly installed Lord Protector on 16th December, 1653, to govern with the aid of a permanent Council and a Parliament, which was to be summoned every three years. One can see dimly through this that the country was not yet ready to assimilate a state of democracy, such as we know today: that it still felt the need for the guidance of one hand, advised by a parliament. A coinage, now designated as patterns, was prepared for Oliver Cromwell as Protector. Most of its denominations are dated 1656 or 1658. The Protectorate came to an end with the death of Cromwell on 3rd September, 1658, before the 'Oliver Cromwell' coinage could have come into general circulation.

Even so the coinage of this Commonwealth/Cromwell period is one full of interest and of problems. Part of the problems were the subject of a Paper at the British Numismatic Society in June 1966, and recorded in the Journal.

There is but one more short period of hammered coinage, that of the first two years of the reign of Charles II, left to be considered. For the purpose of completing the hammered series the coins issued are set out in the form adopted as far as possible for the coins of the hammered period.

Charles II (1660–1685)
Eldest son of Charles I
Hammered coinage (1660–1662)

DENOMINATIONS

Gold: Unite, Double-crown, Crown.
Silver: Halfcrown, Shilling, Sixpence, Groat, Half-groat, Penny.

Basic obv. legend: CAROLUS II D G MAG BRIT FRAN ET HIB REX.

Rarity: Gold, very rare to rare. Silver, very rare to common, but very difficult to find in Extremely Fine condition.

This was the last effort of the hammered coinage. As has already been seen, milled coins had received a certain amount of experimental work, and might have come into general use earlier but for opposition within the mint and the unsettled state of the country.

With the Restoration, and Charles II ascending the throne, great changes were to take place. These changes were not solely confined to the coinage. In 1665 the Great Plague of London swept away large numbers of citizens. This was the last and probably the worst visitation of the Bubonic plague, which had been a constant scourge to the unsanitary medieval cities of England, and London in particular. London was growing in size and population, but without proper water supply, drainage and pest control. Indeed the effluent of the town was to be poured into the Thames for another two hundred years before proper drainage was to be provided.

As though the Great Plague was not enough, in 1666 came the Great Fire of London, which swept away much of the very City itself and which, disastrous as it was, no doubt cleansed the whole midden of medieval London. A new city had to be built, and it was built on more generous lines, with stone replacing wood and wider streets admitting more sunlight and air. Just as the late war, with all its loss and suffering, gave damaged cities the chance to rebuild on more modern lines, so the Great Fire laid the foundations of a City that was to last till 1940.

The new coinage was already in being as the new City began to rise. New ideas were afoot in the reign of Charles II, and a start was made with the re-building of medieval ideas and medieval England.

During the short hammered coinage period of the reign the gold Unite, Double-crown and Crown appeared for the last time. Though the names of the silver pieces remained the coins themselves were 'modernized'. The first mechanical revolution in our coinage took place, the whole structure of the denominations was simplified, and a chapter of coinage history over one thousand years long closed. Modern England was being born.

SUMMARY

In dealing with the hammered coinage of England we have bridged a vast period of time. In the briefest possible way a guide has, it is hoped, been given to the collector. Having come so far, the reader will appreciate the large number of collecting themes that exist in this one period alone. A few have been offered, such as the Penny, which has come through with us from the beginning. Because of the complexities of our hammered coinage, reflecting the panorama of a country's history, nothing more than a guide to possibilities has been given. Thus, only a brief guide can be given concerning further books which the collector will have to consult. From the following standard works the collector will not only be able to study the series in greater detail, but will find in them the large bibliography on which they are based and thus be able to get to the roots of any particular facet of hammered coin collecting which may have had an interest for him. The springboard into further research of English hammered coinage consists basically of two planks:

BROOKE, G. C. *English Coins.*
NORTH, J. J. *English Hammered Coinage. Vol. I. Early Anglo-Saxon to Henry III, circa* 650–1272.
Vol. II, Edward I to Charles II, 1272–1662.

These two works will give the collector all he needs in following and dealing with our hammered coinage. Both contain exhaustive bibliographies to help the collector who would plumb the depths of a thousand years of coinage history.

Since the publication of North's work the following books or Papers have appeared, and are recommended for further reading:

BLUNT, C. E., LYON, C.S.S. & STEWART, B.H.I.H. *The Coinage of Southern England*, 796–840. British Numismatic Journal, 1963.

DOLLEY, R. H. M. *Anglo-Saxon Pennies.*

DOLLEY, R. H. M. *Viking Coins of the Danelaw and of Dublin.*

DOLLEY, R. H. M. *The Norman Conquest and the English Coinage.*

MACK, R. P. *Stephen and the Anarchy*. B.N.J., 1966.

NORTH, J. J. *The Coinage of Edward I and II.*

POTTER, W. J. W. & WINSTANLEY, E. J. *The Coinage of Henry VII.* B.N.J. 1961, 1962 & 1963.

POTTER, W. J. W. *The Coinages of Richard II, Henry IV and Henry V.* B.N.J. 1959 & 1960.

PURVEY, F. *The Pence, Halfpence and Farthings of Richard II of the mints of London, York and Durham.* B.N.J. 1962.

CHAPTER FIVE

Milled Coinage, Phase One

During the many years through which we have travelled in tracing briefly the story of our coinage England has become Britain. James I, as has been seen, united the thrones of England and Scotland, and during the reign of Queen Anne (1702–1714) the political union of the two ancient kingdoms was achieved. We have not yet reached this second stage, but it is close upon us. When Charles II was restored to the throne of England, Scotland still had its separate coinage, with which we shall deal in due time. As has been suggested, the seeds of modern Britain were sown in travail during that reign. Just as great changes came upon the country, so great changes came upon the coinage.

It has been seen that various experiments connected with the production of coinage by machinery had been going on for a very long time. But for mistrust within the Tower mint and but for civil war, milled coins might well have been accepted long before 1662. Enough has been written elsewhere about the reasons why milled coinage was adopted, and enough has been said elsewhere about the primitive machines from which these coins were produced. It will therefore be assumed that the collector has studied this part of the subject. Thus we can come at once to the coinage itself.

The milled coinage of England; Britain after Queen Anne: falls quite easily into two phases. Phase One, now under consideration, started with the introduction of milled coins in 1662, and continued till the Royal Mint, housed in the Tower of London from remote times till August 1812, moved to its new buildings on Little Tower Hill. The move had been undertaken in stages, and the date given is that when 'finally the balance of the premises was surrendered for housing sick and wounded soldiers, and the Mint keys formally handed to the constable.' (Craig, *The Mint*). Reference to the sick and wounded soldiers recalls the fact that in 1812 the Napoleonic wars were in full swing and that hospitals as we now know them were non-existant.

Phase one of our milled coinage therefore covers the period

1662–1812. The Tower mint in which it was struck consisted of a series of rooms or departments which lay roughly in a half circle just inside the main walls of the Tower. From the point at which the visitor of today enters the Tower, the mint offices extended from the river, round the inside of the ramparts, gradually extending over the centuries till they reached the river at the eastern end of the outer walls.

In this age of factory planning and of time and motion studies, such an arrangement for a 'factory' (for the Mint is none other), must seem inconvenient and wasteful of effort. In fact there had been little 'planning' in the modern industrial sense, the Mint, 'just growed'. From this inconvenient arrangement of industrial premises the coins in phase one of our milled coinage were produced.

In the earlier pages of this book stress was laid on the fact that it was impossible to present the various coinages in neat packages. With the re-organization of the denominations into a compact series such a representation now becomes possible. We will attempt to use such a presentation to the full.

Milled Coinage, phase one. 1662–1816

THE KINGS AND QUEENS

Charles II (1660–1685)
Eldest son of Charles I and Henrietta Maria.
James II (1685–1688)
Second son of Charles I and Henrietta Maria: younger brother of Charles II, Lord High Admiral and much respected for his seamanship. *vide* Pepys.
William and Mary (1689–1694)
Joint monarchy. William, son of William II, Prince of Orange and Mary, daughter of Charles I of England. Queen Mary, daughter of James II, when Duke of York.
William III (1694–1702)
Son of William II, as above.
Anne (1702–1714)
Second daughter of James II (as Duke of York) and Anne Hyde.
George I (1714–1727)
Son of Ernest Augustus of Hanover and Sophia, daughter of

Frederick V, Elector Palatine, and grand-daughter of James I of England. (Hence the somewhat tenuous link that brought him to the throne of Great Britain).

George II (1727–1760)
Son of George I.

George III (1760–1820)
Son of Frederick, Prince of Wales and grandson of George II.

THE COINAGE

With the advent of milled coinage a large number of denominations, particularly the more complicated gold, disappeared. A certain amount of streamlining took place both in the number of denominations and their relationship to each other.

DENOMINATIONS

Gold: Five Guineas, Two Guineas, Guinea, Half Guinea, Third Guinea, Quarter Guinea.

Silver: Crown, Halfcrown, Shilling, Sixpence, Fourpence, Threepence, Twopence, Penny.

Copper: (and sometimes tin). Halfpenny, Farthing.

Not all the denominations shown were struck in every reign.

In this range of coinage the Guinea was the unit or pound piece. It is said to have taken its name from the fact that the metal from which it was made came from Guinea in Africa, and from the Gold

Plate 47 *Silver. Sixpences*
1–2 Charles II, 1660–1685. One type only. **3–4** James II, 1685–1688. One type only. **5–6** William and Mary, 1689–1694. One type only, struck in 1693 and 1694. The unusual placing of the date once more gave trouble to the die-cutter. In 1693 a variety is known with the 3 over a 3 upside down. **7–13** William III, 1694–1702. Here again, as with the previous silver denominations of the reign, there are a large number of main differences and almost endless small varieties. The differences in the five busts are obvious enough. The provincial mint letters, B C E N Y and y occur with bust 1 (7), 2 (8), and 4 (10). Bust 3 (9) occurs only once on an extremely rare piece of 1696. The coin may have been a pattern. An example is in the British Museum. Obverse 5 (11) has a small plume below the bust, as on the Shilling. It was only used once, in 1700: as the Shilling: on an extremely rare piece. The two reverse types are distinguished in the main by the early harp (12) and the late type of harp (13). While the first type has large crowns above the four shields, on the second type the crowns may be either large or small. **14–16** Queen Anne, 1702–1714. One obverse type only, with VIGO added in 1703. Two reverse types, pre-Union and post-Union. Both types may be plain, with plumes or with roses and plumes in the angles between the shields.

1

2

3

4

5

6

7

8

9

10

11

12

13

14

15

16

1

2

3

4

5

6

7

8

9

10

11

12

13

14

15

16

Coast African regions in general. The design was simple, the obverse being occupied by the head of the monarch and the reverse by a shield or shields of arms, in various forms. The coins bore their date of issue in Arabic figures (apart from the Gothic Crowns and Florins) and can thus be set down in classified form.

FIVE GUINEAS

Charles II (1660–1685)

Five main obverse types:

1 With pointed truncation to neck. Lovelock on shoulder.
2 Similar with an elephant below signifying that the gold came from the Africa Company.
3 Similar, but with an elephant and castle, having the same significance.
4 With rounded truncation and no lovelock on shoulder.
5 Similar, with elephant and castle.

Reverse type:

One only. Four crowned shields of arms, of England, Scotland, France and Ireland. Four sceptres in saltire with four interlinked Cs in the centre of the field.

Dates of issue:

1668	Obv.	type	1.	1674	Obv.	type	1.
	,,	,,	2.	1675	,,	,,	1.
1669	,,	,,	1.		,,	,,	2.
	,,	,,	2.		,,	,,	3.
1670	,,	,,	1.	1676	,,	,,	1.
1671	,,	,,	1.		,,	,,	3.
1672	,,	,,	1.	1677	,,	,,	1.
1673	,,	,,	1.		,,	,,	3.

Plate 48 *Silver. Sixpences*
1–4 George I, 1714–1727. The difference between the two obverse types is that the lettering on the second is slightly smaller than that on the first. This obverse appears to have been used only in 1723 in conjunction with reverse two: S S C. Large lettering on pieces of this date are rare. Reverse two (4) was only used in 1723. **5–11** George II, 1727–1760. Three obverse types, young head, old head and old head with LIMA added in 1745 and 1746 only. The differences in the four reverse types will, by now, be obvious to the reader. **12–16** George III, 1760–1820. The second obverse type belongs to Milled Coinage, phase two. The difference between the first (14) and second (15) reverses is as for the Shilling; with and without hearts in the arms of the Electorate. The third reverse (16) occurs only with the second obverse.

Dates of issue:

1678	Obv. type 1.	1681	Obv. type 5.
	,, ,, 3.	1682	,, ,, 4.
	,, ,, 4.		,, ,, 5.
1679	,, ,, 4.	1683	,, ,, 4.
1680	,, ,, 4.		,, ,, 5.
	,, ,, 5.	1684	,, ,, 4.
1681	,, ,, 4.		,, ,, 5.

James II (1685–1688)

Two main obverse types:

1 Plain.

2 With Elephant and castle.

Two main reverse types:

1 Four crowned shields of arms, England, Scotland, France and Ireland. Four sceptres in saltire, placed in the wrong order.

2 As above, but the sceptres in the correct order.

Dates of issue:

1686	Obv. type 1.	Rev. type 1.
1687	,, ,, 1.	,, ,, 2.
	,, ,, 2.	,, ,, 2.
1688	,, ,, 1.	,, ,, 2.
	,, ,, 2.	,, ,, 2.

William & Mary (1688–1694)

Two main obverse types:

1 Plain.

2 With elephant and castle.

Reverse type:

Shield of arms, crowned.

Date of issue:

1691	Obv. types 1 and 2.	1693	Obv. types 1 and 2.
1692	,, ,, 1 ,, 2.	1694	,, ,, 1 ,, 2.

William III (1694–1702)

Three main obverse types:

1 Bust of first type.

2 Similar, with elephant and castle.

3 Bust of second type, usually known as the 'fine work' type on account of the much greater clarity of detail.

Reverse type:
Four crowned shields of arms, England, Scotland, France and Ireland. Four sceptres in saltire. Lion of Nassau in centre of flan.

Dates of issue:
1699 Obv. types 1 and 2.
1700 Obv. type 1.
1701 Obv. type 3.

Anne (1702–1714)
Four main obverse types:
1 With the word VIGO under the bust, signifying that the metal was part of the small amount of gold captured at the Battle of Vigo Bay, 1702.
2 Similar, but without the word Vigo.
3 Same bust but lettering of legend larger.
4 A new, broader bust.

Four main reverse types:
1 Four shields of arms, crowned; England, Scotland, France and Ireland. Four sceptres in saltire, a rose in the centre of the flan.
2 After the political union with Scotland. The shields of arms now are, England and Scotland dimidiate, France, England and Scotland dimidiate, Ireland. Star of the Most Noble Order of the Garter in centre of flan.
3 Similar, but with broader crowns and larger lettering.
4 Similar to 2, with small crowns but larger lettering.

Dates of issue

1703	Obv.	type	1.	Rev.	type	1.
1705	”	”	2.	”	”	1.
1706	”	”	2.	”	”	1.
	”	”	2.	”	”	2.
1709	”	”	3.	”	”	3.
1711	”	”	4.	”	”	4.
1713	”	”	4.	”	”	4.
1714	”	”	4.	”	”	4.

George I (1714–1727)
One obverse type only, with head to right.
One reverse type only. Four shields of arms, crowned. England and Scotland dimidiate, France, Ireland and Hanover.

Dates of issue:

1716	1720
1717	1726

George II (1727–1760)

Four main obverse types:

1 Young head, plain.

2 Similar, with E I C below, signifying that the metal was provided by the Honourable East India Company.

3 Old head, with the word LIMA below. The significance of the word has been so often misexplained that the reader is directed to consult Spink & Son's Numismatic Circular, 1965–6–7, for the facts, set out in a series of notes by Anthony Thompson and the author, under the title, 'Why Lima'.

4 Similar, but without Lima.

Reverse types:

One only. Crowned shield of arms.

Dates of issue:

1729 Obv. types 1 and 2.	1741 Obv. type 1.
1730 Obv. type 1.	1746 ,, ,, 3.
1731 ,, ,, 1	1748 ,, ,, 4.
1735 ,, ,, 1.	1753 ,, ,, 4.
1738 ,, ,, 1.	

Plate 49 *Milled Coinage, phase two,* 1816 *to date. Gold*

1–2 George III, 1760–1820. Sovereign, the ancestor of the present coin of that name, first struck in 1817, with St. George and dragon, by Benedetto Pistrucci, in its original form, within the Garter border. **3–4** George IV, 1820–1830. Two Pound piece, 1823, probably the only coin of this denomination struck for and actually put into circulation. **5–8** The two types of Sovereign of George IV. Numbers 5 and 7 couple to form type one, by Pistrucci, with the obverse which the king so much disliked. Numbers 6 and 8 couple to form type two, the head by Wyon, after Chantrey's bust; the reverse by Wyon. **9** William IV, 1830–1837. One type of Sovereign only. The reverse was similar to that of George IV, type two, but had no legend apart from the date, ANNO 1831 (till 1837). **10–14** Queen Victoria, 1837–1901. The five obverse types of Sovereign. The first (10) the young head; the second (11) similar, but with a different wreath. Obverse three (12) again similar but with a new legend. When obverse three was coupled to reverse three in 1871 (see below) the whole legend had to be concentrated on the obverse. Obverse four (13) is the 1887 Jubilee head and obverse five (14) the old head. **15–17** The three reverse types. Reverse two (16) was used only once, in 1843, coupled with obverse two (11), also used once only, (very rare). Reverse three (17) was first used in 1871 and after 1874 was the only type used. From then onwards the St. George and dragon became the traditional reverse of the Sovereign. **18–19** Edward VII, 1901–1910. One type only.

1

2

3

4

5

6

7

8

9

10

11

12

13

14

15

16

17

18

19

1

2

3

4

5

6

7

8

9

10

11

12

13

14

15

16

17

18

19

20

George III (1760–1820)

There were no Five Guinea pieces struck in this reign.

It will be appreciated that in listing the Five Guinea pieces struck during phase one of the milled coinage, only the main varieties have been given. Quite a lot of minor varieties occur. These take such forms as misplaced letters in the edge legends, dates overstruck on those of the previous year, and similar minor varieties.

Some twenty years ago it could have been said that the Five Guinea pieces fell into a number of rarity catagories. In proportion with other issues, some were reasonably scarce. It is probably true to say that at the present time all these pieces are very rare and expensive. They could and do still form a collecting theme, with the Two Guinea pieces about to be catalogued, but only for a collector of ample means. Of all the Five Guinea pieces that of Queen Anne with VIGO below the bust is probably the greatest rarity. It commands four figures in auction sales.

TWO GUINEAS

Charles II (1660–1685)

Four main obverse types:

1 With pointed truncation to neck, lovelock on shoulder.
2 Similar, but with elephant below bust.
3 Rounded truncation, no lovelock.
4 Similar, with elephant and castle below bust.

Reverse, type 1 only:

Plate 50 *Gold. Half Sovereigns*

1–2 George III, 1760–1820. The first Half Sovereign, of one type only, struck in 1817, 1818 and 1820. **3–7** George IV, 1820–1830. Two obverse types, the first (3) by Pistrucci, the second (4) by Wyon after Chantrey's bust. Three reverse types, the first (5) with rose, shamrock and thistle emblems surrounding the shield; the second (6) with a plain ungarnished shield with emblems below; the third (7) a similar square shield, garnished. **8–11** William IV, 1830–1837. Two obverse and two reverse types, which marry up. 8 and 10 make the small size Half Sovereign, struck only in 1834. 9 and 11 make up the normal size piece. A variety exists in 1836 with a slightly larger head of the king. It was struck from the die normally used for the Sixpence. **12–16** Victoria, 1837–1901. Three obverse types, young head (12); Jubilee head (13); old head (14). The reverse types: shield (15), St. George and dragon after Pistrucci (16). Young and Jubilee heads couple with reverse one; old head with reverse two. **17–18** Edward VII, 1901–1910. One type only. **19–20** George V, 1910–1936. One type only.

Four shields of arms, crowned, England, Scotland, France and Ireland. Four sceptres in saltire, four interlinked Cs in centre of flan.

Dates of issue:

1664 Obv. type 1.
,, ,, 2.
1665 ,, ,, 1.
1669 ,, ,, 1.
1671 ,, ,, 1.
1675 ,, ,, 3.
1676 ,, ,, 3.
,, ,, 4.
1677 ,, ,, 3.
1678 ,, ,, 3.
,, ,, 4.
,, ,, 5.
(This piece is so rare that though it is known it was not listed above under the main obverse types.)

1679 Obv. type 3.
1680 ,, ,, 3.
1681 ,, ,, 3.
1682 ,, ,, 3.
,, ,, 4.
1683 ,, ,, 3.
,, ,, 4.
1684 ,, ,, 3.
,, ,, 4.

James II (1685–1688)

One obverse and reverse type only, the reverse as for the Five Guineas, with sceptres correctly placed.

Dates of issue:

1687
1688
This piece is believed only to exist with the 8 superimposed on the 7, traces of which figure can be seen.

William & Mary (1688–1694)

Two main obverse types:

1 With an elephant and castle below the busts.
2 With no elephant and castle.

Reverse, type 1 only:

Crowned shield of arms.

Dates of issue:

1691 Obv. type 1.
1693 ,, ,, 1.
,, ,, 2.
1694 ,, ,, 2. the 4 over 3.
,, ,, 1. ,, 4 ,, 3.

William III (1694–1702)

One obverse and reverse type only. The obverse bust strongly resembles the 3rd obv. of the £5 5s., the 'fine work' type. The reverse is similar to the larger denomination but the crests of the sceptres are more pronounced and the harp in the arms differs completely.

Date of issue:
1701 only.

Anne (1702–1714)

One obverse and reverse type only. The obv. is similar to type 2 of the £5 5s., the rev. to the post-union type 2 of the larger denomination.

Dates of issue:

1709	1713
1711	1714

George I (1714–1727)

One obverse and reverse type only, similar to the £5 5s.

Dates of issue:

1717	1726
1720	

George II (1727–1760)

Three main obverse types:

1 Young head.
2 An intermediate, older head.
3 Old head.

Two main reverse types:

1 A crowned shield of arms, as used on a pattern £2. 2s. struck in 1733, and only used once in the currency issue.
2 Similar, but with a different shape of crown and a somewhat squarer shield.

Dates of issue:

1734 Obv. type 1. Rev. type 1.
1734 „ „ 1. „ „ 2.
1735 „ „ 1. „ „ 2.
1738 „ „ 1. „ „ 2.

Dates of issue:
1739 Obv. type 1. Rev. type 2.
1739 „ „ 1. „ „ 2.
1740 „ „ 2. „ „ 2.
1748 „ „ 3. „ „ 2.
1753 „ „ 3. „ „ 2.

George III (1760–1820)
There were no Two Guinea pieces struck during this reign.

It can be observed once more that, some years ago the Two Guinea pieces were catalogued under various degrees of rarity. Now all such pieces are very rare and costly. Possibly the rarest of them all apart from the legendary 1678, obv. type 5, is the 1734, obv. and rev. 1 piece, which was extremely rare at any cataloguing period. Not a collecting theme in themselves, the Two Guineas march with the Five Guineas as coins that should be represented in the cabinet of the more opulent collector.

For purposes of comparison it should be stated that the Five and Two Guinea pieces of this period were not usually to be found in general circulation. The parallel is, perhaps, that at the present time few people carry £100 notes in their wallets. The fine and rare pieces just described probably represented the millions with which the financiers of the time bargained, just as now they bargain over the possession of Sovereigns, Twenty-Dollar pieces and gold bars, moved from one strongroom to another.

The same cannot be said of the Guineas and Half Guineas, about to be dealt with. The Guinea was the pound unit, and can be considered as a coin actually passing from hand to hand in increasing numbers till, when we reach the reign of George III, it appears to

Plate 51 *Silver. Crowns*
1–2 George III, 1760–1820. The only type of Crown struck in this reign, with the original conception of St. George and dragon within the Garter, as designed by Pistrucci. **3–4** George IV, 1820–1830. The only type of Crown struck in this reign; the St. George enlarged and the Garter eliminated. William IV, 1830–1837. No Crowns struck for general circulation; only patterns exist. **5–8** Victoria, 1836–1901. Four obverse types: young head (5); 'Gothic' obverse (6); Jubilee head (7); old head (8). **9–11** Three reverse types. Type one (9) couples with young head (5); type two (10) couples with 6 to produce the 'Gothic' Crown; type three (11) couples with 7 and 8 to produce the Jubilee Crown and the old head Crown.

1

2

3

4

5

6

7

8

9

10

11

EDWARDVS VII DEI GRA: BRITT: OMN: REX FID: DEF: IND: IMP:

1

1902

2

GEORGIVS V DEI GRA: BRITT: OMN: REX

3

GEORGIVS V. DG. BRITT: OMN: REX. FD. IND: IMP:

4

FID: DEF: IND: IMP:
1927
CROWN

5

CROWN 1935

6

VICTORIA DEI GRATIA

7

1887
BRITT: REG: FID: DEF:

8

have been a fairly common coin. From the collector's point of view the so-called Spade Guinea was once the commonest of all the Guineas. The fact that both Guineas and Half Guineas are now scarce or rare pieces rests on various factors. Of the many types issued during phase one of the milled coinage, some have always been rare. Such pieces aside, the logical process of calling in and melting down Guineas and Half Guineas of earlier reigns, and re-issuing the same metal as a coin of a later reign is a fairly obvious method of economic conservation of assets, reducing the outlay needed to purchase new metal. Though, as we shall see when looking at the silver coins of this Charles II–George II/III period, a certain amount of this metal was still being produced in Britain, gold mining in the British Isles had ceased to be an economic method of metal production. The existence of the Elephant or Elephant and Castle mark, and the very name of the Guinea itself does much to underline this assumption. Naturally the bullion market could always supply a certain amount of 'second-hand' gold. In an age when gold domestic plate was still in limited use, certain of it, when broken or damaged would find its way to the melting pot and so, probably, to the mint through the hands of the bullion dealers and goldsmiths. If this is so its identity has been lost, submerged among the imported Guinea gold.

If we accept the assumption that the Guinea and Half Guinea were coins in reasonable day-to-day use, it will follow that many more types and varieties were issued than was the case with the Five and Two Guinea pieces. While the Guineas and Half Guineas form a possible collecting theme open to the rich but not necessarily opulent collector, their many types prevent them from being catalogued in the same detail as has been done with the larger denominations.

Thus we have arrived once more at the point where we must cut back on detail. The collector may look for varieties similar to those of the larger denominations, but carried several stages further,

Plate 52 Silver. Crowns. Four Shillings
1–2 Edward VII, 1901–1910. One type only, struck in 1902. **3–6** George V, 1910–1936. Two obverse are reverse types. Obverse type one (3) couples with reverse type one (5); obverse type two (4) couples with reverse type two (6) to produce the Jubilee Crown, struck in 1935 only. **7–8** Victoria, 1837–1901. An attempt at a Four Shilling piece or Double Florin, struck only in 1887, 1888, 1889 and 1890.

since more dies and more variations follow the greater demand for the basic unit coin and its subdivisions. Elephants and Castles, pointed and rounded truncations, young and old heads continue to appear. On the reverses similar types: the four shields of arms, or the single crowned shield parallel the reverses used in the various reigns on the larger denominations.

GUINEAS

Charles II.

Nine obverse types:

1 Pointed truncation.
2 Similar with elephant below.
3 Pointed truncation with deep indentation.
4 Similar with elephant below.
5 Pointed truncation deeply indented, the front steeply sloping.
6 Similar with elephant below.
7 Rounded truncation, reaching to the edge of the coin, the face more lined.
8 Similar with elephant and castle below.
9 Similar with elephant only below.

One reverse type:

Four crowned shields of arms, sceptres in saltire, interlinked Cs in the centre; as for the larger denominations.

Dates of issue:

1663	Obv.	types	1 and 2.	1674	Obv.	types	7 and 8.
1664	,,	,,	3, 4, 5, and 6.	1675	,,	,,	7 and 8.
1665	,,	,,	5 and 6.	1676	,,	,,	7 and 8.
1666	,,	,,	5.	1677	,,	,,	7, 8 and 9.
1667	,,	,,	5.	1678	,,	,,	7, 8 and 9.
1668	,,	,,	5 and 6.	1679	,,	,,	7 and 8.
1669	,,	,,	5.	1680	,,	,,	7 and 8.
1670	,,	,,	5.	1681	,,	,,	7 and 8.
1671	,,	,,	5.	1682	,,	,,	7 and 8.
1672	,,	,,	5 and 7.	1683	,,	,,	7 and 8.
1673	,,	,,	5 and 7.	1684	,,	,,	7 and 8.

Notes. All these Guineas are now very or extremely rare. Many minor varieties exist. The tie on the king's hair varies in its position and in 1673 and 1675 a variety is known reading CRAOLVS. The new coinage had still to settle down into a standard pattern.

James II

Four main obverse types:

1 Bust of the king.
2 Similar, with elephant and castle below.
3 A new bust, thinner and with the king's nostrils more prominent.
4 Similar, with elephant and castle below.

One reverse type:
Four crowned shields of arms, sceptres in saltire, nothing in the centre.

Dates of issue:

1685 Obv. types 1 and 2.	1687 Obv. types 3 and 4.
1686 ,, ,, 1, 3 and 4.	1688 ,, ,, 3 and 4.

Notes. 1687 with 7 over 6 is known. All now very rare.

William & Mary

Three obverse types:

1 Jugate busts.
2 Similar, with elephant and castle below.
3 Similar, with elephant only.

One reverse type:
Crowned shield of arms.

Dates of issue:

1689 Obv. types 1 and 2.	1692 Obv. types 1, 2 and 3.
1690 ,, ,, 1 and 2.	1693 ,, ,, 1 and 2.
1691 ,, ,, 1 and 2.	1694 ,, ,, 1 and 2.

Notes. The date 1694, the 4 over 3, is known. All dates now very rare.

William III

Five obverse types:

1 First bust.
2 Similar, with elephant and castle below.
3 Second bust.
4 Similar, with elephant and castle below.
5 Third bust of the 'fine work' type, see note under Five Guineas.

Three reverse types:
Basic layout, four crowned shields of arms, sceptres in saltire, lion of Nassau in the centre. Variations:

1 small or normal figures in the date.
2 larger figures and lettering.
3 The harp in the Irish arms is scrolled and the crowns above the four shields are smaller.

Dates of issue:

1695	Obv.	type	1.	Rev.	type	1.
	,,	,,	2.	,,	,,	1.
1696	,,	,,	1.	,,	,,	1.
1697	,,	,,	2.	,,	,,	1.
	,,	,,	3.	,,	,,	1.
1698	,,	,,	3.	,,	,,	1.
	,,	,,	3.	,,	,,	2.
	,,	,,	4.	,,	,,	1.
1699	,,	,,	3.	,,	,,	1.
	,,	,,	4.	,,	,,	1.
1700	,,	,,	3.	,,	,,	1.
	,,	,,	4.	,,	,,	1.
1701	,,	,,	3.	,,	,,	3.
	,,	,,	4.	,,	,,	3.
	,,	,,	5.	,,	,,	3.

Notes. A considerable number of varieties are known which are not significant enough to establish a main type. Large and small lions occur in the English shield of arms and similar minor varieties are numerous.

Anne

Five main obverse types:
1 Bust of the Queen.
2 Similar, with VIGO below (silver from the large amount captured at the Battle of Vigo Bay, 1702).
3 Similar, bust with an elephant and castle in place of VIGO.
4 A new bust, the Queen's hair fillet with a single curl each side.
5 Similar, with elephant and castle below.

Two reverse types:
1 Before the political union with Scotland: four crowned shields of arms, England and Scotland dimidiate, France, England and Scotland dimidiate, Ireland. Four sceptres in saltire, Star of the Garter in the centre.

2 Four crowned shields of arms, England, Scotland, France and Ireland. Four sceptres in saltire, a rose in the centre. These two reverse types are the pre- and post-union with Scotland arms.

Dates of issue:

1702	Obv.	type	1.	Rev.	type	1.
1703	,,	,,	2.	,,	,,	1.
1705	,,	,,	1.	,,	,,	1.
1706	,,	,,	1.	,,	,,	1.
1707	,,	,,	1.	,,	,,	1.
	,,	,,	1.	,,	,,	2.
	,,	,,	3.	,,	,,	2.
	,,	,,	4.	,,	,,	2.
1708	,,	,,	1.	,,	,,	2.
	,,	,,	4.	,,	,,	2.
	,,	,,	5.	,,	,,	2.
1709	,,	,,	4.	,,	,,	2.
	,,	,,	5.	,,	,,	2.
1710	,,	,,	4.	,,	,,	2.
1711	,,	,,	4.	,,	,,	2.
1712	,,	,,	4.	,,	,,	2.
1713	,,	,,	4.	,,	,,	2.
1714	,,	,,	4.	,,	,,	2.

Notes. There are no minor varieties catalogued but close observation under high magnification might well reveal slight differences of the main die classifications. All dates are now very rare.

George I

Seven obverse types:

1 Head large with a profusion of hair curls. The hair tie has two ends.

2 Slightly smaller head. A lock of hair extends over the shoulder, the hair tie has two ends.

3 Third type of head in lower relief. The lock of hair does not extend over the shoulder.

4 Fourth type of head. The hair tie now has one end and a loop. A lock of hair extends over the shoulder.

5 Similar, with elephant and castle.

6 A smaller head showing the king looking older. The hair tie has two ends, no lock of hair on shoulder.

7 Similar, with elephant and castle.

Two reverse types:

1 Four crowned shields of arms. The legend includes the abbreviation PR EL=Prince Elector. This reverse is used only once.

2 Similar, but without PR. Its absence has allowed for slightly larger lettering and minor differences.

Dates of issue:

1714	Obv.	type	1.	Rev.	type	1.
1715	,,	,,	2.	,,	,,	2.
	,,	,,	3.	,,	,,	3.

1716–1721, inclusive, all Obv. type 4. Rev. type 2.

1721	Obv.	type	5.	Rev.	type	2.
1722	,,	,,	4.	,,	,,	2.
	,,	,,	5.	,,	,,	2.
1723	,,	,,	4.	,,	,,	2.
	,,	,,	6.	,,	,,	2.

1724–1726 Obv. type 6. Rev. type 2.

1726	Obv.	type	7.	Rev.	type	2.
1727	,,	,,	7.	,,	,,	2.

Notes. The reader will have noted that in this, as in some previous reigns, two types of coin can sometimes appear in one year, *vide* 1726. All these Guineas are now very rare. Further close study might well reveal some uncatalogued minor varieties.

George II

Eleven obverse types:

1 First young head, legend in small letters.

2 Similar, but with larger lettering.

3 Second young head: the whole portrait is narrower and the crown of the king's head smaller.

4 Similar, with E I C (=East India Company metal) below truncation.

5 Similar bust, no E I C , lettering of legend slightly larger.

6 Similar, with E I C .

7 An older portrait, known as the intermediate head, the legend lettering small.

8 Similar, with E I C below.
9 Similar, larger lettering, no E I C.
10 Similar, with LIMA below head. For explanation of LIMA see Five Guineas.
11 Old head of the king, large legend lettering.

Five reverse types:

1 Large crowned shield of arms, crowding the legend at 'seven o'clock'.
2 Smaller shield, tapered at the bottom to clear the legend.
3 A squarer shield, the crown larger and more rounded on the spandrils, forcing the figures of the date apart.
4 Similar, with slightly larger legend lettering.
5 Still larger lettering.

Dates of issue:

1727	Obv.	type	1.	Rev.	type	1.
	,,	,,	2.	,,	,,	2.
1728	,,	,,	2.	,,	,,	2.
1729	,,	,,	3.	,,	,,	3.
	,,	,,	4.	,,	,,	3.
1730	,,	,,	3.	,,	,,	3.
1731	,,	,,	3.	,,	,,	3.
	,,	,,	4.	,,	,,	3.
1732	,,	,,	3.	,,	,,	3.
	,,	,,	4.	,,	,,	3.
	,,	,,	5.	,,	,,	3.
	,,	,,	6.	,,	,,	3.

1733–1738 inclusive, all Obv. type 5. Rev. type 3.

1739	Obv.	type	7.	Rev.	type	4.
	,,	,,	8.	,,	,,	4.
1740	,,	,,	7.	,,	,,	4.
1743	,,	,,	7.	,,	,,	4.
1745	,,	,,	9.	,,	,,	4.
	,,	,,	10.	,,	,,	4.
1746	,,	,,	9.	,,	,,	4.

1747–1753 and 1755–1756, 1758–1760, all Obv. type 11. Rev. type 5. (Not struck in 1754 and 1757).

Notes. While, subject to any further very close study, there are no minor varieties to look for, the eleven obverse and five reverse types give a varied picture. The various differences listed are quite clear and constitute quite distinct types.

George III

Six obverse types:

1 First head, somewhat narrow with a moderate amount of hair at the back of the neck, the forward point of the truncation touching the edge of the flan.

2 A somewhat fuller head, more hair at the back of the neck, rounded truncation touching the edge of the flan.

3 Similar, but with much more hair. The rounded truncation and the curls below the neck reach to the edge of the flan.

4 Fourth head, the king older with puffy cheeks and receding hair, rounded truncation to edge of flan and hair curling under back of truncation.

5 Fifth head, similar to the last but slightly smaller, rounded truncation to edge of flan but less hair behind head and no large curl below truncation.

6 Entirely new portrait, the king's head far rounder, hair short, neck long, truncation pointed.

Four Reverse types:

1 Crowned shield of arms, the figure 1s in the date are curved, as, roughly, j.

2 Similar, but the 1s in the date are Roman figures.

3 A complete re-design. The shield of arms is now plain and pointed, shaped as a trenching spade, thus the title, spade Guinea.

4 A further complete re-design. Crowned shield of arms within the Garter. Thus known as the Garter type. As will be seen from the date list, this reverse marries with reverse 6 only.

Dates of issue:

1761 Obv. type 1. Rev. type 1.
1763 ,, ,, 2. ,, ,, 1.
1764 ,, ,, 2. ,, ,, 1.

Plate 53 Silver. Halfcrowns

1–2 George III, 1760–1820. Type one, sometimes called the 'bull head' type. **3–4** Type two, both obverse and reverse redesigned. **5–6** George IV, 1820–1830. Two obverse types, the first (5) by Pistrucci and disliked by the King. The second (6) by Wyon after Chantrey's bust. **7–9** Three reverse types. Obverse one (5) couples with reverse one (7) and with reverse two (8). Obverse two (6) couples with reverse three (9).

GEORGIUS III DEI GRATIA
1816

1

BRITANNIARUM REX FID: DEF:

2

GEORGIUS III DEI GRATIA
1818

3

BRITANNIARUM REX FID: DEF:

4

GEORGIUS IIII D: G: BRITANNIAR: REX F: D:

5

GEORGIUS IV DEI GRATIA
1828

6

ANNO 1820

7

ANNO

8

BRITANNIARUM REX FID: DEF:

9

1

2

3

4

5

6

7

8

9

10

11

12

13

14

1765–1773 inclusive, all Obv. type 3. Rev. type 1.
1774–1779, 1781–1786, all Obv. type 4. Rev. type 2. (not struck in 1780).
1787–1799, all Obv. type 5. Rev. type 3.
1813 Obv. type 6. Rev. type 4.

Notes. Subject, once again, to much closer study, there are no minor varieties catalogued. The obverse designs are the work of three famous engravers, Yeo, T. Pingo and Marchant. The Spade Guinea, which captured the imagination of many writers of fiction, was once almost more than common. Now, like most gold coins of milled coinage phase one, it commands a high price. The Guinea of 1813, the last ever struck is sometimes known as the military Guinea. It was said to have been struck specially for the troops embarking for France in that year. Napoleon had been defeated in Russia but still had to meet his Waterloo, in 1815.

HALF GUINEAS

Charles II

Three main obverse types:
1 Head of the king, with pointed truncation.
2 Larger head, with rounded truncation.
3 Similar, with elephant and castle below.

One reverse type:
Four crowned shields of arms, sceptres in saltire, interlinked Cs in the centre.

Dates of issue:
1669–
1672 Obv. type 1.
1672–
1676 „ „ 2.
1676 „ „ 3.
1677 Obv. type 2 and 3.
1678 „ „ 2 and 3.
1679 „ „ 2.
1680 „ „ 2 and 3.

Plate 54 Silver. Halfcrowns
1–2 William IV, 1830–1837. One type only. **3–5** Victoria, 1837–1901. Three obverse types: young head (3); Jubilee head (4); old head (5). **6–8** Three reverse types. Type one (6) couples with obverse one (3); type two (7) couples with obverse two (4); type three (8) couples with obverse three (5). **9–10** Edward VII, 1901–1910. One type only. **11–12** George V, 1910–1936. Two obverse types. **13–14** Two reverse types. Type one (13) couples with obverse type one (11) and with obverse type two (12) in 1926 and 1927. Type two (14) couples with obverse two (12) in 1927 and after.

Dates of issue:

1681 Obv. type 2.	1683 Obv. type 2 and 3.
1682 ,, ,, 2 and 3.	1684 ,, ,, 2 and 3.

Notes. 1678 with 8 over 7 is known. All these pieces are now rare.

James II

Two main obverse types:
1 Head of the king.
2 Similar, with elephant and castle below.

One reverse type:
Four crowned shields of arms, sceptres in saltire.

Dates of issue:

1686 Obv. type 1.	1687 Obv. type 1.
1686 ,, ,, 2.	1688 ,, ,, 1.

William & Mary

Three main obverse types:
1 Jugate busts of the Joint Monarchs, somewhat thin and narrow
2 Fuller, broader busts.
3 Similar, with elephant and castle, the castle almost obliterated, below.

One reverse type:
Crowned shield of arms.

Dates of issue:

1689 Obv. type 1.	1692 Obv. type 2 and 3.
1690 ,, ,, 2.	1693 ,, ,, 2.
1691 ,, ,, 2 and 3.	1694 ,, ,, 2.

Notes. 1693 with 3 over 2 is known.

William III

Two main obverse types:
1 Head of the king.
2 Similar, with elephant and castle below.

Two reverse types:
1 Four crowned shields of arms, sceptres in saltire, lion of Nassau in centre.
2 Similar, but the harp in the Irish arms is larger.

Dates of issue:

1695	Obv.	type	1.	Rev.	type	1.
	,,	,,	2.	,,	,,	1.
1696	,,	,,	2.	,,	,,	1.
1697	,,	,,	1.	,,	,,	2.
1698	,,	,,	1.	,,	,,	2.
	,,	,,	2.	,,	,,	2.
1700	,,	,,	1.	,,	,,	2.
1701	,,	,,	2.	,,	,,	2.

Anne

Two main obverse types:

1 Bust of the queen.

2 Similar, with VIGO below.

Two reverse types:

1 four crowned shields of arms, sceptres in saltire.

2 Similar, but the arms of England and Scotland demidiate, known as the post-union type.

Dates of issue:

1702	Obv.	type	1.	Rev.	type	1.
1703	,,	,,	2.	,,	,,	1.
1705	,,	,,	1.	,,	,,	1.
1707	,,	,,	1.	,,	,,	2.

1708–1714 inclusive, all Obv. type 1. Rev. type 2.

George I

Three main obverse types:

1 Head of the king, the hair tie with two ends, a lock of hair on the shoulder.

2 Similar, with elephant and castle below.

3 A smaller bust, showing the king older, no lock of hair on the shoulder.

One reverse type only:

Four crowned shields of arms, sceptres in saltire, Star of the Garter in centre.

Dates of issue:

1715 and 1717–1721 inclusive, all Obv. type 1

1721 Obv. type 2.

1772	Obv.	type	1.
1723	,,	,,	1.
1724–			
1727	,,	,,	3.

George II

Five main obverse types:

1 Young head.
2 Similar with E I C below.
3 Intermediate head (by age).
4 Similar, with LIMA below.
5 Old head.

Two reverse types:

1 Crowned shield of arms.
2 Similar, but lettering larger.

Dates of issue:

1728	Obv.	type	1.	Rev.	type	1.
1729	,,	,,	1.	,,	,,	1.
	,,	,,	2.	,,	,,	1.
1730	,,	,,	1.	,,	,,	1.
	,,	,,	2.	,,	,,	1.
1731	,,	,,	1.	,,	,,	1.
	,,	,,	2.	,,	,,	1.
1732	,,	,,	1.	,,	,,	1.
	,,	,,	2.	,,	,,	1.

1733–1739 inclusive, all Obv. type 1. Rev. type 1.

1739	Obv.	type	2.	Rev.	type	1.
1740	,,	,,	3.	,,	,,	1.
1743	,,	,,	3.	,,	,,	1.
1745	,,	,,	3.	,,	,,	1.
	,,	,,	4.	,,	,,	1.
1746	,,	,,	3.	,,	,,	1.

1747–1753 and 1755, 1756, 1759, 1760, all Obv. type 5. Rev. type 2.

Notes. No minor varieties so far catalogued. LIMA and E I C have already been explained.

Plate 55 Silver. Florins
1–2 Victoria, 1837–1901. The so-called 'Godless' Florin of 1849, the first silver Florin struck for Great Britain. **3–4** The 'Gothic' Florin which succeeded the piece above, 1851–1887. **5–6** The Jubilee type Florin, 1887–1892. **7–8** the old head Florin, 1893–1901. **9–10** Edward VII, 1901–1910. One type only, with De Saulles standing Britannia reverse. **11–12** George V, 1910–1936. First type, 1911–1927. **13–14** Second type, 1927–1936.

1

2

3

4

5

6

7

8

9

10

11

12

13

14

1

2

3

4

5

6

7

8

9

10

11

12

13

14

15

16

17

18

19

20

21

George III

Seven main obverse types:

1 Young head with rounded truncation.
2 Similar, but truncation steeper and pointed.
3 A rounder, fuller face, chin very receding, the detail somewhat fogged.
4 Similar, but the detail clearer.
5 Older face, steep, rounded truncation, the crown of the head more pointed.
6 Similar, but the portrait rounder and broader.
7 Entirely new head; rounder, hair short, neck long, truncation pointed.

Four reverse types:

1 Crowned shield of arms, the figure 1 in date curved.
2 Similar, but Roman I in date.
3 Spade-type shield (see Guineas).
4 Crowned shield within the garter, (see Guineas).

Dates of issue:

1762 Obv. type 1. Rev. type 1.
1763 ,, ,, 1. ,, ,, 1.
1764–1766 and 1768–1769, 1772–1774, all Obv. type 2. Rev. type 1.
1774 Obv. type 3. Rev. type 1.
1775 ,, ,, 2. ,, ,, 1.
,, ,, 3. ,, ,, 1.
,, ,, 4. ,, ,, 1.
1776–1779, all Obv. type 4. Rev. type 1.
1781, 1784–1786, all Obv. type 4. Rev. type 2.

Plate 56 Silver. Shillings

1–2 George IV, 1820–1830. (For George III see Plate 46). Two obverse types, as for Halfcrown (see plate 53). **3–5** Three reverse types. Type one (3) couples with obverse one (1); type two (4) couples with obverse one (1); type three (5) couples with obverse two (2). **6–7** William IV, 1830–1837. One type only. **8–12** Victoria, 1837–1901. Five obverse types. Type one (8) young head; type two (9) young head, redesigned and larger; type three (10) small Jubilee head; type four (11) large Jubilee head; type five (12) old head. **13–15** Three reverse types. Type one (13) couples with obverse one (8) and obverse two (9); type two (14) couples with obverse three (10) and obverse four (11); type three (15) couples with obverse five (12). **16–17** Edward VII, 1901–1910. One type only. **18–19** George V, 1910–1936. Type one, 1911–1926. **20–21** Type two, 1926–1936. Type two obverse (20) couples with reverse one (19) in 1926 and 1927.

1787–1791, 1793–1798 and 1800, all Obv. type 5. Rev. type 3.
1801–1803, all Obv. type 6. Rev. type 4.
1804, 1806, 1808–1811 and 1813, all Obv. type 7. Rev. type 4.
Notes. As for Guineas.

From the larger number of issues it will be seen that the collector has more chance of obtaining Guineas and Half Guineas for his collection than he had with the larger denominations. Unless the collector is confining himself entirely to gold, it is obviously not necessary to attempt to acquire the majority of dates listed. Some, in any case, are extremely rare. In a general cabinet of English coins some representative dates of the gold coins listed above are all that is necessary to give a reasonable coverage of the coins of this period.

The small issues of Third and Quarter Guineas are as follows.

QUARTER GUINEAS

George I

One obverse and one reverse type only:
Similar to Half Guineas.
Date of issue: 1718.

George III

One obverse and reverse type only:
Similar to early Half Guineas.
Date of issue: 1762.

THIRD GUINEAS

George III

Two obverse types:

1 Traditional type of laureate head, similar to Half Guineas, but with long neck.
2 Similar to last obverse type of Half Guineas.

Two reverse types:

1 A crown, surrounded by the legend, which contains the date.
2 Similar, the crown of slightly different shape, the date below it.

Dates of issue:
1797–1800 inclusive, all Obv. type 1. Rev. type 1.
1801–1803, all Obv. type 1. Rev. type 2.
1804, 1806, 1808, 1809–1811 and 1813, all Obv. type 2. Rev. type 2.
Notes. The denominations have been given out of order since the Quarter Guineas were issued in an earlier reign than the Thirds.

Most collectors could afford one or two of these rather charming little pieces.

This rounds off the gold issues of phase one. In general, as has been hinted in the notes, the majority of the pieces are now scarce to extremely rare. Even so there are collectors who specialize in gold alone. Reference to the auction sale catalogues over the years will show that they are a sound investment.

In these days of increasing study there is still work that can be carried out by the collector in the search for minor varieties, if sufficient specimens can be got together for close study. All the gold coins listed in phase one, and all those to be listed down to the year 1837, may be bought freely by the collector without the humiliation of state control in the form of the recently, and it is hoped temporary, 'collector's licence'.

We can now take a similarly brief look at the silver coins of phase one of the milled series.

The silver coinage of the period fits into the method of presentation which has so far been adopted since the issue of milled coinage. The donominations have already been listed (page 156). The largest denomination is the Crown, which, as has been seen, first appeared as a silver piece in 1551.

The silver Crown has always been an attractive collecting theme. The milled coins in the series will be described in some detail, since this detail holds much of collector interest. In their design the smaller denominations: Halfcrown, Shilling and Sixpence: were mainly smaller reproductions of the Crown. Very broadly, therefore, what is said of the Crown applies to the smaller denominations down to the Sixpence. The Groat or Fourpence, *et infra*, will be the subject of further remarks.

SILVER

CROWNS

Charles II

Four obverse types:

The first has a rose below the bust but the differences lie mainly in the portraiture.

Two reverse types:

1 Four crowned shields of arms, cruciform, England and France quarterly, Scotland, England and France quarterly, Ireland.

Two interlinked Cs in each angle, Star of the Garter in the centre.

2 Four crowned shields of arms, England, Scotland, France, Ireland. Otherwise, similar.

Dates of issue:
1662 Obv. type 1. Rev. type 1.
„ „ 2. „ „ 1.
1663 „ „ 1. „ „ 2.
1664–1670 inclusive, all Obv. type 2. Rev. type 2.
1671–1678 inclusive, all Obv. type 3. Rev. type 2.
1679 Obv. type 3. Rev. type 2.
„ „ 4. „ „ 2.
1680 „ „ 3. „ „ 2.
„ „ 4. „ „ 2.
1681–1684, all Obv. type 4. Rev. type 2

Notes. Considerable varieties exist within this date framework. The coins have on their edges the legend DECUV ET TUTAMEN ANNO REGNI. . . . 'an ornament and a safeguard' (against clipping) 'in the. . . . year of the reign.' The regnal year does not necessarily coincide with the date of the coin, thus two different regnal dates may appear on the edge. This continues with similar pieces throughout the series. Some of the first obverse type have no rose. A variety of 1666 has an elephant below obverse type 2. A variety of 1680 and 1681 has an elephant and castle below obverse type 4. In 1668, 1669, 1670, 1673, 1675, 1677, 1678, 1680 and 1682

Plate 57 Silver. Sixpences. Groats
1–2 George IV, 1820–1830. (For George III see plate 48). Two obverse types, as for Halfcrowns. **3–5** Three reverse types, as for Shillings. Obverse one (1) couples with reverse one (3) and reverse two (4). Obverse two (2) couples with reverse three (5). **6–7** William IV, 1830–1837. One type only. **8–10** Victoria, 1837–1901. Three obverse types. Type one (8) young head; type two (9) Jubilee head; type three (10) old head. **11–13** Three reverse types. Obverse one (8) couples with reverse one (11); obverse two (9) couples with reverse two (12) and reverse three (12); obverse three (10) couples with reverse three (13). **14–15** Edward VII, 1901–1910. One type only. **16–17** George V, 1910–1936. Two obverse types. **18–19** Two reverse types. Obverse one (16) couples with reverse one (18); obverse two (17) couples with reverse one in 1926 and 1927. Obverse two (17) couples with reverse two (19) from 1927 to 1936. **20–21** William IV. Groat. **22–23** Victoria. Groat. Both the above are additional to the Maundy Groat with figure 4 on the reverse.

1

2

3

4

5

6

7

8

9

10

11

12

13

14

15

16

17

18

19

20

21

22

23

1
3a
2
4
4
5
3
5
7
6
11
8
6
12
9
14
13
10

the date is on some varieties struck over that of the previous year, save for 1675, where the 5 is over 3. The edge dates start in Arabic figures, which change to words. In this case the Arabic edge dates are that of the coin, when a word is used, such as TERTIO, it is that of the regnal year. Differences occur in legend punctuation, and other minor varieties exist. It obviously took some time for the new methods of coining to shake down into a standard pattern.

James II

Two obverse types:

The differences being entirely in the portrait.

One reverse type only.

Four crowned shields of arms, cruciform, England, Scotland, France and Ireland. Star of the Garter in the centre.

Dates of issue:

1686 Obv. type 1.	1688 Obv. type 2.
1687 „ „ 2.	

Notes. Legend punctuation again varies, and a variety of the 1688 piece has the date altered from 1687.

Plate 58

Gold, Five Pound pieces. **1** The 'Jubilee' obverse. Designed by Boehm it was so ill-liked that it led to **2**, the 'Old head' obverse, designed by Brock. The Edward VII obverse **3** of the denomination is shown below. The common reverse of these three pieces, **3a** as also of the proof pieces of the same denomination for George V and George VI, was Pistrucci's St. George and dragon. **4** Gold, Sovereign of Elizabeth II. Pistrucci's St. George reverse has for the moment become the traditional reverse of our theoretical gold coinage. The Crown pieces of George VI. **5**, as issued in the sets of coins struck in 1937 and as issued for circulation. **6**, as issued to mark the Festival of Britain, the introduction of the silver Crown in 1551 and the centenary of the Great Exhibition of 1851. The first is a silver piece, the second cupro-nickel. Note the difference in the style of lettering used on the two pieces. The reverse of the first was an original design by Kruger Grey. That of the second reverted to Pistrucci's design for the reverse of the Crown of George III, but without the Garter frame, which had disappeared by the reign of George IV and has not been used on a Crown since the original issue. A group of eight pieces of George VI. The obverse type is followed by, **7**, the reverse of the silver Halfcrown of 1942, **8**, the reverse of the silver Florin of the same year, **9**, the reverse of the silver Sixpence of 1946, the last of the silver issues, all with the IND IMP title. **10** is the reverse of the redesigned cupro-nickel Sixpence of 1949, **11** the reverse of the cupro-nickel Halfcrown of 1950, **12** the reverse of the Florin of 1949, also cupro-nickel, **13**, the cupro-nickel Shilling 1951, **14** the cupro-nickel Scottish Shilling of 1951, all without the IND IMP title.

William & Mary

One obverse type, one reverse type:

Four crowned shields of arms, England, Scotland, France, Ireland. The letters W M superimposed, in the angles. The lion of Nassau in the centre.

Dates of issue:

1691	1692

Notes. The four figures of the date appear singly, one in each angle below the W M initials. This unique method of stating the date of the coin seems to have caused the die cutter some trouble, since in 1692 the 2 is found superimposed over a 2 which is upside down. 1691, like 1961, can be read either way up.

William III

Four obverse types:

The differences being in the portrait.

Three reverse types:

The now usual four crowned shield of arms, set about a centre point, in this case the lion of Nassau. The main differences (though there were others) are in the harp form of the Irish shield. These have been catalogued as:

1 Early harp, having a bust on the top of the left member of the harp frame.

2 Ordinary harp, with the bust reduced to a head.

3 Late harp, which has no head.

Dates of issue:

1695	Obv.	type	1.	Rev.	type	1.
1696	,,	,,	1.	,,	,,	1.
	,,	,,	2.	,,	,,	2.
	,,	,,	3.	,,	,,	2.
	,,	,,	4.	,,	,,	1.
1697	,,	,,	4.	,,	,,	2.
1700	,,	,,	4.	,,	,,	3.

Notes. Here again the edge readings provide numerous varieties.

Anne

Three main obverse types:

1 With VIGO below bust.

2 Similar, but plain.

3 Broader bust.

Two main reverse types:

1 Four crowned shields of arms, England, Scotland, France, Ireland. Star of the Garter in centre of coin. This reverse can be as above, or can have plumes or roses and plumes in the angles.

2 Four crowned shields of arms, England and Scotland dimidiate, France, England and Scotland dimidiate, Ireland. Used after the political union with Scotland. This reverse can be as above or with plumes or roses and plumes in the angles.

Dates of issue:

1703	Obv.	type	1.	Rev.	type	1.
1705	,,	,,	1.	,,	,,	1, with plumes.
1706	,,	,,	1.	,,	,,	1, with roses and plumes.
1707	,,	,,	1.	,,	,,	1, similar.
1707	,,	,,	2.	,,	,,	2.
1708	,,	,,	2.	,,	,,	2, plain or with plumes.
1713	,,	,,	3.	,,	,,	2, roses and plumes.

Notes. The plumes indicate that the metal was of Welsh origin: the roses and plumes that the metal was supplied by the 'Company for smelting down lead with Pitcoale and Seacoale': VIGO indicates metal from the capture of silver at the Battle of Vigo Bay, 1702.

George I

One obverse type only. F.D.=Fidei Defensor (defender of the Faith) now added to the legend.

Two reverse types:

1 Four crowned shields of arms, England and Scotland dimidiate, France, Ireland, the Electorate. Star of the Garter in the centre. In the angles roses and plumes. In 1723, the letters S S C, signifying that the metal was supplied by the South Sea Company.

Dates of issue:

1716	Rev.	type	1.	1723	Rev.	type	2.
1718	,,	,,	1.	1726	,,	,,	1.
1720	,,	,,	1.				

Notes. 1718 occurs with date altered from 1716, 1720 occurs with date altered from 1718.

George II

Two main obverse types:

1 Young head.

2 Old head. The latter has the word LIMA below on the 1764 issue. See notes for the £5 5s.

Three main reverse types:

Basic: four crowned shields of arms, England and Scotland dimidiate, France, Ireland, Hanover. Star of the Garter in the centre. Variations:

1 Roses and plumes in the angles.
2 Roses in the angles.
3 Plain, with neither. Use of these roses and plumes as for the Crowns of Anne.

Dates of issue:

1732	Obv.	type	1.	Rev.	type	1.
1734	,,	,,	1.	,,	,,	1.
1735	,,	,,	1.	,,	,,	1.
1736	,,	,,	1.	,,	,,	1.
1739	,,	,,	1.	,,	,,	2.
1741	,,	,,	1.	,,	,,	2.
1743	,,	,,	2.	,,	,,	2.
1746	,,	,,	2.	,,	,,	3, with LIMA.
1750	,,	,,	2.	,,	,,	3.
1751	,,	,,	2.	,,	,,	3.

George III

No Crowns of the type so far described were struck in this reign. Before the Crown piece was struck a fundamental reorganization had taken place, affecting not only the coins themselves but the Royal Mint itself. Of this more in its place.

Particular stress has been laid on the Crown piece, both hammered and milled since it is a very popular collecting theme. It is presumed that the collector has understood the various inferences which are to be drawn from the changes in the obverse and reverse designs. In total, the main broad differences in the obverses are changes in the portrait of the monarch. The obverse and reverse letters and symbols reflect the use of metal from various sources and the necessary changes in the shields of arms followed the accession of William III and Mary and the House of Hanover.

Very broadly the Halfcrowns followed the pattern of the Crowns, and were, in some measure, a reduction of that piece. As will be seen, in some instances there are more obverse types which were, as with the Crown, mainly differences in portraiture. The reverse designs followed those of the Crown to some extent but for reasons which will be given, more variations occur. Thus the method of presentation adopted for the Crown cannot strictly be adhered to with its half: a few more notes will be needed.

HALFCROWNS

Charles II

Five main obverse types, all slightly different portraits.
The elephant below bust occurs in 1666, and the elephant and castle in 1681.
One reverse type only, as for the Crown, reverse type 2.
Dates of issue:

1663 Obv. type 1.	1670 Obv. type 3.
1664 ,, ,, 2.	1671 ,, ,, 4.
1666 ,, ,, 3.	1672 ,, ,, 4 and 5.
1667 ,, ,, 3.	1673–1684 inclusive, all Obv. type 5.
1668 ,, ,, 3.	
1669 ,, ,, 3.	

Notes. Overstruck dates occur, as also do mistakes in the lettering of the edge legend. Some extremely rare pieces have plumes (=Welsh silver) on the obverse and/or the reverse. Such rarities are not likely to be seen by the average collector. Many minor varieties of stops in the legends occur as do mis-spellings. Here again the new methods of production and design had not yet settled down into a standard pattern. For the collector of the Halfcrown there is much of interest and many minor varieties to look for.

James II

Two obverse types and one reverse type, as for the Crown.

Dates of issue:

1685 Obv. type 1.	1687 Obv. type 1 and 2.
1686 ,, ,, 1.	1688 ,, ,, 2.

Notes. Overstruck dates occur. In a few rare varieties the V (=U) in JACOBVS is an A upside down.

William & Mary

Two main obverse types:
Difference mainly in the portraiture, which might be described as 'long necks' and 'short necks' of the Joint Monarchs.

Three main reverse types:

1 Crowned shield of arms, in four main cantons, the lion of Naussau in the centre.
2 Similar, but the first and fourth cantons divided into four.
3 Four crowned shields of arms, as for the Crown piece, with W M in monogram in the angles and the date figures below as for the Crown.

Dates of issue:

1689	Obv.	type	1.	Rev.	type	1.
	,,	,,	1.	,,	,,	2.
1690	,,	,,	1.	,,	,,	2.
1691	,,	,,	2.	,,	,,	3.
1692	,,	,,	2.	,,	,,	3.
1693	,,	,,	2.	,,	,,	3.

Notes. Again many minor varieties occur. Differences in punctuation are frequent. There may be no pearls (=dots) on the Crown on reverse type 1, and the caul (=the head lining of the crown: the cap that rests on the head) may be frosted: i.e. covered in small dots, or not frosted: plain. On the third reverse type the die cutter was still in trouble with the unusual arrangement of the date figures, so that 3 recut over 3 upside down occurs.

William III

Two main obverse types:

In 1696 some pieces had a slight variety of obverse 1. Obverse 2 is used once.

Four main reverse types:

1 Small shields of arms.
2 Larger shields, with what is known as the 'early' type of harp.
3 With even larger shields.
4 With plumes (=Welsh silver) in the angles.

Dates of issue:

1696, from London and all the provincial mints: see notes below. 1697, 1698, 1699, 1700, 1701.

Notes. The issues are complicated here by the opening of five branch mints in 1696 to deal with the work which resulted from the calling in of the last of the hammered coinage which was now finally melted down. These provincial mints were at Bristol, B below bust, Chester, C: Exeter, E: Norwich, N: and York, Y or y below bust.

The varieties are so numerous, and in many cases so small that this series of Halfcrowns does not fit accurately into the sequence of obverse and reverse types used so far. One type in 1696 is known with obverse 2, used only in this year. It resembles the 'fine work' type of the Five Guineas, and is so rare that only a very worn specimen has been available for illustration.

The whole series of silver coins of William III are a study in themselves. As such they are dealt with in a monograph by E. R. Jackson Kent, 'Some notes on the Silver Coinage of William III'. Only the dates of issue have therefore been given.

Anne

Three main obverse types, as for the Crown.

Two main reverse types:

1 Before the union with Scotland shields of arms.

2 After the union shields of arms. Both types may have plumes or roses and plumes in the angles. A very rare piece dated 1703 has no VIGO below the bust.

Dates of issue:

(P=plumes on reverse, R and P= roses and plumes on reverse.)

1703	Obv.	type	1.	Rev.	type	1, with Vigo below bust.
1704	,,	,,	1.	,,	,,	1, P.
1705	,,	,,	1.	,,	,,	1, P.
1706	,,	,,	1.	,,	,,	1, R and P.
1707	,,	,,	1.	,,	,,	1, R and P.
	,,	,,	2.	,,	,,	1, R and P.
	,,	,,	3.	,,	,,	2, R and P.
1708	,,	,,	3.	,,	,,	2.
	,,	,,	1.	,,	,,	2, P.
	,,	,,	3.	,,	,,	2, P.
1709	,,	,,	3.	,,	,,	2.
1710	,,	,,	3.	,,	,,	2, R and P.
1712	,,	,,	3.	,,	,,	2, R and P.
1713	,,	,,	3.	,,	,,	2.
	,,	,,	3.	,,	,,	2, R and P.
1714	,,	,,	3.	,,	,,	2, R and P.

George I

One obverse type only.

Two main reverse types:

1 With roses and plumes.

2 With S S C in the angles (=South Sea Company silver).

Dates of issue:

1715	Rev.	type	1.	1723	Rev.	type	2.
1717	,,	,,	1.	1726	,,	,,	1.
1720	,,	,,	1.				

George II

Two main obverse types:

1 Young head.

2 Old head.

Three main reverse types:

1 With roses and plumes in the angles.

2 With roses.

3 Plain in the angles.

Dates of issue:

1731	Obv.	type	1.	Rev.	type	1.
1732	,,	,,	1.	,,	,,	1.
1734	,,	,,	1.	,,	,,	1.
1735	,,	,,	1.	,,	,,	1.
1735	,,	,,	1.	,,	,,	1.
1736	,,	,,	1.	,,	,,	1.
1739	,,	,,	1.	,,	,,	2.
1741	,,	,,	1.	,,	,,	2.
1743	,,	,,	2.	,,	,,	2.
1745	,,	,,	2.	,,	,,	2.
	,,	,,	2.	,,	,,	3, with LIMA below bust.

Plate 59

The coinage of Elizabeth II. **1** the common obverse bust, **2** the common reverse of the cupro-nickel crowns of 1953 and 1960, **3** the obverse of the Coronation Crown of 1953, **4** the 'Churchill' memorial Crown of 1965. On the latter no value is stated. The reasonably traditional obverse and the modern type of reverse hardly go well together, though each is individually a fine piece of coinage design. Examples of the cupro-nickel coinage of Elizabeth II. **5** the obverse types, **6** the Halfcrown of 1958, **7** the Florin of 1963, **8** the English Shilling of 1965, **9** the Scottish Shilling of 1963, **10** the Sixpence of 1960. The continuous legend on the obverse gave it a pseudo-medieval appearance. The beginning of our copper/bronze coinage. **11** a Harington Farthing, James I. **12** a Maltravers Farthing, Charles I. **13** a Charles II copper Halfpenny, 1673. **14** James II tin Halfpenny with copper plug, shaded.

1
2
3
5
4
4
5
6
7
8
9
10
11
11
12
12
13
13
14
14

1
1692
1
GULIELMUS TERTIUS
BRITANNIA
1696
2
2
GEORGIUS III·D·G·REX
6
ANNA REGINA
3
GEORGIUS REX
4
BRITANNIA
1797
6
BRITANNIA
3
BRITANNIA
4
GEORGIUS III·D·G·REX
7
BRITANNIA
1797
7
GEORGIUS II REX
5
BRITANNIA
1729
5
GEORGIUS III·D·G·REX
8
BRITANNIA
1797
8
10
1821
10
GEORGIUS III·D·G·REX
9
BRITANNIA
1797
9
GEORGIUS IV DEI GRATIA
1825
11
BRITANNIAR: REX FID: DEF:
11

Dates of issue:
1746 Obv. type 2. Rev. type 3, with LIMA below bust.
1750 „ „ 2. „ „ 3.
1751 „ „ 2. „ „ 3.

George III
No halfcrowns of the type so far described were issued in this reign. See note under Crowns.

The above lists are but a brief outline of what exists. Many minor varieties occur, especially in the William III pieces. Overstruck dates, mis-spellings, letters upside down in the edge legends, Irish harps with different numbers of strings and similar variations may be looked for. Halfcrowns, back to 1551 if need be, and onwards to the present are a popular collecting theme in themselves.

SHILLINGS
The designs of the Shillings followed very closely those of the Halfcrowns. Space will not permit their presentation in quite such detail. Broadly, the same types of varieties, major and minor, occur, though not necessarily with dates that coincide with those of the Halfcrowns. By now the reader probably knows what to look for, the more detailed descriptions being given in the standard works to be listed at the end of this section.

Charles II
Five main obverse types, one reverse type.

Plate 60 The base metal coinage continued
1 William and Mary, tin Farthing of 1692. **2** William III, copper Halfpenny of 1696. **3** Anne, the famous copper Farthing of 1714, never put into circulation and the origin of many legends as to its value. **4** George I, copper Halfpenny of 1717, sometimes called 'dump' because of its thick dumpy appearance. **5** George II, copper Halfpenny of 1729. **6–9** George III. The famous Boulton and Watt, Soho mint pure copper pieces of 1797. The currency Twopence, weighing 2 oz. *avoir*, and a Penny, Halfpenny and Farthing from some of the many designs considered or adopted. **10** George IV. Farthing, in copper, with the first type obverse. The king objected to the caricature of his portrait as rendered by Pistrucci. The reverse, though fussy by modern standards, is a fine example of the detailed engraving of William Wyon. Dated 1821, this piece is of the first year of issue. **11** George IV. Penny, in copper, 1925. The obverse, the second type, was engraved by Wyon from a bust of the king by Chantrey. The reverse is by William Wyon, and is similar to the Farthing though differing in detail.

Dates of issue:

1663	Obv.	types	1 and 2.	1676	Obv.	types	3.
1666	,,	,,	2 and 3.	1677	,,	,,	3.
1668	,,	,,	2 and 3.	1678	,,	,,	3.
1669	,,	,,	2 and 3.	1679	,,	,,	3.
1670	,,	,,	3.	1680	,,	,,	3.
1671	,,	,,	3.	1681	,,	,,	3.
1672	,,	,,	3.	1682	,,	,,	3.
1673	,,	,,	3.	1683	,,	,,	3 and 5.
1674	,,	,,	3 and 4.	1684	,,	,,	5.
1675	,,	,,	3 and 4.				

Notes. Look for altered dates, plumes on one or both sides, elephant, (1666) or elephant and castle. Some dates are extremely rare.

James II

One obverse and one reverse type only.

Dates of issue:

1685	1687
1686	1688

Notes. Look for altered dates and varieties in punctuation. No extremely rare pieces in this reign.

William & Mary

One obverse and one reverse type only, the latter with the monogram WM and the date figures in the shield angles.

Dates of issue:

1692	1693

Notes. Look for punctuation varieties.

William III

Seven obverse types, one normal reverse type, though a reverse occurs with the shields of Scotland and Ireland transposed: the normal position for Ireland is at nine o'clock. This variety only occurs in 1697. The provincial mints were in operation, as for Halfcrowns.

Dates of issue:

Only the obverse types will be given, save for 1697.

1695 Obv. type 1.

1696 ,, ,, 1. Provincial mint marks, B. C. E. N. Y. and y occur on the obverse in this year.

1696 Obv. type 2.
„ „ 3.
„ „ 3, with C and Y.
1697 Obv. type 1. Rev. type 1.
„ „ 1. „ „ 2.
„ „ 1. „ „ 2.
„ „ 3. „ „ 1.
„ „ 4. „ „ 1.
„ „ 4. „ „ 1, with all provincial mint letters.

An extremely rare variety has the arms of France and Ireland transposed.

1698 Obv. type 4.
„ „ 5.
1699 „ „ 5.
„ „ 6.
1700 „ „ 6.
„ „ 7.
1701 „ „ 6.

Notes. Look for punctuation variations, small lions in the British arms, plumes on reverse, roses on reverse and plume under bust. So many varieties exist that the reader is referred to Jackson Kent, *ante*.

Anne

Four main obverse types, two main reverse types. These concern the pre- and post-Union arms. Plumes or roses and plumes can occur in the angles of both types: or either can occur without them. Dates of issue:

1702 Obv. type 1. Rev. type 1, with VIGO below bust.
1703 „ „ 2. „ „ 1, with VIGO below bust.
1704 „ „ 2. „ „ 1.
1705 „ „ 2. „ „ 1.
1707 „ „ 2. „ „ 1.
„ „ 3. „ „ 2.
1708 „ „ 2. „ „ 2.
„ „ 3. „ „ 2.
1709 „ „ 3. „ „ 2.
1710 „ „ 3. „ „ 2.
„ „ 4. „ „ 2.

Dates of issue:

1711	Obv.	type	3.	Rev.	type	2.
	,,	,,	4.	,,	,,	2.
1712	,,	,,	4.	,,	,,	2.

Plate 61 *The base metal coinage continued*
1 William IV. Penny, in copper, 1834. The obverse was engraved from a bust of the king of Chantrey and is the work of William Wyon. The reverse is William Wyon's rendering of Britannia. **2** Victoria. Penny, in copper, 1841. The whole of this coin was designed and engraved by William Wyon. The obverse had his fine portrait head of the young Queen, signed W.W. on the truncation. The reverse is similar to that by the same artist on Pennies of the two previous reigns. **3** Victoria. Half Farthing, in copper, 1842. Although struck for use in Ceylon, this denomination was made current in Britain from June 1842 till December 1869, in which year the last of the copper coinage was demonetized, leaving only bronze in circulation. **4** Victoria. Penny, in bronze, 1860. This was the first year of issue of the bronze coinage and this piece is often called the 'bun' Penny on account of the Queen's hair style. The whole coin was designed and engraved by L. C. Wyon. Note the lighthouse and ship. The former went through many varieties of appearance in minor detail. As will be seen (**5–9**), both disappeared later, but the lighthouse returned again in 1937, and still remains. It was said there was no room for the ship, though in fact the space for it was still there, partly occupied by the Y in PENNY. Apparently tradition would not allow so fine a ship as the *Queen Mary* to take the place of the now outdated sailing vessel. **5** Victoria. Penny, in bronze, 1898. There was no 'Jubilee head' penny, the design jumping from 'young head' to 'old head' in 1895. Both ship and lighthouse have now disappeared, since Britannia now took up more of the available space. **6, 7** Edward VII–George V. Pennies, in bronze. Father and son on the obverses with a similar design on the reverse. Britannia still crowds out the lighthouse and ship. **8, 9** George VI–Elizabeth II. Pennies in bronze. Father and daughter face each other above a common reverse. Britannia has been modelled on a smaller scale so there is now room for the lighthouse. A little contracting of the legend would have left room for a liner or a battleship: after all we are, or were, a maritime nation, building the world's best ships. Would tradition not allow funnel to replace sail? **10, 11** George VI. Halfpenny and Farthing, in bronze, 1951. Apparently tradition would not allow funnel to replace sail. Already our coinage was looking back to the past and the designer of the Halfpenny, Paget, gave us Drake's *Golden Hind*. Very acceptable, in its way, but had our modern maritime architects no claim to be represented? Perhaps we shall have the *Queen Elizabeth 2* on the coins of 2061. However, we did get one of our native birds, the Wren, smallest of them all, on the Farthing. **12** George VI. Threepence, in nickel-brass, 1951. Introduced in 1937 with the new coinage of the reign this 12-sided piece soon proved useful, in the days when threepence would still buy something. Disliked by some, this thick, chunky coin finally replaced its silver counterpart, which now only remains in use in the series of Maundy coins. **13** Elizabeth II. Threepence, in nickel-brass, 1961. The portcullis first appeared on the coinage of Henry VIII. Apart from recalling the past, what is its purpose now?

1834
1
1841
2
HALF
FARTHING
3
3
4
1860
4
1
2
6
1902
6 – 7
5
1898
5
7
10
1951
10
8
9
1937
8 – 9
1951
FARTHING
11
12
13
1951
12
1961
13

1
1
2
2
3
3
4
4
5
5
6
6
7
7
8
8
9
9
10
10
11
11
12
12
13
13
14
14

Dates of issue:
1713 Obv. type 4. Rev. type 2.
1714 „ „ 4. „ „ 2.

Notes. Look for punctuation varieties and for upside down letters in 1714.

George I

Two main obverse types:

1 The king's hair-tie behind his head has two straight ends.
2 The tie has a loop. With 2 the letters W C C can occur under the bust (=Welsh Copper Company metal).

Four main reverse types:

1 Roses and plumes in the angles.
2 Plain in the angles.

Plate 62 Scottish Coinage

1 David I, 1124–1153. Silver Penny, struck at Roxburgh mint, probably in the early part of the reign. **2** Henry, Earl of Northumberland, 1139–1152. Silver Penny, mint unknown. Henry was the son of David I, was created Earl of Northumberland by the English king, Stephen, in 1139, and died before his father. His sons became Malcolm IV, 1153–1165, and William the Lion, 1165–1214. **3** William the Lion, 1165–1214. Silver Penny, struck at Roxburgh mint. **4** Alexander III, 1249–1285. Silver Penny, struck at Edinburgh mint. **5** John Baliol, 1292–1296. Silver Penny. **6** Robert Bruce, 1306–1329. Silver Penny. The coins of this king have no mint names. **7** David II, 1329–1371. Gold Noble, probably struck soon after 1357. This exceedingly rare piece, of which only five are known, imitated the gold Nobles of the contemporary English king, Edward III, corresponding in weight and fineness to Edward's Fourth Coinage, 1351–1361. **8** Robert II, 1371–1390. Silver Groat, struck at Edinburgh mint, VILLA EDINBVRGH being the inner legend on the reverse. **9** James I, 1406–1437. Gold Demy. The obverse has the lion of Scotland. In the centre of the St. Andrew's cross on the reverse is a tiny I (Jacobus). The value of the piece appears to have been about 9s., the same value as the contemporary English Half-Noble. **10** James II, 1437–1460. Gold Lion. Sometimes called the St. Andrew on account of the reverse, these pieces, first struck in 1451 had a value of 6s. 8d., later raised to 10s. **11** James III, 1460–1488. Gold Rider, probably struck shortly before 1476. By breaking through the ring of beads and the legend at various points the spirited representation of the king on horseback has an almost three-dimensional appearance. In 1491 its value was 23s. **12** James IV, 1488–1514. Gold Unicorn. The numeral 4 appears after the king's name. On this, the British Museum specimen, only the tail of the figure can be seen. Unicorns were first struck in 1486 (James III), and were current for 18s. **13** James V, 1514–1542. Gold Bonnet Piece, 1539. These are the first dated coins of the Scottish series. English coins did not begin to be dated before the silver of 1547–8, Edward VI. Current for 40s. **14** Mary, 1542–1567. Silver Testoon of 1561, coinage period III, during Mary's first widowhood after the death of Francis of France. Current for 5s.

3 S S C in the angles.
4 Plumes and interlinked Cs in alternate angles.

Dates of issue:

1715	Obv.	type	1.	Rev.	type	1.
1716	,,	,,	1.	,,	,,	1.
1717	,,	,,	1.	,,	,,	1.
1718	,,	,,	1.	,,	,,	1.
1719	,,	,,	1.	,,	,,	1.
1720	,,	,,	1.	,,	,,	1.
	,,	,,	1.	,,	,,	2.
1721	,,	,,	1.	,,	,,	1.
	,,	,,	1.	,,	,,	2.
1722	,,	,,	1.	,,	,,	1.
1723	,,	,,	1.	,,	,,	1.
	,,	,,	1.	,,	,,	3.
	,,	,,	2.	,,	,,	3.
	,,	,,	2.	,,	,,	1.
	,,	,,	2.	,,	,,	4.
1724	,,	,,	2.	,,	,,	1.
	,,	,,	2.	,,	,,	4.
1725	,,	,,	2.	,,	,,	1.
	,,	,,	2.	,,	,,	4.
1726	,,	,,	2.	,,	,,	1.
	,,	,,	2.	,,	,,	4.
1727	,,	,,	2.	,,	,,	1.

Notes. Look for punctuation varieties, arms of France at twelve o'clock (very rare [1723 1–3]), and overstruck dates.

George II

Two main obverse types:
1 Young head.
2 Old head, sometimes with LIMA below. (See Crowns).

Four main reverse types:
1 With plumes in angles.
2 With roses and plumes alternate.
3 Plain.
4 Roses only.

Dates of issue:

1727	Obv.	type	1.	Rev.	type	1.
	,,	,,	1.	,,	,,	2.
1728	,,	,,	1.	,,	,,	2.
	,,	,,	1.	,,	,,	3.
1729	,,	,,	1.	,,	,,	2.
1731	,,	,,	1.	,,	,,	1.
	,,	,,	1.	,,	,,	2.
1732	,,	,,	1.	,,	,,	2.
1734	,,	,,	1.	,,	,,	2.
1735	,,	,,	1.	,,	,,	2.
1736	,,	,,	1.	,,	,,	2.
1737	,,	,,	1.	,,	,,	2.
1739	,,	,,	1.	,,	,,	4.
1741	,,	,,	1.	,,	,,	4.
1743	,,	,,	2.	,,	,,	4.
1745	,,	,,	2.	,,	,,	3, LIMA.
	,,	,,	2.	,,	,,	4.
1746	,,	,,	2.	,,	,,	3, LIMA.
1747	,,	,,	2.	,,	,,	4.
1750	,,	,,	2.	,,	,,	3.
1751	,,	,,	2.	,,	,,	3.
1758	,,	,,	2.	,,	,,	3.

Notes. Look for punctuation varieties, overstruck dates 1746 and 1750 and a large o in date 1750. No great rarities in this reign.

George III

Three main obverse types, all quite distinctive.

Four main reverse types:

1 Crowned shields of arms, as normal type so far.
2 Uncrowned shields of arms, the limbs of the Star of the Garter elongated into the angles, a crown above each point.
3 Similar, but the arms of the Electorate have no tiny hearts above the lion rampant in the second quarter.
4 Large crowned shield of arms within the Garter, occupying the whole flan.

Dates of issue:

1763	Obv.	type	1.	Rev.	type	1.
1787	,,	,,	2.	,,	,,	2.

Dates of issue:

1787 Obv. type 2. Rev. type 3.

1798 ,, ,, 2. ,, ,, 3.

1816, 1817, 1818, 1819 and 1820 all Obv. type 3. Rev. type 4, phase two of the milled coinage.

Notes. Obverse type 3 coupled with reverse type 4 takes the Shilling into phase two of the milled coinage, to be dealt with *post* as a separate section. The 1798 Obverse type 2, reverse type 3 piece is known as the Dorrien & Magens shilling, was struck from bullion sent to the mint from a private source, was recalled and is extremely rare. There are not a large number of minor varieties to look for.

SIXPENCES

These follow closely the types of the Shilling. They can be regarded as a collecting theme, but are mostly added by the collector to his cabinet as an addition to his collection of the milled series, rather than as a collecting theme on their own. Only dates issued will therefore be given.

Charles II. 1674, 1675, 1676, 1677, 1678, 1679, 1680, 1681, 1682, 1683. 1684.

James II. 1686, 1687, 1688.

William & Mary. 1693, 1694.

William III. 1695, 1696, 1697, 1698, 1699, 1700, 1701.

Anne. 1703, 1705, 1707, 1708, 1710, 1711.

George I. 1717, 1720, 1723, 1726.

George II. 1728, 1731, 1732, 1734, 1735, 1736, 1739, 1741, 1743, 1745, 1746, 1750, 1751, 1757, 1758.

George III. 1787 (in phase two 1816, 1817, 1818, 1819, 1820).

Notes. As with the Halfcrowns and Shillings there are the usual varieties to look for. Charles II, overstruck dates: James II, similar in 1687: William & Mary, 3 over 3 upside down in 1693: William III, the provincial mint letters, punctuation variations, arms wrongly placed, upside down letters, plumes on reverse, roses on reverse, plumes under bust in 1700: Anne, pre- and post-Union shields, plumes and roses and plumes on reverse: George I, overstruck date in 1720, small letters on obverse in 1723, with S S C on reverse: George II, young and old head, overstruck dates, plain reverse, plumes on reverse, roses and plumes on reverse, and roses only on reverse: George III, as for the Shillings.

The major denominations of the silver coinage issued under phase one of the English milled series have thus been listed. Much more detail could have, and probably should have been given had space permitted. Since this book is but a guide the reader is, once again, counselled to refer to the standard works on this subject. These are *The Milled Coinage of England*, and *The English Silver Coinage from 1649* and similar works in which every detail of the series is given.

Under phase one of the English milled series there still remain to be dealt with the minor silver issues. These consist of the Fourpence or Groat, the descendant of the original Groat introduced with the Fourth Coinage of Edward III in 1351; the Threepence which appeared circa 1550, Edward VI; the Half Groat or Twopence which came with the Groat under Edward III, and the Penny, still with us since the eighth century.

A large number of collectors collect these four denominations under the heading of Maundy money. The story of this ancient charitable ceremony was dealt with in *The Beginner's Guide to Coin Collecting* (Pelham Books), p. 30, ff. Maundy money is a collecting theme, and a complete series from 1662 till 1969 forms a collection of considerable value.

It has to be remembered that when phase one of our milled coinage commenced in the reign of Charles II, these four small silver coins were, in theory at least, in day-to-day use. They passed out of such use with the gradual introduction of copper and bronze Pennies, Halfpennies and Farthings. The point at which the four small silver denominations began to be set aside for the Maundy Thursday ceremony is postulated by Brooke in his standard work, *English Coins*. Dealing with the introduction of milled coinage, he writes, 'The common belief that the sixpence was the lowest denomination now struck for ordinary currency, and that the smaller coins were made for Maundy distribution, is incorrect. The penny, which was the only coin distributed as Maundy, was struck under ordinary indenture and circulated. It was not till 1729, or possibly 1731, that the pieces of 4d., 3d., and 2d. were used as Maundy, and only since that date have they and the silver penny ceased to circulate as currency. Maundy money is, of course, and always has been, legal tender. The term "Maundy money" is only applicable in and after the reign of George II.'

So far as the coins themselves are concerned, those collectors who make them their theme have elected to start the Maundy series with the last hammered coinage of Charles II. Taking the story back to front, at the present time the silver 4d., 3d., 2d. and 1d., the only silver coins which we still have, are issued each year for the Maundy ceremony. Though they are legal tender, they are now struck for no other purpose than that of the Maundy distribution. What will happen to these four denominations after decimalization remains to be seen. Back as far as 1822, George IV, each of these four denominations has been issued every year. Before 1822 this was not so. Thus, in 1779 only the Penny was struck and in 1762 only the Threepence. In the majority of years back to Charles II, last hammered issue, all four denominations appeared, but there are several instances over the period when one or more denomination is missing.

The collector of Maundy money will not, therefore, be able to obtain a set of four pieces for every year from the last hammered issue of Charles II down to 1969. This fact is therefore accepted by the collector, whose complete Maundy collection may have only a Penny to represent one particular year.

Since Maundy money settled down into sets of four coins in about 1822 the issue of such pieces has been limited. These limits have become more stringent since the reign of Victoria. At the present time only the actual pensioners and a number of officials connected with the ceremony receive Maundy money. Thus, these four pieces have become some of the rarest coins to be issued. In 1965 only 1,221 pieces were issued for the denominations of Fourpence to Twopence and only 1,143 Pennies were issued.

Over the centuries the appearance of the coins has differed little. The head of the monarch naturally occupies the obverse, and the reverse, apart from some of the earlier issues, usually shows the value in Roman, later Arabic figures. Even within this rare series their are greater rarities, and minor varieties. The Penny of 1689 is a great rarity, but about the rarest pieces in the series are the 2d., 3d. and 4d. of 1765, (George III). It is possible that a Penny may exist, but it had not been seen as late as 1950.

As a whole, therefore, Maundy money is a rare series. A complete set, from the hammered series of Charles II down to 1969 is not only an interesting collecting theme, but is a good investment. Nor does the value lie entirely in the coins of previous centuries.

Sets of Maundy money of the present Queen command high prices, as may be realized by the issue figures given above. Some 1,200 coins go just nowhere among the millions of collectors at the present time.

We thus come to the end of a very brief account of the milled coinage of England, phase one. As has been said, at this point in time the Royal Mint was moved from its traditional home in the Tower of London, and established in its own buildings on Little Tower Hill, from which location it is about to move to Wales.

The milled coinage phase two reflects the industrial revolution. The Mint was not slow to take advantage of the prime mover in this revolution: steam power. Since the necessary facilities for the generation of such power could not be accommodated in the antiquated premises occupied in the Tower, the Mint for the first time in its history was given its own premises, and could exist as an entity; The Royal Mint.

CHAPTER SIX

Milled Coinage, Phase Two

Phase two of the story of our milled coinage saw two great reforms. The first, the removal of the Mint to its own premises, was mentioned in the last chapter. It had taken some five hundred years for the Mint to be displaced from the Tower of London, where it must have existed on sufferance for many generations. Now in 1816 it was established in its own 'house' designed by Smirke and still standing, and could go about its business hindered by none. In some measure the move was brought about by the energetic Birmingham manufacturer Matthew Boulton, who, after years of campaigning, had at last convinced the Treasury that in his steam-powered mint at Soho he could, with his improved minting machinery, produce more accurate coins in shape and weight than could the Royal Mint.

Boulton's improvements needed the then dangerous power supplied by the steam engine, which needed copious supplies of fire and water to generate its energy. Enquiries were made to find out if such a monster could be accommodated in the Tower, but it was felt that such risks could not be taken. The army, long in superior control of the fortress, now squeezed the mint out of its domain. If the Mint wanted to set itself on fire or blow itself up with steam engines it should not do so in the Tower.

The second great reform affected the coinage itself. For economic reasons too complex to be dealt with here, the coinage had run into a very poor state. The whole monetary system had to be reformed, as it had been in 1662, and this reform, coinciding with the removal of the Royal Mint, now took place. Why and how it was carried out is told in detail by Craig in 'The Mint', as well as by many other writers.

So far as the collector is concerned a new coinage appeared. The Guinea, for so long the pound unit, with its multiples and fractions, disappeared, to be replaced by the new Pound, now reverting to an ancient name, the Sovereign. The revaluation of the pound unit left the Guinea worth 21s., and from this period dates the custom of offering the customer an article priced in Guineas, a polite, snob-value way of demanding an extra shilling in the pound.

In the silver range the denominations remained the same, from Crown to Penny, but now there was a copper range of Penny, Halfpenny and Farthing, which will be dealt with in its place.

Milled Coinage, phase two, from 1816

THE KINGS AND QUEENS

George III (1760–1820)
Already detailed.
George IV (1820–1830)
Eldest son of George III. Made Prince Regent during his father's illness.
William IV (1830–1837)
Third son of George III.
Victoria (1837–1901)
Only child of the Duke of Kent, who was a son of George III, and the Princess Louisa Victoria of Saxe-Coburg.
Edward VII (1901–1910)
Eldest son of Victoria.
George V (1910–1936)
Second son of Edward VII.
Edward VIII (1936)
Eldest son of George V, uncrowned, abdicated 11th December, 1936.
George VI (1936–1952)
Second son (Duke of York) of George V. Succeeded his elder brother on the latter's abdication.
Elizabeth II (1952–)
Eldest daughter of George VI.

THE COINAGE

The coinage which was put into circulation after the reform carried out during the reign of George III, and issued from the new Royal Mint on Tower Hill is not difficult to deal with. The Sovereign, or One Pound Piece was the gold unit, with multiples of Five- and Two Pounds, which, so far as can be traced, never circulated. In the reign of Victoria it is said that these two pieces were struck from gold specially purchased by the Mint for the purpose. In that reign they were struck as proofs in the specimen sets of 1887 and 1893, and as normal coins made for collectors, not for general use. The Sovereign was subdivided into the Half Sovereign, value ten shillings.

The silver; after 1946 cupro-nickel; range consisted of the Crown, Halfcrown, Florin or Two Shillings; introduced in the reign of Victoria as a step towards decimalization; the Shilling, Sixpence and Threepence, together with the Fourpence, Twopence and Penny which, with the Threepence were used for Maundy Money, which remain our only silver coins at the present day.

In 1797–1799 the ancestors of our present bronze Penny, Halfpenny and Farthing, the latter no longer struck, appeared. They will be dealt with separately, as stated above.

GOLD

FIVE POUNDS

George III

No issue, apart from a few pattern pieces.

George IV

No issue, apart from a few pattern or proof pieces.

William IV

No issue.

Victoria

Two main obverse types:

1 Jubilee head, 1887.

2 Old head, 1893.

One reverse type:

St. George and dragon.

Dates of issue:

1887, 1: and 1893, 2, struck as proof and currency pieces, the latter never circulating, as far as is known.

Edward VII

Issued as frosted proofs (i.e. dull finish) only, in 1902.

Obverse. Head of the king, reverse, St. George.

George V

Issued as proofs only in 1911. Type as Edward VII, but with head of George V.

Edward VIII

No issue. It is said that about two sets of the whole coinage of Edward VIII were issued as proofs, to keep the coinage record in being. If this is so such sets were never seen by the public.

George VI

Issued as proofs only in 1937. Type as George V, but with head of George VI.

Elizabeth II

No issue. Remarks as for Edward VIII.

TWO POUNDS

George III

No issue.

George IV

Issued in 1823. Obverse: head of king. Reverse: St. George.

William IV

No issue.

Victoria

As for Five Pounds.

Edward VII

As for Five Pounds.

George V

As For Five Pounds.

Edward VIII

As above.

George VI

As for Five Pounds.

Elizabeth II

As above, for Edward VIII.

SOVEREIGNS

George III

One type only. Obverse: head of George III. Reverse: St. George and dragon within the Garter.

Dates of issue:

1817	1820
1818	

George IV

Two main types:

1 Head of George IV by Pistrucci. Reverse: St. George, no Garter as border.

2 Head of George IV by Wyon based on Chantrey's bust of the king. Reverse: Crowned shield of arms.

Dates of issue:

1821 type 1.	1825 type 2.
1822 ,,	1826 ,,
1823 ,,	1827 ,,
1824 ,,	1828 ,,
1825 ,,	1829 ,,
	1830 ,,

William IV

One type only.

Obverse: head of William IV.

Reverse: crowned shield of arms.

Dates of issue:

1831	1835
1832	1836
1833	1837

Victoria

Five main obverse types:

1 Young head.

2 Young head with different wreath.

3 Young head with new legends.

4 Jubilee head.

5 Old head.

Three main reverse types:

1 Crowned shield of arms.

2 The same, but shield narrower.

3 St. George

Dates of issue:

1838, 1839, 1841, 1842, 1843, all Obv. type 1. Rev. type 1.

1843 Obv. type 2. Rev. type 2.

1844, 1845, 1846, 1847, 1848, 1849, 1850, 1851, 1852, 1853, 1854, 1855, 1856, 1857, 1858, 1859, 1860, 1861, 1862, 1863, 1864, 1865, 1866, 1868, 1869, 1870, 1871, all Obv. type 1. Rev. type 1.

1871 Obv. type 3. Rev. type 3.
1872 „ „ 3. „ „ 1.
„ „ 3. „ „ 3.
1873 „ „ 3. „ „ 1.
„ „ 3. „ „ 3.
1874 „ „ 3. „ „ 1.
„ „ 3. „ „ 3.
1876 „ „ 3. „ „ 3.
1878, 1879, 1880, 1884, 1885, all Obv. type 3. Rev. type 3.
1887, 1888, 1889, 1890, 1891, 1892, all Obv. type 4. Rev. type 3.
1893, 1894, 1895, 1896, 1898, 1899, 1900, 1901, all Obv. type 5. Rev. type 3.

Notes. Varieties to look for, 1856–1859 with narrow date figures. 1864–1879, with die numbers. During this period small numbers were placed on the dies partly to determine how long a die lasted in use.

Edward VII

One type only.
Obverse: head of Edward VII.
Reverse: St. George.
Dates of issue:

1902	1907
1903	1908
1904	1909
1905	1910
1906	

Notes. No main varieties to look for.

George V

One type only.
Obverse: head of George V.
Reverse: St. George, as for Edward VII.
Dates of issue:

1911	1915
1912	1916
1913	1917
1914	1925

Notes. No main varieties to look for. The 1925 issue was not put into circulation.

Edward VIII

No issue, see notes above. (p. 203).

George VI

No issue for general circulation. Proofs only, see notes above (under Five Pounds).

Elizabeth II

One type only.
Obverse: head of Elizabeth II.
Reverse: St. George.
Dates of issue:

1957	1962	1965
1958	1963	1966
1959	1964	1967
		1968

Notes. These Sovereigns were not struck for general circulation. Their purpose was partly to keep the technicians at the Royal Mint familiar with the special skills needed to strike gold coins, partly keep the coin in being, since in the Middle East many keep their savings in actual Sovereigns, and partly to make acceptable to those people a Sovereign showing a female head. An ancient prejudice had existed against Sovereigns which did not show a male head.

HALF SOVEREIGNS

George III

One type only.
Obverse: head of George III.
Reverse: crowned shield of arms.

Dates of issue:

1817	1820
1818	

George IV

Two main obverse types:

1 Head of George IV by Pistrucci.
2 Similar, by Wyon after Chantrey. (See Sovereigns above).

Three main reverse types:

1 Oval crowned shield of arms with shamrock and thistle garniture.

2 Square crowned shield of arms.
3 Square garnished crowned shield of arms.

Dates of issue:

1821	Obv.	type	1.	Rev.	type	1.
1823	,,	,,	1.	,,	,,	2.
1824	,,	,,	1.	,,	,,	2.
1825	,,	,,	1.	,,	,,	2.
1826	,,	,,	2.	,,	,,	3.
1827	,,	,,	2.	,,	,,	3.
1828	,,	,,	2.	,,	,,	3.

William IV
One obverse type:
Head of William IV, but the coin in two sizes.
1 Small.
2 Large, i.e. normal size.
One reverse type:
Garnished crowned shield of arms.
Dates of issue:
1834 Obv. type 1. Rev. type 1.
1835, 1836, 1837, all Obv. type 2. Rev. type 2.

Victoria
Three main obverse types:
1 Young head.
2 Jubilee head.
3 Old head.
Two main reverse types:
1 Crowned shield of arms.
2 St. George.
Dates of issue:
1838, 1839, 1841, 1842, 1843, 1844, 1845, 1846, 1847, 1848, 1849, 1850, 1851, 1852, 1853, 1854, 1855, 1856, 1857, 1858, 1859, 1860, 1861, 1863, 1864, 1865, 1866, 1867, 1869, 1870, 1871, 1872, 1873, 1874, 1875, 1876, 1877, 1878, 1879, 1880, 1883, 1884, 1885, 1886, all Obv. type 1. Rev. type 1.
1887, 1888, 1889, 1890, 1891, 1892, 1893, all Obv. type 2. Rev. type 1. 1893, 1894, 1895, 1896, 1897, 1898, 1899, 1900, 1901, all Obv. type 3. Rev. type 2.

Edward VII

One type only.

Obverse: head of Edward VII.

Reverse: St. George.

Dates of issue:

1902	1907
1903	1908
1904	1909
1905	1910
1906	

George V

One type only. Obverse: head of George V. Reverse: St. George, as for Edward VII.

Dates of issue:

1911	1914
1912	1915
1913	

After 1915 no Half Sovereigns were struck. Gold no longer circulated. Subject to notes above concerning proof issues struck to

Plate 63 Scottish Coinage, continued

1 Mary, 1542–1567. Silver Ryal, 1567, coinage period V, after the death of Darnley. Struck in this year only. Current for 30s. The countermark', a crowned thistle, was added during the next reign and the pieces reissued at the enhanced value of 36s. 9d. **2** James VI, 1567–1625 (James I of England, 1603–1625). Gold, Twenty Pound Piece, 1576. This large, handsome and very rare piece weighed one ounce Scottish. The earliest issue of the reign, the piece was once considered to be a medal, on account of its size. **3** James VI. Gold Ducat or Four Pound Piece, 1580. Struck on this date only. **4** James VI. Gold Lion Noble, 1586. Current at £3 15s. sometimes called the Scottish Angel since it corresponded in size and weight to the English coin of that name. Note the similarity of the lion on the obverse with that on Kruger Gray's English 'Scottish' Shilling of 1937. **5** James VI. Gold Hat piece, 1591. This piece, current at £4 must have had a short life. In the same year all the gold money in circulation was called in, save for the Thistle Noble (not illustrated). **6** James VI. Gold Rider, 1594. Current for £5 the Act which ordered the striking of this piece and its half was that which called in all the other gold coins save the Thistle Noble. The equestrian figure is not so spirited as was that of James III of 118 years before. James VI was a much more nervous man, probably on account of his adventurous peril-surrounded early life. **7** James VI. Silver Thirty Shilling Piece, 1585. This fine portrait piece was drawn by Lord Seyton's painter and the dies made by Thomas Foulis. There was a similar Forty Shilling Piece. **8** James VI. Billon Plack, 1583–1588. Current for 8d. **9** James VI. Billon Hardhead, 1588. Current for 2d.

3
3
4
4
1
1
5
5
2
2
6
7
7
6
8
8
9
9

1
1
4
2
2
5
5
4
3
3
6
6
7
8
8
7

keep the coinage record in being, no further Half Sovereigns were minted at the Royal Mint, London. The milled coinage, phase two, gold coins, is therefore, ended.

SILVER after 1946 *cupro-nickel.*
CROWNS

George III

One main type only.

Obverse: head of George III.

Reverse: St. George and the dragon within the Garter, the whole design by Pistrucci.

Plate 64 Scottish Coinage, continued

1 James VI, 1567–1625 (James I of England, 1603–1625). Gold Unit, of the second coinage period, after James's accession to the English throne. Current for £12 Scottish or 20s. English. Grueber points out, 'The proportionate current value of the Scottish and English coins at this time was at 12 to 1. Thus the unite or twenty shillings English was equivalent to £12 Scottish, and the English shilling to the twelve shillings Scottish.' **2** James VI. Copper Turner or Twopence, 1614. In the English series of copper pieces of James VI and I mention was made of the money the king made out of the concession. The same thing was going on in Scotland for, says Grueber, 'This copper coinage, which was first issued in 1614, was ordered out of the king's pity and commiseration for the poor without any kind of consideration of profit for himself. Yet its current value per stone was at £26 13s. 4d. as against its metal value of £17 1s. 4d.' **3** Charles I, 1625–1649. Gold Unit or Sceptre, second issue. Current for £12 Scottish, 20s. English. The dies were by Briot, appointed master of the Scottish mint in 1635. He was assisted by Falconer, his son-in-law. Struck by the mill and screw press, this early mill coin was made from gold by the African Company from bullion obtained from Guinea. Note the 'signature', a thistle and ϖ. **4** Charles I. Silver Three Pound Piece or Crown, first issue. Current for 60s. Scottish, 5s. English. **5** Charles I. Silver Two Shillings, first issue. **6** Charles I. Silver Twelve Shillings, third issue, from January 1637. Another early mill piece by Briot/Falconer, this time with the latter's 'signature', ᅲ. Very similar to the English Shilling, its equivalent, the XII in this case standing for shillings instead of pence. **7** Charles I. Silver Sixty Shillings, fourth issue. Another fine early mill piece by Briot, this time, apparently, without Falconer's assistance. Note the 'signature', now turned round so that the thistle stands upright. These fine pieces give some idea of what the English coinage of the period might have been like but for the Civil War and the Commonwealth. **8** Charles II, 1660–1684. Silver Four Merk Piece, 1674. From dies by Joachim Harder, graver at the Edinburgh mint, the stamps being made by Thomas Simon, whom we saw in connection with the English coinage of the period. Falconer, now Sir John, has his initial below the bust. Charles II appointed him principal Warden of the Mint. The LIII above 4 in the centre of the reverse is the value, 53s. 4d.

Dates of issue:

1818 1820

1819

George IV

One main type only.

Obverse: head of George IV.

Reverse: St George, no Garter border, the design 'after' Pistrucci.

Dates of issue:

1821 1822

William IV

No issue. Dies for this piece were prepared but only a few patterns were struck.

Victoria

Four main obverse types:

1 Young head.
2 'Gothic' bust.
3 Jubilee head.
4 Old head.

Three main reverse types:

1 Crowned shield of arms.
2 'Gothic' type, basically four crowned shields of arms with emblems in the angles and 'Gothic' lettering.
3 St. George, after Pistrucci.

Dates of issue:

1844, 1845, 1847, all Obverse type 1. Reverse type 1.

1847 Obv. type 2. Rev. type. 2.

1887, 1888, 1889, 1890, 1891, 1892, all Obv. type 3. Rev. type 3.

1893, 1894, 1895, 1896, 1897, 1898, 1899, 1900, all Obv. type 4. Rev. type 3.

Notes. The regnal dates on the edge legend vary in the old head types. The DECVS ET TUTAMEN edge legend is used in 1844 and on the old head types. The edge of the Jubilee type is grained.

Edward VII

One main type only.

Obverse: head of Edward VII.

Reverse: St. George.

Dates of issue:
1902 only

George V

Two main obverse types:
1 Head of George V.
2 Similar, but slightly smaller, remodelled head.

Two main reverse types:
1 A crown with date above, within a wreath.
2 A modernized form of St. George and dragon.

Dates of issue:
1927, proofs only.
1928, 1929, 1930, 1931, 1932, 1933, 1934, 1935, 1936, the last two years, Obv. type 2. Rev. type 2, respectively.

Notes. The Crowns of George V are the rarest in the whole Crown series, so far as numbers struck but not so far as numbers which survive of other reigns. As a coin for daily use the piece had almost passed out of circulation. No Crown was issued with the new coinage in 1911, and but for the protests of numismatists the piece might have ceased to be struck. With the remodelled coinage of 1927 the Crown reappeared, in this year as a proof only. It continued to be struck, as shown in the date list, but only in very small numbers. A larger issue was made in 1935, (type 2), to mark the Jubilee of the King. At this point it seems to have been realized that the Crown could be issued as a commemorative piece, as will be seen.

The small issue of Crowns in 1936, struck after the death of George V are often considered, with reasonable precedent, as the issue of Edward VIII.

Edward VIII

No issue, but see notes above.

George VI

One main obverse type:
Head of George VI.

Two reverse types:
1 Crowned royal arms, with supporters.
2 St. George, after Pistrucci. The head on the second issue is very slightly smaller, to allow for a continuous legend.

Dates of issue:

1937 Obv. type 1. Rev. type 1. In silver.

1951 ,, ,, 1. ,, ,, 2. In cupro-nickel.

Elizabeth II

Two obverse types:

1 The Queen on horseback.

2 Bust of the Queen.

Two reverse types:

1 Four plain shields of arms, rose, shamrock, leek and thistle in the angles, crown in the centre. The leek divides the date.

2 Sir Winston Churchill.

Dates of issue:

1953 Obv. type 1. Rev. type 1.

1960 ,, ,, 2. ,, ,, 1.

1965 ,, ,, 2. ,, ,, 2.

Plate 65 Scottish Coinage, continued

1 Charles II, 1660–1684. Silver Dollar, 1682. Struck from dies by Jan Roettier, with Sir John Falconer's initial in front of the bust. Very similar to the contemporary English Crown save that the arms are in different sequence: 1, Scotland; 2, England; 3, France; 4, Ireland. Thistles occupy the angles instead of interlinked c's, a pair of these having taken the place of the Star of the Garter in the centre. **2** Charles II. Copper Bawbee or Sixpenny Piece, 1679. Supposed to have derived its name from the French *bas billon.* **3** James VII, 1684–1688 (James II of England, 1685–1688). Silver Forty Shilling Piece, 1687. Note that James used his English titles (reverse legend) while Charles had used his Scottish. The value, 40 appears below the bust. There was a similar 60s. piece. **4** William and Mary, 1689–1694. Silver Forty Shilling Piece, 1693. Again with the value, 40, below the busts which, like those of Charles and James, face the opposite way to that of the English coinage. There was also a similar 60s. piece. **5** William II, 1694–1702 (William III of England, same dates). Gold Pistole, 1701. The first gold coinage in Scotland for three reigns. Note that William placed no numerals after his name on his Scottish coinage. Note also the sun rising above the sea, the crest of the Darien Company, who had imported the gold from Africa. It is said that the ship which brought the gold was also called the *Rising Sun,* which seems quite probable if it were owned by the Company. Struck only in 1701, with the Half-Pistole of the same date, this short-lived gold coinage was the last in the Scottish series. The Pistole was current for £12 Scottish. **6** William II. Silver Forty Shilling Piece, 1696. **7** Anne, 1702–1714. Silver Halfcrown, 1708, coinage period II, after the Act of Union implementation. Similar to the English contemporary Halfcrown but with the Edinburgh mint mark below the bust.

1
1
2
2
3
3
4
4
5
5
6
6
7
7

DOUBLE FLORINS

Victoria

One obverse type:
Jubilee head.

One reverse type:
Four crowned shields of arms, sceptres in saltire, Star of the Garter in the centre.

Plate 66 Irish Coinage

1 John, as Lord of Ireland, 1177–1199. Silver Halfpenny, struck at Dublin mint. The name of the moneyer, NICOLAS ON DWE=Dublin, appears on the reverse. **2** John, as King, 1199–1216. Silver Penny struck at Dublin mint. Unlike the English Pennies of this king, his name, IOHANNES REX appears clearly on the coin. **3** Henry III, 1216–1272. Silver Penny struck at Dublin mint. Struck after 1248, in which year dies were ordered from London and sent to Dublin. They were to be the 'Long Cross' reverse type, but the obverse was to have the king in a triangle instead of a circle. **4** Edward IV, 1461–1483. Silver Groat struck at Dublin mint. The king's name does not appear at all on this piece. **5** Edward IV. Silver Double-Groat, fourth issue, 1467–1470, struck at the Dublin mint. **6** Edward IV. Silver Groat, struck at Dublin mint, *c.* 1465–1467. Known as the 'English type', the mint name forms the inner legend on the reverse. **7** Henry VII. Silver Groat, 'Three Crown Coinage', *c.* 1485–1490. The arms on the obverse are those of England. On either side is a tiny shield bearing a saltire (x). This is the arms of Gerald Fitzgerald, Earl of Kildare, Lord Chief Justice of Ireland. For his services he was given unlimited control of the mints and their officers and all the profits arising from the coinage. **8** Richard III, 1483–1485. Silver Groat, second issue ('Three Crown Coinage'), after 1483. **9** Henry VII, 1485–1509. Silver Groat, struck at the Dublin mint, second period. **10** Henry VIII, 1509–1547. Silver Sixpence, Dublin. Posthumous issue. Issued under an indenture granted in 1544–5 to Sir Martin Bowes, this coinage was struck in London and exported to Dublin. **11** Mary, 1553–1554. Silver Shilling, 1553. The first issue of the Shilling for Ireland. **12** Philip and Mary, 1554–1558. Billon Groat, 1556. Struck in accordance with an indenture of 6 December, 1554 to Sir Edward Peckham, Treasurer of the English mint. This and the Shilling, a similar piece, were struck in London from base money brought into England by Philip. The coinage was then exported to Dublin. **13** Elizabeth I, 1558–1603. Silver Shilling, first issue. Peckham received a further indenture in 1558, under which this coinage was struck in London and exported to Ireland. The coins were made from base money current in England: remember Henry VIII and the debased state of the English coinage. It was at this period that the Tower Mint was enlarged by new buildings. At first known as the 'upper mint' the buildings which had been erected to deal with the English recoinage necessitated by the recalling of the base money, were later turned over to the production of the coinage for Ireland and were known as the 'Irish mint' till the eighteenth century. **14** James I, 1603–1625. Silver Shilling, second issue.

Dates of issue:

1887	1889
1888	1890

Notes. Struck in this reign only. The piece was discontinued as it was too nearly the size of the Crown, then in general use. The only known varieties are that in 1887 some coins have a Roman I in the date and in 1888 and 1889 some pieces have a 1 for the second I in the Queen's name.

HALFCROWNS

George III

Two main obverse types:

1 Bust of George III: sometimes known as the 'bull head' type.
2 Head of king: smaller, legend larger.

Two reverse types:

1 Crowned shield of arms within the Garter and the Collar of the Garter.
2 Similar, but redesigned; no Collar.

Dates of issue:

1816, 1817, both Obv. type 1. Rev. type 1.
1817, 1818, 1819, 1820, all Obv. type 2. Rev. type 2.

Notes. The change in obverse design resulted from the dislike of the first type. This was designed by Pistrucci in jasper, and engraved by T. Wyon. Pistrucci, then scarcely competent to engrave on steel, accused Wyon of spoiling his design.

George IV

Two main obverse types:

1 Large head of George IV.
2 Smaller head, without wreath.

Three reverse types:

1 Crowned shield of arms, with rose, thistle and shamrock.
2 Square crowned shield of arms within the Garter and the Collar of the Garter.
3 Shield of arms, crowned, helmeted and garnished, motto on ribband below.

Dates of issue:

1820, 1821, 1823, all Obv. type 1. Rev. type 1.

1823, 1824, both Obv. type 1. Rev. type 2.

1825, 1826, 1828, 1829, all Obv. type 2. Rev. type 3.

Notes. The change in obverse design was caused by the king's dislike of Pistrucci's portrait. The second portrait is taken from Chantrey's bust of the king.

William IV

One type only:
Obverse: head of William IV.
Reverse: Crowned and mantled shield of arms.

Dates of issue:

1834	1836
1835	1837

Victoria

Three main obverse types:

1 Young head.
2 Jubilee head.
3 Old head.

Three reverse types:

1 Crowned shield of arms, sprigs of olive to left and right, small national emblems below.
2 Crowned shield of arms within the Garter and the Collar of the Garter.
3 Pointed crowned shield of arms within the Collar of the Garter.

Dates of issue:
1839–1846 inclusive, 1848–1850, 1874–1887, all Obv. type 1. Rev. type 1.
1887–1892, all Obv. type 2. Rev. type 2.
1893–1901, all Obv. type 3. Rev. type 3.

Notes. The long gap between 1850 and 1874 was due to the introduction of the Florin. It was thought that this coin, a first step towards decimalization, might supersede the Halfcrown.

Edward VII

One type only:
Obverse: head of Edward VII.
Reverse: crowned shield of arms within the Garter.

Dates issued:
1902–1910 inclusive.

George V

Two main obverse varieties, the head being smaller in the second. Two reverse types:

1 Crowned shield of arms within the Garter.

2 Narrow-waisted shield, no Garter or crown, a lance-rest in the top left side of the shield.

Dates of issue:

1911–1926 inclusive, all Obv. type 1. Rev. type 1.

1926, 1927, Obv. type 2. Rev. type 1.

1927–1936, all Obv. type 2. Rev. type 2.

1936 Obv. type 2. Rev. type 2.

Edward VIII

No issue, see notes above.

George VI

One obverse type:

Head of George VI.

One reverse type:

Narrow-waisted shield of arms, hung by a ring from a nail. No lance rest.

Dates of issue:

1937–1951 inclusive.

A 1952 piece was recently discovered (1967).

Notes. Though of one type the issue falls into three catagories. (i) Silver, 1937–1946, (ii) Cupro-nickel, 1947–1948, (iii) Cupro-nickel, 1949–1952, without IND IMP in the legend. This omission followed self-government in India. It applies to all other denominations.

Elizabeth II

One type only:

Obverse: bust of Elizabeth II.

Reverse: crowned shield of arms dividing E R.

Dates issued:

1953–1968 inclusive

Notes. Though of one type the issue falls into two catagories. (i) 1953, with BRIT OMN in legend, (ii) all other dates without BRIT OMN. This applies to all other denominations.

FLORINS

Victoria

Four main obverse types:

1 'Gothic' bust.

2 Similar bust but larger since the size of the coin was increased after the first year of issue.

3 Jubilee head.

4 Old head.

Four main reverse types:

1 'Gothic' reverse with four crowned shields of arms, rose, thistle, rose, shamrock in the angles, rose in the centre.

2 Similar, but larger, cross moline in centre.

3 Four crowned shields of arms, sceptres in saltire, Star of the Garter in the centre.

4 Crown above three shields of arms, England, Scotland and Ireland, placed 2 and 1, superimposed on sceptres in saltire, rose, shamrock and thistle in the spaces, surrounded by the Garter.

Dates of issue:

1849 Obv. type 1. Rev. type 1.

1851–1860 inclusive, all Obv. type. 2. Rev. type 2.

1862–1881, all Obv. type 2. Rev. type 2.

1883–1887, all Obv. type 2. Rev. type 2.

1887–1892, all Obv. type 3. Rev. type 3.

1893–1901, all Obv. type 4. Rev. type 4.

Notes. 1849 had the date in Arabic figures on the obverse. D.G. was omitted, earning the name of Godless Florin for the piece. So strong was public feeling on this point that the design was altered at once. In 1851, the next issue, the size was expanded and the design accordingly, D:G: reappeared, the lettering was of roughly Gothic type: in printing circles it would probably be set as 'black letter': and this piece is that usually known as the Gothic Florin. The date was inscribed in Roman numerals, often giving rise to the idea that the piece is undated when it appears today. Close examination of the obverse will show that a ring of trefoilated arches is placed just within the protective rim. These vary in number over the years, 48, 42, 38, and 33 having been recorded. BRITT in the legend sometimes has only one T: on some pieces the artist's initials, W.W.

(William Wyon), appear and on others they are omitted. From 1864 till 1878 the practice of numbering dies, referred to above under Sovereigns, was continued. Many numbers, up to 228 have been recorded, but information is probably far from complete on this point, and may never now be finalized, short of a search of the Royal Mint Records. There are minor varieties of stops. There are no particular varieties recorded for the Jubilee and Old head types.

Edward VII

One type only:

Obverse: head of Edward VII.

Reverse: Britannia, standing on the prow of a ship, the sea beyond.

Dates of issue:

1902–1910 inclusive.

Notes. The work of the artist de Saulles, the standing figure of Britannia proved to be a well-liked reverse type. De Saulles appears to have developed it from his reverse design for the British Dollar, which first appeared in 1895.

George V

Two main obverse varieties, the head being smaller on the second.

Two reverse types:

1 Four crowned shields of arms, sceptres in saltire, Star of the Garter in the centre.

2 Four plain shields of arms in saltire, sceptres cruciform, G in the centre.

Dates of issue:

1911–1927 inclusive, all Obv. type 1. Rev. type 1.

1927–1933, all Obv. type 2. Rev. type 2.

1935, 1936, Obv. type 2. Rev. type 2.

Edward VIII

No issue, but see notes above.

George VI

One type only:

Obverse: head of George VI.

Reverse: a crowned stemmed rose, thistle and shamrock to left and right; G R similar.

Dates of issue:
1937–1951 inclusive.

Notes. See notes under Halfcrowns for changes in metal and legend during the reign.

Elizabeth II
One type only:
Obverse: bust of Elizabeth II.
Reverse: In the centre a full-blown rose, surrounded by a ring composed of thistles, leeks and shamrocks, the legend fitted into the spaces among the emblems.

Dates of issue:
1953–1968 inclusive.

Notes. Though the author has had the pleasure of meeting one of the two artists whose initials appear on the reverse as the designers of that part of the Florins of Elizabeth II, he cannot truly compliment the artist on the design. This is of little moment, since other works of this most eminent man, in the fields of sculpture, statues and gem cutting will long pay tribute to his skill. When the designs of the coinage of the present reign were first published in 1953 the popular press, almost without exception, showed the reverse of the Florin in any position but that which was correct. In fact this is probably the first coin struck for Britain in which the initials of the joint reverse designers determine which way the reverse should be viewed. These minute initials are set on either side of a leek in the ring of national emblems mentioned above. Thus the word SHILLINGS in the legend is the 'base' from which the design should be viewed. The date, so often on past precedent in the 'six o'clock' position, thus appears at 'three o'clock', leading the casual viewer into error. As confirmation: when the coin is correctly viewed, FID DEF occur at eleven and one o'clock respectively. See notes under Halfcrowns for change of legend.

SHILLINGS

George III
The final type, Obv. type 3. Rev. type 4, 1816–1820 have already been listed in phase one.

George IV

Two main obverse types:

As for Halfcrowns.

Three reverse types:

1 As Halfcrown.

2 Square crowned shield of arms within the Garter.

3 A crown surmounted by a lion, national emblems below.

Dates issued:

1821 Obv. type 1. Rev. type 1.

1823–1825 inclusive, Obv. type 1. Rev. type 2.

1825–1827 and 1829, Obv. type 2. Rev. type 3.

Plate 67 Irish Coinage, continued

1 Charles I, 1625–1649. Silver Crown, Inchiquin Money, 1642. Called after Lord Inchiquin, Vice-President of Munster, who appears to have had no connection with the issue. As in England, silver plate was donated to the King's cause, and this is probably a piece of such plate. The reverse is stamped with the same weight, the stamp being at the rounded end of the piece. **2** Charles I. Silver Halfcrown, Ormonde Money, 1643. Called after James, Duke of Ormond, and again made from domestic silver plate. **3** Charles II, 1649–1685. Silver Halfcrown 1649 (?) Ormonde proclaimed Charles II in all the places where he had authority within about 14 days of the execution of Charles I. These pieces are supposed to have been struck by Ormonde: the reverse is very similar to the last coin. **4** Charles II. Copper Halfpenny, called the St. Patrick's Halfpenny. There appear to be no authentic records about this piece. There was also a similar Farthing. At one time they were assigned to the previous reign. No mention is made of any metal but copper, but the author had seen a St. Patrick's Farthing in gold, which passed through Wallis and Wallis's Lewes sale room in the early 1960s. **5** James II, 1685–1688. Brass or copper Crown, called Gun Money, 1690. Made from old brass guns and probably any brass and copper available: some say bells were melted down too. A good deal of metal would be needed for the Gun Money series, since it is said that something over £1,000,000 of it was issued. **6** James II. Brass or copper Halfcrown, called Gun Money, 1689. Note the value in pence (xxx) and the date and month, Feb: of issue. Large numbers of varieties abound among the dies. **7** James II. Pewter Halfpenny, 1690. Grueber says that small pieces of prince's metal were inserted on both sides. This metal is an alloy of copper and zinc, i.e. brass, so the supply of old brass cannon for coin making must have been running short. **8** William and Mary, 1689–1694. Copper Halfpenny, 1693. Issued between 1690 and 1694, the Halfpenny was the only Irish issue of the reign. William sealed the fate of the Gun Money after the Battle of the Boyne by reducing the Crowns and large Halfcrowns (they came in two sizes) to one Penny value each, the small Halfcrowns to three farthings and the Shillings and Sixpences to one farthing each. Halfpennies in copper dated 1695 and 1696 were also the only special currency for Ireland issued during the reign of William III, 1694–1702. No money was struck for Ireland under Queen Anne, 1703–1714. **9** George I, 1714–1727. Copper Halfpenny, 1722. **10** George II, 1727–1760. Copper Halfpenny, 1736.

1
2
2
3
4
3
5
6
6
7
8
8
9
9
10
10

VOCE POPULI
1
HIBERNIA 1760
1
GEORGIUS III D:G REX
2
HIBERNIA 1805
2
GEORGIUS III DEI GRATIA REX
3
BANK OF IRELAND TOKEN 1804 SIX SHILLINGS
3
GEORGIUS IV D:G REX
4
HIBERNIA 1822
4
éIRe 1951
5
CORÓIN leat 2/6d
5
FLÓIRIN 2s
5
1s SCILLING
5
6d Reul
5
leat Reul 3d
5
SAORSTÁT ÉIREANN 1928
5
1d PINGIN
5
éIRe 1966
6
Deich SCILLING
6
½d leat PINGIN
5
¼d FEOIRLING
5

William IV

One type only:

Obverse: head of William IV

Reverse: A wreath and small crown. ONE SHILLING in the field.

Dates issued:

1834–1837 inclusive.

Victoria

Five main obverse types:

1 Young head.
2 Young head, larger.
3 Jubilee head.
4 Jubilee head, larger.
5 Old head.

Three reverse types:

1 As William IV.
2 Square crowned shield within the Garter.
3 Three crowned shields of arms, England, Scotland and Ireland, placed two and one, within the Garter, national emblems in the spaces.

Dates of issue:

1838, 1839, both Obv. type 1. Rev. type 1.

1839–1846, 1848–1887 inclusive, all Obv. type 2. Rev. type 1.

1887–1889, Obv. type 3. Rev. type 2.

Plate 68 *Irish Coinage, continued*
1 George II, 1727–1760. Copper Halfpenny, 1760, called the 'Voce Populi' halfpenny. A token issue, from Dublin, unofficial and called into being by the sudden cessation of regal issues in 1755. **2** George III, 1760–1820. Copper Penny, 1805, second issue. From dies made by Küchler and with all the marks of Boulton's Soho mint style, from which mint they came. **3** George III. Silver Bank of Ireland Six Shillings, 1804. Following the lead of the Bank of England, the Bank of Ireland issued its own silver currency for a period, for much the same reasons. These pieces were struck from Spanish Pieces of Eight, or Dollars, at Boulton's Soho mint. **4** George IV, 1820–1830. Copper Penny, 1822. This and a similar Halfpenny were the last coins struck for Ireland under British rule. In 1823 the coinage was entirely assimilated to that of Great Britain's till southern Ireland became a republic. **5** The Republic of Ireland. Set of coins, of various dates. The obverse design is common to all, but the legend changes. In silver, nickel and bronze. **6** Republic of Ireland. The recently issued silver Ten Shilling piece. It is said that it is not much liked. This piece dated 1966.

1889–1892 Obv. type 4. Rev. type 2.

1893–1901, all Obv. type 5. Rev. type 3.

Notes. Some slight varieties of head in the 1860–1880 period. 1848 has the 8 over 6, 1856 has a variety with smaller head and lettering. Dies numbered from 1864–1879. A variety of 1867 and another of 1879 has no die number.

Edward VII

One type only:

Obverse: head of Edward VII.

Reverse: a crown surmounted by a lion.

Dates issued:

1902–1910 inclusive.

George V

Two main obverse varieties, the head being smaller in the second.

Two reverse types:

1 A crown surmounted by a lion.

2 Similar, modernized.

Dates issued:

1911–1926 inclusive, all Obv. type 1. Rev. type 1.

1926 Obv. type 2. Rev. type 1.

1927 ,, ,, 2. ,, ,, 1.

1927–1936 inclusive, all Obv. type 2. Rev. type 2.

Edward VIII

See notes above.

George VI

One obverse type:

Head of George VI.

Two reverse types:

1 A crown surmounted by a lion, the English reverse type.

2 A crown surmounted by a Scottish lion, with sword and sceptre, the Scottish reverse type.

Dates of issue:

1937–1951 inclusive. See notes under Halfcrowns for change of metal and legend.

Notes. The Scottish reverse type was introduced in 1937 as a compliment to the Queen Consort, now Queen Elizabeth the Queen Mother. A Scottish type has been struck for every year since in which the English type appeared. It does not count as a Scottish coin and was not struck in Scotland.

Elizabeth II

One main obverse type:
Bust of Elizabeth II.
Two reverse types:
1 Crowned shield of the arms of England dividing the date.
2 Crowned shield of Scottish arms dividing the date.

Dates of issue:
1953–1965 inclusive.

Notes. The Scottish type appeared each year with the English type. See notes under Halfcrowns for change of legend.

SIXPENCES

In most reigns these followed closely the designs of the Shillings.

George III

Issues of 1817–1820 detailed under phase one.

George IV

Types as the Shillings.

Dates of issue:
1821 Obv. type 1. Rev. type 1.
1824–1826 Obv. type 1. Rev. type 2.
1826–1829 inclusive, all Obv. type 2. Rev. type 3.

William IV

Type as the Shilling.

Dates of issue:
1831 1834–1837 inclusive.

Victoria

Three obverse types:
1 Young head.
2 Jubilee head.
3 Old head.
Three reverse types:
1 A wreath with a crown above, SIX PENCE in two lines in the field.
2 Crowned shield of arms within the Garter.

3 Similar to type 1, but a crown of different shape, making it appear to be set lower vis-à-vis the wreath.

Dates of issue:
1838–1846 inclusive, 1848–1887, all Obv. type 1. Rev. type 1.
1887 Obv. type 2. Rev. type 2.
„ „ 2. „ „ 3.
1888–1893, all Obv. type 2. Rev. type 3.
1893–1901, all Obv. type 3. Rev. type 3.

Notes. In 1848 there is a variety with the second 8 over 7. Die numbers were in use from 1864 till 1879. The years 1866, 1871, 1877 and 1879 occur with no die numbers. In 1878 a variety reads DRITANNIAR and in 1880 the Queen's hair is thinner, and is in longer waves with no lock on her cheek. This continues after 1880 to the end of obverse type 1. In 1884 a die variety has SIX PENCE in larger letters with more space from the date. The 1887 obverse type 2, reverse type 2 was discontinued in that year since when gilded it could pass as a Half Sovereign. Collectors will note that the reverses of the two coins are really substantially different, but the general public is easily deceived. Even so two varieties of reverse type 2 exist, one with the initials of the artist, J.E.B. (Joseph Edgar Boehm) on the truncation while the second has these initials below the truncation. In spite of the recall, 1887 obverse type 2, reverse type 2 is not rare and gilt specimens are fairly frequently seen.

Edward VII
One type only:
Obverse: head of Edward VII.
Reverse: wreath and crown and SIX PENCE.

Dates of issue:
1902–1910 inclusive.

George V
Two main obverse varieties, the head on the second being smaller.
Two reverse types:
1 A crown surmounted by a lion.
2 A design composed of six sprigs of acorns and oak leaves, the legend fitted into the spaces.

Dates of issue:
1911–1926 inclusive, all Obv. type 1. Rev. type 1.
1926 Obv. type 2. Rev. type 1.
1927 ,, ,, 2. ,, ,, 2.
1927–1936 Obv. type 2. Rev. type 2.

Notes. In 1925 a variety had a new beading and a broader rim on the obverse, which continued into 1926. In 1930 the obverse has a narrower edge.

Edward VIII
No issue, see notes above.

George VI
Two main obverse types, the head on the second being slightly larger.
Two reverse types:
1 The royal cypher, GRI crowned and dividing the date.
2 The cypher GR VI crowned and dividing the date.
Dates of issue:
1937–1947 inclusive, all Obv. type 1. Rev. type 1.
1948–1952, all Obv. type 2. Rev. type 2.

Notes. See under Halfcrowns for change of metal and legend.

Elizabeth II
One type only:
Obverse: head of Elizabeth II.
Reverse: a design composed of a rose, thistle, shamrock and leek.
Dates of issue:
1953–1968 inclusive.

Notes. See notes under Halfcrowns for change of legend.

GROATS

In the reign of William IV the Groat or Fourpence was revived at the suggestion of Joseph Hume. This piece was additional to the Maundy Groat. The two are quite distinct, the Hume pieces having a seated figure of Britannia on the reverse. The issue continued into the reign of Victoria, but was then discontinued. The obverse type in both reigns was the usual head of the monarch.

William IV and Victoria

Dates of issue:

1836–1849 inclusive. 1851–1856

Notes. No varieties for William IV, 1847 is known with the 7 over 6. 1856 may exist.

Some lists continue this piece over a further range of dates. A Groat continued to be struck for British Guiana till quite recent years and was formerly of the same type as that for Great Britain. It was not struck primarily for this country after 1855–1856.

This leaves only the four Maundy pieces unlisted. The reader is referred to the closing paragraphs of phase one for brief details of this series. All reigns issued silver Threepences, reverse type crowned 3 down to 1927. These have been included in Maundy money though of course they circulated alone. From 1927 to 1944 the silver Threepence for general circulation had its own reverse type. After 1944 none were struck. This only now leaves the Maundy Threepence, still struck in silver with the crowned 3 reverse. The silver pieces from 1927 to 1944 are hardly likely to form a collecting theme.

Bibliography

The story of phase two is based on *The Milled Coinage of England, 1662–1946* and on Jackson-Kent's *Notes on the Coinage of William III.* After 1946 details have been obtained from *The Standard Catalogue of British Commonwealth Coins* (B. A. Seaby's Ltd.) and from *The Guide Book and Catalogue of British Commonwealth Coins, 1798–1967* by J. Remick and Somer James (Regency Coin & Stamp Co. Ltd., Winnipeg).

CHAPTER SEVEN

English Copper and Bronze Coinage

This is a series of coins which has passed through a considerable change in appreciation from the collector's point of view. Some thirty or more years ago it was hardly regarded as a collecting theme. Now it is not only a collecting theme, but has been shown to be one of considerable interest and importance. How this came about is a possible illustration of the fact that where there is no proper reference book there is little collector's interest, though students may be working on the subject. From such students' work comes the standard catalogue, and with it collector's interest. Also reflected in this particular story is the fact of rising coin values and broadening interest by an increasing number of collectors. Perhaps this can be further explained on the basis of some recollection.

Some thirty years ago, with many fewer collectors, with lower coin values, and thus with more coins to be shared among the collecting interest, English copper coins were included in a general cabinet of the whole English series. In 1886 and 1898, D. T. Batty, in the course of publishing a very useful general catalogue of the whole English series devoted two volumes, iii and iv, to the subject. In 1893 Hyman Montagu, whose coin collection will always remain one of the greatest of his age, produced his second edition of *Copper, Tin and Bronze Coinage of England.* The works of these two authors were reasonably adequate for the interest in English copper and bronze coinage as it then stood, but were far from complete by the modern exacting standards of research and cataloguing. Further back still, Ruding had included the series in his *Annals of the Coinage of Great Britain,* third edition, 1840, and the series had some mention over the years in the Gentleman's Magazine between 1731 and 1868. Snelling in the 1760s devoted some of his writing to the subject: H. A. Grueber naturally included the series in his *Handbook of the Coins of Great Britain and Ireland in the British Museum,* published in 1899, and a number of Papers appeared, and were to appear, on various aspects of the subject. No one, however, had taken the series really seriously, or realized its potential. Copper and bronze coins were still cheap, minor issues not considered worthy of serious research.

Ernest Bramah, better known for his works of popular fiction, had produced a handy little book, *English Regal Copper Coins*, in 1929, which dealt with modern issues. At the same time Henry Garside was studying the series, mainly post 1860, in great detail and published his work in 1920, with a Supplement in 1925.

Garside was probably the first man to commence a study of British copper and bronze coinage in minute detail. So great was the detail into which he delved that as late as 1935: the series still being considered a minor one: his work was received with some amusement. So much effort spent on a series of so little importance. He was in advance of his time.

Garside's method of cataloguing these so common coins was one which had been followed before: and very much so since: that of obtaining huge quantities of every denomination and studying each piece in detail. The number of berries in the monarch's wreath, the number of dots in the border, the form and size of the then traditional lighthouse on the pieces: these and other minute details were all catalogued, and this method has been faithfully followed in recent years by the many who study with equal intensity the various small die varieties on modern coins in almost every series.

At Garside's death the author transported his collection from his home in south-west London to the West End, and its sheer bulk made the springs of Spink & Son's Rolls-Royce van groan under its weight. The collection was in cabinets, in bags, in tins, wrapped up in rolls of newspaper, bursting through envelopes. Much of it was in uncirculated specimens, just as Garside had received it from the bank. Numerically it was so great that the then market for the series just could not absorb it, and a great deal of it was paid in at face value. Few collectors took seriously this minor series. Those who did obtained some very fine coins, but the great bulk was more than the market could be expected to assimilate. Today the collection would be worth a minor fortune.

All Garside's efforts had not been lost. Working quietly in the background, the author of the now standard work, *English Copper, Tin and Bronze Coins in the British Museum*, 1588–1958, had appreciated the work that had been done, and seen the need for a proper catalogue; appreciated the potential interest of the series and seen in it something of its importance. Thus, after many years of devoted work, was born the British Museum Catalogue of the series. The fact that it contains some hundreds of examples not in the British Museum collection but in the collection of the author, who first catalogued them during his researches, obtains but the merest mention in the Introduction.

It is easy to write appreciatively of the work of a friend, but the fact remains that Wilson Peck's catalogue is a monumental work in the true sense of the word. Since its publication in 1960 interest in the series has surged upward, not only because the Catalogue was published, and much of its information filtered off into handy guides to the series, but also because it appeared at the moment when coin values were rising sharply and, perhaps above all, when numismatics as a whole was commanding a vastly increased interest. Cause and effect went hand in hand till now almost everyone who handles any quantity of coinage is taking a more serious look at the money thus in circulation, even down to the once almost disregarded 'coppers'. These have now come into their own as a collecting (as well as a speculative) theme.

With this standard catalogue and its many satellites easily and frequently cheaply to hand there is no real point in giving great details of its considerable number of dates and die varieties here. A little of the background history may stimulate an interest since, like the story behind any coin or series of coins, there much history lies.

The beginnings of the British series of copper and bronze coinage have their origins in the need for smaller denominations of coin than were being struck by the Royal Mint. We have seen something of the Pennies, marked with a cross, for conveniently dividing them into Half-Pennies and Quarter-Pennies: Farthings. We have also seen how such methods of mutilating a coin opened the way to clipping: to pieces of short weight.

In the centuries long past, whose coinage we have briefly reviewed in the first section of this book, only gold and silver were in use as coinage metals. We have seen something of the methods used to produce small change, in the cutting of Pennies and in the provision of Halfgroats; twopence; and Threefarthing pieces. But such methods failed to meet the legitimate needs of the general population as money began to spread into its hands.

Peck, B.M.C. p. 7, gives the general picture. 'To sum up: all the evidence suggests that the shortage of official small change was fairly general during the three centuries which have been under review and that this state of affairs was well known to the authorities, who seem to have been singularly indifferent to the many difficulties and hardships it caused among the poorer classes in all their small transactions, which in aggregate probably constituted a considerable part of their total expenditure. The Tudor monarchs in particular must surely have known that several European states were by this time issuing pieces of small change in billon, copper, or brass, yet there is no evidence that any of them except Elizabeth ever even contemplated a similar coinage for England. The use of tokens and foreign coins was admittedly an infringement of the royal prerogative, but this in no way exonerates the king or his councillors for their failure to provide what was, after all, a very necessary adjunct to the main currency. Instead, their almost invariable reaction to these illegal issues had been merely to make ineffective laws against their use, and to continue to pin their faith in the occasional issue of small silver when complaints of its shortage became too pressing to be ignored. But in the end even this standby failed, for by Edward VI's reign the size of the farthing had so diminished that its mintage in the restored standard silver under Elizabeth was found to be quite impracticable.'

It was against this background that our base metal coinage began to come into being. During the reign of Elizabeth I various patterns for a copper coinage appeared. These took the form of Halfpennies, Pennies and Twopenny pieces, and were struck in such metals as base silver, silver, copper, pewter and one, the Twopence, in gold, silver and copper. These pieces are from very rare to practically unique. The matter was not proceeded with at this time, and it was not until the next reign, James I, that any base metal pieces began to appear for general use.

Even so the matter still dragged on, and while several proposals for copper tokens were put forward between 1607 and 1612, nothing materialized. James, as king of Scotland, on which throne he sat, it will be remembered, before he ascended that of England, knew perfectly well the advantages which followed the issue of copper pieces in Scotland. Then, says Oman, (*The Coinage of England*), he finally 'conceived the unhappy idea of placing the issue of such money in the hands of private persons' who, 'as holders of the monopoly, could be heavily charged for the privilege and yield him, so it was estimated, a profit of £35,000. The plan was finally drawn up on 10 April 1613 and set out in a proclamation dated 19 May 1613'. (Ruding, quoted from Peck).

The original authority was conferred by letters patent on John, Lord Harington of Exton, for a period of three years. Scarcely had the patent been granted than Harington died. It then passed to his son, who also died a few months later. It then devolved upon Lady Anne Harington, the widow of Lord Harington, who gave it up in 1614, when it was taken up by the Duke of Lennox, later Duke of Richmond and Lennox, who appears to have employed two agents responsible for the actual manufacture. Finally, when Lennox died in 1624 the patent passed jointly to his widow, Frances, Dowager Duchess of Richmond, and Sir Francis Crane. By 1634 (Charles I), Lord Maltravers held the patent with Crane.

From all this graft and granting of patents there emerged a series which has become known as the Royal and Rose Farthing Tokens. At first they were issued in tinned copper, looking when first struck reasonably like silver (c.f. the Ancient British tin, i.e. speculum coins, *ante*). Later the pieces were issued in copper. The series as a whole was never well received, the authorities in some counties refusing to accept them at all, despite considerable pressure from official sources to keep the pieces in circulation.

The pieces were roughly round and later oval. The basic original design was, obverse, a crown with two sceptres in saltire behind it, reverse, a crowned harp. The Rose series, issued later under Charles I, had a crowned rose on the reverse. Peck lists some seventy-one different privy-marks used at various times throughout the issue of these pieces. H. A. Seaby, in his *British Copper Coins and their values, part I, Regal Coins*, catalogues the series for handy reference under the following types:

James I

Type 1 Harrington (sic): small size.
Type 2 Harrington normal size.
Type 3 Lennox.
Type 4 Lennox, oval.

Charles I

Type 1 Richmond, round.

Type 2 transitional, with double-arched crowns.
Type 3 Maltravers.
Type 4 Richmond, oval
Type 5 Maltravers, oval.

Rose types
Type 1 Double-arched crowns, double rose.
Type 2 Single-arched crowns, single rose.
Type 3 Sceptres below crown (not behind).

This profusion of types, added to the seventy-one privy- marks offer a quite interesting small field of study. While values average around twenty shillings for a common specimen in F–VF Condition, some pieces are quite rare and valued in pounds. Not a great deal of attention was paid to them till Peck sifted both them and their history.

Though their intrinsic value was but a fraction of their face value, this did not prevent a crop of counterfeits appearing. Only reference to Peck and considerable study of minute varieties can sort these counterfeits from the genuine pieces.

Methods of production once more harked back to the Ancient British speculum series, in that the pieces were made in strips, and at least one sheet with about eighty-one tokens ready to be cut has been recorded. These two examples of production methods gave rise to some thought, but it appears that the strips and/or sheets were produced by passing the metal between two rollers, engraved incuse with the designs, thus producing the design in relief on the sheet or strip. Copper being relatively soft, this method of production produced quite a clearly defined piece, the tokens then being punched out from the strips or sheets, which usually gave them a slight convexity. A strip of uncut pieces is preserved in the British Museum.

Towards the end of 1644 the issue ceased, and during the Commonwealth and Protectorate, 1648/9–1659, their absence gave rise to a considerable issue of private copper or brass tradesmen's tokens. These pieces, of which there are many thousands, form a study in themselves and a collecting theme of particular interest to anyone interested in local trades, local history and like subjects. Known briefly as Seventeenth Century Tokens, they almost became accepted as official. Something was said of them in the

Beginner's Guide, p. 128 ff. The government of the period seems to have progressed no further than the striking of an interesting series of pattern Farthing tokens and a few currency Farthing tokens, together with some pattern regal Farthings during the protectorate; all very rare or practically unique pieces.

At the Restoration, the matter of small change began to receive more serious attention. Patterns were produced for a proposed regal copper coinage and by 1672 Halfpennies and Farthings began to go into general circulation. As pointed out above, the silver Penny was still in production as the normal small value coin of the period.

The copper coins introduced in the reign of Charles I had the seated figure of Britannia, then facing left, as the reverse design. This lady had appeared centuries before on Roman coins, but from her reintroduction in 1672 she has remained the traditional reverse for copper and bronze coins, though latterly she only appears on the Penny. She now appears on the 50 New Penny pieces.

The first copper coins were struck on blanks imported from Sweden, but in 1684 tin Farthings appeared. The idea behind their issue was to assist the ancient Cornish tin trade, which had then, as now, fallen on hard times. A plug of copper was inserted in the centre of the coin with the idea of making forgery more difficult. Even so quite a large number of forged lead pieces appeared. This was one of the reasons why these pieces were discontued.

The Halfpennies and Farthings continued to be struck during the reign of James II (1685–1688), and on into the reign of William and Mary (1689–1694), the last pieces being issued in 1692. Like all tin coins they looked very attractive when new and well struck, but deteriorated rapidly in use, such that really fine specimens are now rare pieces.

Three main types of Halfpenny and two main types of Farthing were issued in copper during the reign of William III (1694–1702).

In the reign of Anne (1702–1714) no copper coins were struck for circulation. There was by now a considerable amount of copper, and presumably tin, in circulation, so striking was suspended. At this period Isaac Newton was Master of the Mint. His scientific mind concerned itself not only with astronomy but with economics. On the subject of copper coinage he postulated three requirements. These were, (i) 'the coins should contain their intrinsic value of *pure* copper, less only the cost of making and issuing them'; (a theory which Matthew Boulton was later in part to support), (ii) 'that the *entire* process of coining should be undertaken by the Mint from ingots of raw metal, instead of purchasing ready-made blanks as previously', (*vide ante*, the Swedish copper; tin was now apparently out), and (iii) 'that the quantity of coin issued should be directly related to actual requirements.' (The quotations are from Peck).

Unfortunately this ran Newton into technical troubles. The fact that one of his requirements, that the copper should be without any alloy, and the fact that the horse-driven rolling mills at the Mint produced insufficient power to reduce the size of the castings so required to the necessary thickness for coining, produced coins which failed to stand up to the 'hammer test'. This 'hammer test' which now seems somewhat primitive, was the only test known at that time which was accepted as the test of pure copper. When struck, the pure copper coins were heated to redness and then hammered: when this was done the coins split. Though many tests were carried out under Newton's direction, this failure was not overcome.

Notwithstanding, towards the end of the reign some copper Farthings were produced, and will be found catalogued under the date 1714. Had Queen Anne lived a few months longer they might well have been put into circulation. In fact they were not, but their existence, and their absence from general circulation seems to have given rise to the nineteenth century legend that an Anne Farthing was worth a small fortune: an idea which still lives in the minds of some people who come into possession of a specimen. The story is told by Peck, quoting an account by J. Henry, and is an illustration of the gullibility of the public in such matters. (Even today there has only to appear in the press an article on the subject of the rarity of the 1933 Penny for dealers to be offered specimens by the public, all of which turn out to be Halfpennies). Nothing more than trial pieces and patterns were issued in copper during the reign of Anne, and Peck concludes the matter, 'Many believe that the Farthing dated 1714 was actually issued for circulation, but Craig, who had access to the latest relevant records, states emphatically that 'Queen Anne's farthings . . . and her double-headed halfpence were but strays from these experiments.'

Only Halfpennies and Farthings were struck in copper during

the reigns of George I, George II and the first part of the reign of George III. They were still inadequate in quantity and many forgeries were in circulation. Token coins again appeared, to form a series usually referred to as the Eighteenth Century Tokens. Like those of the previous century they are a subject and a collecting theme in themselves.

Meantime Matthew Boulton, with his steam-powered mint and his improved machinery had been campaigning for a better coinage, as mentioned above, and for a proper copper coinage to meet public need and thus put out of business the forgers of copper coins. Boulton noted how many forged coins he received in change at toll gates and similar places on his journeys about the country. With his private Soho mint to back him, he spared no effort to impress on the government of the day the fact that a higher standard of coin production was needed and that a copper coinage was essential.

In this latter he was finally awarded a contract for the minting of Twopenny and Penny pieces in pure copper, and from this contract came the so-called 'cartwheel' pieces. Struck in 1797, they were large and heavy, and by 1799 the Twopence was discontinued and the Pennies, Halfpennies and Farthings were redesigned and lightened in weight. These early Soho issues were the foundation on which the copper denominations of Penny, Halfpenny and Farthing were laid, a series which were to last in this metal till 1860, when bronze took the place of copper.

By the reign of George IV (1820–1830), the three denominations had settled into a form which was to be familiar till the present time: till the demonetization of the Farthing and the final extinction of the trinity under decimalization. A collector seeing any of these denominations would recognize them easily today, even though their value was not at this time, nor for some time to come, to be stated on them. Their value, ONE PENNY, HALF PENNY and FARTHING was not to be their reverse legend till the bronze pieces came into use in 1860.

The design of the three pieces in the reign of George IV was of a high order. The ancestor of Britannia as we know her today on our Pennies, facing right, first appeared on these issues. She appeared to best advantage on the Farthing where all the proportions seem in harmony. The enlargement of the design to fit the Halfpenny and Penny are perhaps not quite so pleasing. From the number of carefully preserved and not infrequently gilded Farthings of George IV that one sees it is possible to conclude that it was a popular piece which pleased the eye. It was a loan issue till 1825, when all three denominations began to be struck with Chantrey's bust of the king: the Farthing not appearing in this second issue till 1826.

Little more than the head of the monarch was changed for the issues of William IV and Victoria, and it was not till the issue of bronze coins in 1860 that the whole design was greatly altered by L. C. Wyon, and the pieces as we now know them were established. They have passed through various alterations during the interval. Ship and lighthouse have come and gone. The latter has come again since 1937. Britannia disappeared from the Halfpenny in 1937 and from the Farthing in the same year when the coinage of the new reign, that of George VI, appeared. Her place had been taken by a ship, inspired by the Golden Hind of Drake, on the former, and by Britain's smallest bird, the Wren, on the latter. But till their moment of extinction their ancestry was clear.

Such a brief account of our copper and bronze coinage has made it look, perhaps, too simple and lacking in interest and variety. This is not in fact the case. The British Museum Catalogue referred to is some 640 pages long and needed fifty plates to illustrate it. It took years to produce, and has proved for all time to come that the British series of copper and bronze coinage is one of great interest, of infinite variety and with a background story of quite exceptional interest. The series is a collecting theme, and a most rewarding one.

One more fact of interest must be recorded before this less than adequate treatment of a fine series of coins is brought to a close. From 1860 onwards our bronze coinage had settled into the Penny–Halfpenny–Farthing groove for so long that no one ever expected it to be changed, or an addition to be made to it. It was therefore a surprise and to many a shock when in 1937 the nickel-brass, twelve-sided, thick, chunky Threepence appeared. It took time for this coin to gain popularity. For the first time since the oddly-shaped siege pieces of the Civil War a coin that was not intended to be circular was put into circulation. True, the Empire of India had square and serrated coins in the reign of George V, but they were 'foreign' pieces, struck in metals like nickel, which had never been used for home coinage in general circulation. The silver Threepence, though nominally in daily use, was suffering the fate of the silver Penny. It was too small, too easily lost and too insignificant to be accepted by a modern bustling world. Yet in 1937 three pennies in one piece still had a use, and for once in our numismatic history such a fact was accepted. A Threepence of reasonable size was put into circulation.

Even so it got off to a rather poor start. It was said that the Scots, who still liked and used its silver counterpart, would have none of it. It was complained that it would not 'stack', as indeed it will not above about four pieces. 'Penny-in-the-slot' machines would not accept it, though they might soon have done so but for World War II. In 1937 threepence would still carry you some distance on London's Underground system, where slot machines for tickets abounded. Some slot machine manufacturers had been given a 'trial run' of the new piece before it was proclaimed and added to our currency: which accounts in part for the fabulous Edward VIII dodecagonal pieces.

The authorities persisted with the new coin, the Royal Mint continued to churn out some forty million pieces a year. World War II gave plenty of more important things to worry about and by the time this vast wave of insanity was over the new coin had proved its worth and become accepted. Even in these days of depreciated values it is still a useful coin, and it killed off its silver rival, apart from the 'Maundy Threepence', when silver coins ceased to be struck after 1946. It will last till the end of the present system: the first coin for centuries that really departed from tradition. Then when our coinage has been decimalized and the dodecagonal piece is being recalled, collectors will suddenly realize that it was a short-lived coin, with less than forty years of history. It will then become a collecting theme.

Readers who have come thus far with our story will appreciate that any one series of coins contains many minor varieties. On the broad view designs change; between reigns and during reigns; as the monarch gets older, as economic conditions decree changes in metals in which coins are produced and as coinages change their scales of denomination to meet changing needs. These main changes constitute various broad types into which the coins of a reign or the coins of a period fall. Within these broad outlines occur the many minor varieties. We have seen such varieties as those of punctuation, mistakes in die cutting, numbered dies, provincial mint marks and the like. The British series of copper and bronze coins is no exception, and is full of those small minor varieties which are of such interest to the collector.

In the belief that readers have assimilated the significance of such matters we have been steadily cutting back on detail. This has been necessary in view of the many centuries of coin production which these pages have attempted to cover. Now, in bringing our story, and our guide, towards its conclusion, only a date list of copper and bronze coins can be given. This series abounds in collector interest and is a collecting theme.

In earlier pages it has been said that more detailed research could well reward the collector. In the series of copper and bronze coinage of Britain there is not quite so much scope for the student. The British Museum Catalogue has covered ninety-nine-and-a-half per cent of the possible varieties. The odd half per cent still appears so that the B.M.C. is a challenge to the collector. Varieties not recorded in this massive work were readily received by its author, clinically analysed, and accepted or rejected. As in all fields of coin collecting there is still work to be done: major or minor: and in this work the most humble of collectors can play his part.

Date list of copper, tin and bronze coinage, Charles II to date

Charles II

COPPER HALFPENNIES	COPPER FARTHINGS	TIN FARTHINGS
1672	1672	1684
1673	1673	1685
1675	1674	
	1675	
	1679	

James II

TIN HALFPENNIES	TIN FARTHINGS
1685	1684
1686	1685
1687	1686
	1687

William & Mary

TIN HALFPENNIES	TIN FARTHINGS
1689	1689
1690	1689/90*
1691	1690
1691/2*	1691
1692	1692
COPPER	COPPER
1694	1693
	1694

* These have the first date on the reverse and the second on the edge. The Farthing also occurs with 1690 on the reverse and 1689 on the edge.

William III

COPPER HALFPENNIES	COPPER FARTHINGS
1695	1695
1696	1696

COPPER HALFPENNIES	COPPER FARTHINGS
1697	1697
1698	1698
1699	1699
1700	1700
1701	

Anne

FARTHINGS

1714 (officially never put into circulation).

George I

HALFPENNIES	FARTHINGS
1717	1717
1718	1718
1719	1719
1720	1720
1721	1721
1722	1722
1723	1723
1724	1724

George II

HALFPENNIES	FARTHINGS
1729	1730
1730	1731
1731	1732
1732	1733
1733	1734
1734	1735
1735	1736
1736	1737
1737	1739
1738	1741
1739	1744
1740	1746

HALFPENNIES	FARTHINGS
1742	1749
1743	1750
1744	1754
1745	
1746	
1747	
1748	
1749	
1750	
1751	
1752	
1753	
1754	

George III

HALFPENNIES (first issue)	FARTHINGS (first issue)
1770	1771
1771	1773
1772	1774
1773	1775
1774	
1775	

Second issue, from Soho mint.

TWOPENCE	PENNY
1797	1797

Third issue, from Soho mint.

	HALFPENNIES	FARTHINGS
	1799	1799

Fourth issue, from Soho mint.

PENNIES	HALFPENNIES	FARTHINGS
1806	1806	1806
1807	1807	1807

George IV

PENNIES	HALFPENNIES	FARTHINGS	
1825	1825	1821	Half Farthings and Third Farthings were struck, but not for circulation in Great Britain.
1826	1826	1822	
1827	1827	1823	
		1825	
		1826	
		1827	
		1828	
		1829	
		1830	

William IV

PENNIES	HALFPENNIES	FARTHINGS	
1831	1831	1831	Half Farthings and Third Farthings were struck, but not for use in Great Britain.
1834	1834	1834	
1837	1837	1835	
		1836	
		1837	

Victoria

Copper issues

PENNIES	HALFPENNIES	FARTHINGS	HALF FARTHINGS
1841	1838	1838	1839
1843	1841	1839	1842
1844	1843	1840	1843
1845	1844	1841	1844
1846	1845	1842	1847
1847	1846	1843	1851
1848	1847	1844	1852
1849	1848	1845	1853
1851	1851	1846	1854
1853	1852	1847	1856
1854	1853	1848	
1855	1854	1849	
1856	1855	1850	
1857	1856	1851	

PENNIES	HALFPENNIES	FARTHINGS	HALF FARTHINGS
1858	1857	1852	(current 1842–
1859	1858	1853	1869) Third
1860	1859	1854	Farthings and
	1860	1855	Quarter
		1856	Farthings were
		1857	struck, but not
		1858	for use in Great
		1859	Britain.
		1860	

Bronze issues

PENNIES	HALFPENNIES	FARTHINGS
1860	1860	1860
1861	1861	1861
1862	1862	1862
1863	1863	1863
1864	1864	1864
1865	1865	1865
1866	1866	1866
1867	1867	1867
1868	1868	1868
1869	1869	1869
1870	1870	1872
1871	1871	1873
1872	1872	1874
1873	1873	1875
1874	1874	1876
1875	1875	1877
1876	1876	1878
1877	1877	1879
1878	1878	1880
1879	1879	1881
1880	1880	1882
1881	1881	1883
1882	1882	1884
1883	1883	1885
1884	1884	1886
1885	1885	1887

PENNIES	HALFPENNIES	FARTHINGS
1886	1886	1888
1887	1887	1890
1888	1888	1891
1889	1889	1892
1890	1890	1893
1891	1891	1894
1892	1892	1895
1893	1893	1896
1894	1894	1897
1895	1895	1898
1896	1896	1899
1897	1897	1900
1898	1898	1901
1899	1899	
1900	1900	
1901	1901	

Edward VII

PENNIES	HALFPENNIES	FARTHINGS
1902	1902	1902
1903	1903	1903
1904	1904	1904
1905	1905	1905
1906	1906	1906
1907	1907	1907
1908	1908	1908
1909	1909	1909
1910	1910	1910

George V

PENNIES	HALFPENNIES	FARTHINGS
1911	1911	1911
1912	1912	1912
1913	1913	1913
1914	1914	1914
1915	1915	1915
1916	1916	1916
1917	1917	1917

PENNIES	HALFPENNIES	FARTHINGS
1918	1918	1918
1919	1919	1919
1920	1920	1920
1921	1921	1921
1922	1922	1922
1926	1923	1923
1927	1924	1924
1928	1925	1925
1929	1926	1926
1930	1927	1927
1931	1928	1928
1932	1929	1929
1933	1930	1930
1934	1931	1931
1935	1932	1932
	1933	1933
	1934	1934
	1935	1935

Edward VIII

The coins dated 1936 have the portrait and titles of George V. Since that king died in January the coins belong to the reign of Edward VIII. Our new coinage for any one year usually begins to appear in about the month of March. (See also p. 211).

PENNY	HALFPENNY	FARTHING
1936	1936	1936

George VI

PENNIES	HALFPENNIES	FARTHINGS
1937	1937	1937
1938	1938	1938
1939	1939	1939
1940	1940	1940
1944	1941	1941
1945	1942	1942
1946	1943	1943
1947	1944	1944

PENNIES	HALFPENNIES	FARTHINGS
1948	1945	1945
1949	1946	1946
1950	1947	1947
1951	1948	1948
	1949	1949
	1950	1950
	1951	1951
	1952	1952

Elizabeth II

PENNIES	HALFPENNIES	FARTHINGS
1953	1953	1953
1961	1954	1954
1962	1955	1955
1963	1956	1956
1964	1957	Last issue of this denomination.
1965	1958	
1966	1959	
1967	1960	
	1962	
	1963	
	1964	
	1965	
	1966	
	1967	

Nickel-Brass Threepence

George VI	*Elizabeth II*
1937	1953
1938	1954
1939	1955
1940	1956
1941	1957
1942	1958
1943	1959
1944	1960
1945	1961

1946	1962
1948	1963
1949	1964
1950	1965
1951	1966
1952	1967

It will be appreciated that the above lists are only of the dates on which the various denominations were issued. They will give the collector some idea what to look for.

Apart from such items as the 1933 Penny, the 1954 Penny, the twelve-sided Threepence of Edward VIII, and the Penny, Half-penny and Farthing in the same series, none of which the collector is ever likely to see, there are few great rarities in the currency series, apart from die varieties and similar small differences. Some of these are very rare, but the collector can build up a fully representative collection of copper, tin and bronze coins for quite a reasonable investment of capital.

As was pointed out in an earlier chapter, the Penny, in various shapes and forms has come with us through the entire story since the date of its inception as a denomination. It is now a silver Maundy piece and a bronze currency coin. At the risk of repetition it can be pointed out once more that it is a collecting theme of major interest.

The patterns and proofs in the copper, tin and bronze series are frequently of very great rarity. As with all such pieces in any series they are an interesting study in themselves, but are mostly expensive items. Only Peck's British Museum Catalogue lists them all and illustrates the majority. Its full title is *English Copper, Tin and Bronze Coins in the British Museum, 1558–1958*, published by the Trustees of the British Museum.

CHAPTER EIGHT

Scottish Coinage

It still comes as a surprise to some collectors that the one-time separate kingdom of Scotland had its own separate coinage. There has always been an interchange of money between the two kingdoms, and the earliest coins to circulate in Scotland before the twelfth century were mainly Anglo-Saxon and English Pennies and Northumbrian Stycas.

The series has the advantage from the collector's point of view of being a complete entity since, after the union of the two kingdoms in the reign of Queen Anne, no further Scottish coins were issued, the last date being 1706.

As might be expected, in many ways the numismatic history of Scotland had its parallel with that of England. The series starts with the hammered issues, provincial mints came and went and milled coinage was finally established under Charles II. Many denominations unknown in England were used during the period of some 680 years of Scottish coinage. The familiar pattern of major and minor varieties, differences in size and weight, pattern and proof pieces and so forth will be found in the series.

The major works of reference on the subject are, Burns, *The Coinage of Scotland*, and Stewart, *The Scottish Coinage*, the second edition of which is now in print. A very useful quick-reference to the series is Seaby's *Standard Catalogue of the Coins of Great Britain and Ireland* (1958) which preceded the present *Standard Catalogue of British Coins*. The series is also dealt with in Grueber's *Handbook of the Coins of Great Britain and Ireland in the British Musuem*, 1899, and further back still by Lindsey, in his *Coinage of Scotland*. For all practical purposes Stewart is the main work for the collector.

The following list of coins struck in Scotland is based upon Seaby's catalogue mentioned above. For those who may be taking up the story at this point it might be well to repeat one or two observations already written in earlier pages.

This list is but the bare skeleton of what the collector may look for in the Scottish series. Like all series of coins, and series of hammered coins in particular, the various pieces, denominations and varieties will not necessarily fit snugly under a compact set of headings. This makes the subject more interesting, both for the collector and for the author. So far as the series allows it will be presented under a number of general headings, but these will have to be departed from as occasion demands. Remarks will be added where they will be helpful. The coinage of Scotland starts with David I.

The Hammered Coinage of Scotland

David I, 1124–1153

Metal	*Denomination*	*No. of types, value, etc.*	*Remarks*
Silver	Penny	Four	Types I–III vary in workmanship, which is often rough. IV is known as the English type. All rare to extremely rare.

Henry, Earl of Northumberland, 1139–1152

Silver	Penny	Three	All extremely rare (E.R.)

Malcolm IV, 1153–1165

Silver	Penny	Five, type II divided into *a* and *b*	Of great rarity

William the Lion, 1165–1214

Silver	Penny	Three issues, the second divided into two types	Common to very rare

Alexander II, 1214–1249

Silver	Penny	One, with five obverse varieties	

Alexander III, 1249–1285

Silver	Penny	Three types: head alternatively r. or l.	First coinage
		Nine varieties, A to I	Second coinage In variety, the king's

Metal	*Denomination*	*No. of types, value, etc.*	*Remarks*
			name is XESCOSSIE Commonest Pennies in this series, obtainable for a few pounds.
Silver	Halfpenny	Similar to Penny	
Silver	Farthing	Similar to Penny	
		John Baliol, 1292–1296	
Silver	Penny	As type I above. Obverse legend JOHANNES DIE GRA	Some with CIVITAS SANDRE=St. Andrew's mint
Silver	Halfpenny	Two main types	Some from St. Andrews
		Robert Bruce, 1306–1329	
Silver	Penny, Halfpenny, Farthing	As Alexander III type C	
		David II, 1329–1371	
Silver	Penny, Halfpenny, Farthing	Similar to Alexander III type C	First issue
Gold	Noble	Similar to that of Edward III of England	Second issue 1357–1367. E.R.
Silver	Groat	Types A to D	Differences mainly in portrait.
	Halfgroat	Types A to C	Similar differences
	Penny	Types A to D	Similar differences

Metal	*Denominations*	*No. of types, value, etc.*	*Remarks*
Silver	Groat Halfgroat Penny		Third issue
		Robert II, 1371–1390	
Silver	Groat, Halfgroat, Penny, Halfpenny	Two types of each, second with B behind head	
		Robert III, 1390–1406	
Gold	Long-cross Lion Demy, or Demi-Lion	Of two types	Heavy coinage, First issue
Silver	Groat, Halfgroat, Penny, Halfpenny		Weights: Lion, 61 grs: Groat, 46 grs.
Gold	Short-cross Lion	Similar to L.C. Lion	
Silver	Demy, Groat, Halfgroat, Penny, Halfpenny		Heavy coinage, Second issue
Gold	Lion	Of two types	Weights: Lion,
Silver	Demy Groat	Of two types Three varieties	38 grs., groat, 28 grs.
		James I, 1406–1437	
Gold	Demy Half-demy	Of three types	
Silver	Groat	Two varieties	Billon=base
Billon	Penny Halfpenny	Types A to C	metal mixture of silver and copper
		James II, 1437–1460	
Gold	Demy	Two varieties	First coinage
Silver	Groat	Two main varieties	

Metal	*Denominations*	*No. of types, value, etc.*	*Remarks*
Billon	Penny		
Gold	Lion		Second coinage
Silver	Groat, Penny		first issue
Gold	Lion, Half-lion	Of two types	Second coinage second issue
Silver	Groat, Halfgroat, Penny	Of three types	

James III, 1460–1488

Gold	Rider Half-rider Quarter-rider	Of two types	So called from king being on horseback
	Unicorn	Of two types	Obverse Unicorn
	Half-unicorn	Of two types	to 1
Silver	Groat Halfgroat		Silver coinage, first issue, *c.* 1470
Billon	Plack, Half-plack, Penny	Plack=3d., later 2d.: from Fr. *plaque*	
Silver	Groat, Halfgroat		Silver coinage,
Billon	Penny		second issue, *c.* 1473
Silver	Groat, Halfgroat, Penny		Silver coinage, third issue,
Billon	Penny		*c.* 1475
Silver	Groat, Halfgroat, Penny		Silver coinage, fourth issue, *c.* 1480
Silver	Groat	Three main varieties	Silver coinage, fifth issue, *c.* 1484
Silver	Groat, Halfgroat		Silver coinage,
Billon	Penny		sixth issue, *c.* 1485

Metal	*Denominations*	*No. of types, value, etc.*	*Remarks*
Copper	Farthing	Of two varieties	
	Penny	Of Bishop Kennedy of St. Andrews	
	Farthing		

James IV, 1488–1513

Metal	*Denominations*	*No. of types, value, etc.*	*Remarks*
Gold	Unicorn	Of three varieties	
	Half-unicorn		
	Lion	Of three varieties	
	Half-lion	Of two varieties	
Silver	Groat, Halfgroat		Silver coinage, first issue, *c.* 1489–90
Silver	Groat		Silver coinage, second issue, *c.* 1491
Silver	Groat, Halfgroat, Penny		Silver coinage, third issue, after 1492
Silver	Groat		Silver coinage, fourth issue, E.R.
Billon	Plack	Of six varieties	
	Half-plack	Of two varieties	
	Penny	Of two issues and four types	

James V, 1514–1542

Metal	*Denominations*	*No. of types, value, etc.*	*Remarks*
Gold	Unicorn, Half-unicorn		First coinage, 1513–1526
Billon	Plack		
Gold	Unicorn or Ecu	Value 20/–: of two varieties	Second coinage, 1526–1539

Metal	*Denomination*	*No. of types, value, etc.*	*Remarks*
Silver	Groat	Of four types	
	Third-groat		
Gold	Bonnet piece,	So called from	Third coinage,
	⅔ Bonnet piece,	type of king's	1539–1542
	⅓ bonnet piece	hat	
Billon	Bawbee,	Bawbee = 1½d.,	
	Half-bawbee,	later raised to	
	Quarter-bawbee	6d.	

Mary, 1542–1567
('Mary, Queen of Scots')

Gold	Abbey Crown or	Value 20/–	First coinage,
	Ecu, Twenty		before marriage
	Shillings, 1543		to Francis,
	Lion, 1553	Value 44/–	1542–1553
	Half-lion		
Silver	Testoon		Second coinage,
Billon	Bawbee		1554–1555
	Half-bawbee		
Silver	Testoon		
	Half-testoon		
Billon	Penny	Of four varieties	
Gold	Lion		Third coinage,
	Ryal or £3 piece		1555–1558
	Half Ryal		
Silver	Testoon		
	Half-testoon		
Billon	Plack	Value 4d.	
	Lion or hardhead	Value 1½d.	
	Penny		
Gold	Ducat	Of highest rarity	Fourth coinage,
Silver	Testoon		1558–1560,
	Half-testoon		during marriage
Billon	12d. Groat or		to Francis, as
	nonsunt		Dauphin
	Lion or hardhead		

Metal	*Denomination*	*No. of types, value, etc.*	*Remarks*
Silver	Testoon Half-testoon		Fifth coinage, 1560–1561, Francis as King of France
Silver	Crown Testoon Half-testoon	Value 23/– With portrait With portrait	Sixth coinage, 1561–1565, Mary as widow
Silver	Ryal or 'Crookston' dollar ⅔ Ryal, ⅓ ryal	Value 30/–	Seventh coinage, Mary and Darnley 1565–1567
Silver	Ryal, ⅔ ryal, ⅓ ryal		Eighth coinage, 1567

James VI, 1567–1625 (James I of England)

Silver	Ryal or sword dollar ⅔ ryal, ⅓ ryal	Value 30/–	First coinage, 1567–1571, before accession to English throne.
Gold	£20 piece		
Silver	Noble or half-merk Half-noble or Quarter-merk or Forty-penny piece Thistle dollar or Double Merk Thistle Half-dollar	Value 6s. 8d.	Second coinage, 1572–1580
Gold	Ducat, Four pound piece or Noble		

Metal	*Denomination*	*No. of types, value, etc.*	*Remarks*
Silver	Sixteen shillings		Third coinage,
	Eight shillings		1580–1581
	Four shillings		
	Two shillings		
Gold	Lion noble or		Fourth coinage,
	Scottish angel	Value 75/–	1582–1589
	⅔ Lion noble		
	⅓ Lion noble		
Silver	Forty-shillings		
	Thirty-shillings		
	Twenty-shillings		
	Ten-shillings		
Billon	Plack	Value 8d.	
	Half-plack		
Gold	Thistle noble	Value £7 6s. 8d.	Fifth coinage,
Billon	Hardhead	Value 2d.	1588–1589
	Half-hardhead		
Gold	Hat piece	Value £4. So called from the style of the hat.	Sixth coinage, 1591–1594
Silver	Balance half-merk	Value 6s. 8d.	
	Balance quarter-merk	So called from the 'balance' = scales, on obverse	
Gold	Rider	Value £5. So	Seventh coinage,
	Half-rider	called from the king on horse-back	1593–1601
Silver	Ten-shillings		
	Five shillings		
	Thirty-penny piece		
	Twelve-penny piece		

Metal	*Denomination*	*No. of types, value, etc.*	*Remarks*
Billon	Saltire plack	Value 4d.	
Copper	Twopence		
	Penny		
Gold	Sword and Sceptre piece.		Eighth coinage, 1601–1604
	Half Sword and Sceptre piece		
Silver	Thistle-merk	Value 13s. 4d.	
	½ thistle-merk		
	¼ thistle-merk		
	⅛ thistle-merk		
Gold	Unit or Sceptre	Value £12 Scot. or 20/– Eng.	Ninth coinage, 1605. First after accession to English throne
	Double-crown		
	Britain-crown		
	Halfcrown		
	Thistle-crown		
Silver	Sixty-shillings	Value 5/– Eng.	
	Thirty-shillings		
	Twelve-shillings		
	Six-shillings		
	Two-shillings		
	Shilling		
	Half-shilling	Value ½d. Eng.	
Gold	Unit		Tenth coinage, 1610–1625, second after accession to English throne.
	Double-crown		
	Britain-crown		
	Halfcrown		
Silver	Sixty-shillings		
	Thirty-shillings		
	Twelve-shillings		
	Six-shillings		
Copper	Turner or Twopence	1614 and 1623 Two issues, different in legend	
	Penny		

Charles I, 1625–1649

Metal	*Denomination*	*No. of types, value, etc.*	*Remarks*
Gold	Unit or Double angel	Bust of James but new legend	First coinage, 1625–1636
	Double-crown		
	Britain-crown or Five merk		
Silver	Sixty-shillings or Crown sterling	James on horse, new legend	
	Thirty-shillings		
	Twelve-shillings		
	Six-shillings	1625–1634	
	Two-shillings		
	Shilling		
	Half-shilling		
Copper	Turner	Value 2d., two issues	
	Penny		
Silver	Half-merk		Second coinage, 1636, Briot's hammered issue
	Forty-penny piece		
	Twenty-penny piece		
Gold	Unit		Third coinage, divided into five issues: this, 1, by Briot
	Double-crown or half-unit		
	Britain-crown		
	Halfcrown		
Silver	Sixty-shillings		
	Thirty-shillings		
	Twelve-shillings		
	Six-shillings		
	Half-merk		
	Forty-pence		
	Twenty-pence		
Silver	Thirty-shillings		Third coinage. *section* 2, intermediate issue
	Twelve-shillings		
	Forty-pence		
	Twenty-pence		

Metal	*Denomination*	*No. of types, value, etc.*	*Remarks*
Silver	Twelve-shillings Six-shillings Forty-pence Twenty-pence		Third coinage *section 3*, by Falconer with privy-mark F.
Silver	Thirty-shillings Twelve-shillings Six-shillings Twenty-pence		Third coinage, *section 4*, Falconer's 2nd issue, with F
Silver	Thirty-shillings Twelve-shillings Twenty-pence		Third coinage, *section 5*, by Falconer, no F
Silver	Three-shillings Two-shillings		Fourth coinage, 1642
Copper	Turner or Bodle		

This ends the Scottish hammered issues. There were no Commonwealth or Cromwell issues in Scotland.

Space has allowed no more than a list of coins issued in this most interesting series. Readers will no doubt have been interested in the colourful names of some of the denominations and their relative values when set against English issues. Much more detail could have been given had space allowed. It is hoped that what has been written may stimulate some collectors to investigate further the hammered coinage of Scotland. We must press on with the equally brief listing of the milled coinage of Scotland.

The Milled Coinage of Scotland

Charles II, 1660–1684

Metal	*Denominations*	*Dates of issue, value, etc.*	*Remarks*
Silver	Four Merks	Value, 53s. 4d. Three varieties, (i) 1664 (ii) 1665–1673, (iii) 1674–1675	First coinage, 1664–1675

Metal	*Denomination*	*Dates of issue, value, etc.*	*Remarks*
	Two Merks	Three varieties. (i) 1664, (ii) 1664–1673, (iii) 1673–1675	
	Merk	Three varieties. (i) 1664–1673, (ii) 1672–1673, (iii) 1674–1675	
	Half-merk	(i) Varieties. (ii) 1664–1673, Similar, counter-marked 1665, (iii) 1675 F below bust, (iv) 1675, plain	
Bronze	Turner or Bodle		
Silver	Dollar		Second coinage, 1675–1682
	Half-dollar		
	Quarter-dollar		
	Eighth-dollar		
	Sixteenth-dollar		

Charles II was crowned king of Scotland in 1651 and, owing to the Commonwealth period in England as we have seen, did not come to the throne of England till the restoration in 1660. The silver pieces, down to the Eighth-dollar are similar in general appearance to the English issues, but vary in interesting detail.

The obverses have the laureate bust of the king, to right, but with a mantle and armour not present on the English series. There is sometimes a thistle above the bust, and sometimes below. The third main variety has F below the bust, the mark of Sir John Falconer, Master of the Mint.

The reverses also vary. Four shields of arms, Scotland, England and France quarterly, Scotland and Ireland are on the smaller denominations altered to Scotland, England, France and Ireland. On the larger denominations the shields are plain, and there are interlinked Cs in the angles, with a crown above. The value, such as the Four merks, 53s. 4d., is shown in the centre as LIII above 4: the Merk being XIII above 4. In the second coinage the crowns are above the shields which now show the arms as described second above, there are thistles in the angles and two interlinked Cs in the centre. In this coinage also the reverse legend includes the Scottish title, SCO.

The outstanding point about the second coinage, however, is that the armoured bust to right has been replaced by a draped bust to left, looking more akin to its English counterpart. The 'about face' during a reign will strike the collector of milled English coins as unusual, since in that series it rarely occurs, save in a few instances, c.f. base-metal coins of Charles II and James II.

James VII, 1686–1688
(James II of England)

Metal	*Denominations*	*Dates of issue*	*Remarks*
Silver	Sixty-shillings	Later striking	Proof only
	Forty-shillings		
	Ten-shillings		

All three pieces have a draped bust of the king to right, the opposite way to that of the English coinage of this reign. The value, 60, 40 and 10 respectively, appears below. On the two larger pieces the reverse has a crowned shield of arms, Scotland, England and France quarterly, Ireland and Scotland. The smaller piece has the four crowned shields of arms, Scotland, England, France and Ireland, with a St. Andrew's cross, terminated with a thistle, rose, fleur and harp respectively. (Readers will note that in describing four shields of arms thus placed they are given clockwise: a large shield of arms quartered is described in the heraldic manner, $\begin{array}{|cc}1&2\\3&4\end{array}$ The SCO in the legend has disappeared, but an edge legend is now used. It reads NEMO ME IMPUNE LACESSET, No one shall hurt me with impunity, followed by the regnal year. In the next reign the edge legend becomes PROTEGIT ET ORNAT, It protects and adorns, and in the reign of Anne, after the Union, the DECUS ET TUTAMEN legend is used.

William & Mary, 1689–1694

Metal	*Denomination*	*Dates of issue*	*Remarks*
Silver	Sixty-shillings		
	Forty-shillings		
	Twenty-shillings	1693–1694	
	Ten-shillings	1690 (i) Small shield, English crown, 1690 (ii) Large shield, Scottish crown, 1691–1694	
	Five-shillings	1691	
Copper	Bawbee		
	Bodle		

The jugate busts of the Joint Monarchs occupy the obverse, with the value below on the silver pieces. The busts face left, the opposite way to the English series. On the reverse of the first four silver pieces the single crowned shield of arms appears, the arms being Scotland, England and France quarterly, Ireland, Scotland, with an inescutcheon of the Lion of Nassau. The Five-shillings has the Royal cypher WM as reverse. In the copper issues the Bawbee has a thistle on reverse and the Bodle the cypher as obverse and the thistle as reverse.

William III, 1694–1702

Metal	*Denomination*	*Dates of issue*	*Remarks*
Gold	Pistole	1701 Value £12 Scot.	Metal from the Darien Company
	Half-pistole	Similar	
Silver	Sixty-shillings	1699	Extremely rare
	Forty-shillings	1695–1698	
	Twenty-shillings	1695–1699	
	Ten-shillings	1695–1702	
	Five-shillings	1695–1702	

Metal	*Denomination*	*Dates of issue*	*Remarks*
Copper	Bawbee or sixpence	1695–1697	
	Bodle or twopence	1695	Legend GVLIELMVS REX
		1695	Legend GVLIELMVS R
		1695	Legend GVL REX

Readers will note the first milled gold issue in this series. The obverses of the gold and silver pieces have the bust of William III to left, the opposite way to the English series. The reverses of the larger pieces have the crowned shield of arms which on the two gold pieces have a crowned W and R to left and right. There is an interesting story behind the gold pieces, c.f. Stewart.

Anne, 1702–1714

Metal	*Denomination*	*Dates of issue*	*Remarks*
Silver	Ten-shillings	1705	Legend reads REG
		1706	Legend reads REGINA
	Five-shillings	1705	Three legend readings
		1706	

The obverse has the bust of the Queen to left, as on the English series, with the value below. The reverse is occupied by the shield of arms surmounted by the Scottish crown.

After the union of the two kingdoms in 1707 it was ordered that 'from and after the Union the Coin shall be of the same standard and value throughout the United Kingdom, as now in England, and a mint shall be continued in Scotland under the same rules as the mint in England'. The Scottish issues were of silver only, no gold or copper being coined. They are distinguished by having an E or an

E and a star under the bust. The post-union issues were therefore as follows:

Silver	Crown	E below bust	1707, 1708
	Halfcrown	,,	1707–1709
	Shilling	,,	1707–1709
	Shilling	E and star	1707–1709
	Sixpence	E below bust	1707 and 1708
	Sixpence	E and star	1708 and 1709

The Shillings have three varieties of bust and the Sixpences two. This was the last coinage to be struck in Scotland. The present Scottish Shilling is not struck in Scotland, nor is it a Scottish piece. It was issued for reasons already given. The Edinburgh mint ceased operation after 1709 and in 1817 the buildings were sold. The office of Governor of the Mint of Scotland was abolished in the same year.

Dies for a Silver Crown piece were made in 1716, when Prince James, the Elder Pretender, made his second attempt to recover the English throne. They were made in Paris by Norbert Roettier, but no pieces seem to have been struck from them till 1828, when the dies, now in the British Museum, came into the hands of a coin dealer. The piece styles James as James VIII. Dies were also prepared for one or two denominations on the occasion of James's first attempt to recapture the throne.

On his map of the Scottish mints, Stewart shows the following, given from north to south:
Forres, Inverness, Aberdeen, Montrose, Forfar, Dundee, Perth, St. Andrews, Stirling, Montrose, Kinghorn, Dumbarton, Linlithgow, Edinburgh, Dunbar, Glasgow, Berwick-on-Tweed, Lanark, Kelso, Ayre, Jedburgh, Dumfries, Carlisle. There were also some ecclesiastical privilege mints, such as Crossraguel Abbey. As with the English series, the provincial mints were in operation during the hammered period, the last of them, Stirling, ceasing to operate after the reign of Mary.

CHAPTER NINE

The Coinage of Ireland

Like Scotland, Ireland had, for a long period, its own separate coinage. Though several books have been published on the more recent coinage of Eire, post 1928, nothing has been published in book form on the whole Irish coinage for many years, though there is at least one book in preparation.

The working material on this series will be found in a book about to go to press, with the tentative title of *A Catalogue of Irish Coins, 995–1968.* Meantime Grueber's British Museum Catalogue, mentioned above, can still be used, but with great caution. Much later research has resulted in many reattributions. (See note, p. 280.)

The series starts with hammered issues. Though there were various coins in use from about A.D. 1000, the series is frequently taken up by collectors in the time of John (1177–1216), when he was Lord of Ireland. He did not come to the English throne till 1199.

John, 1171–1216

Metal	*Denomination*	*Remarks*
Silver	Halfpenny	First coinage 1185. Profile type. Obverse has bust facing right, reverse has cross potent with fleur-de-lis in each angle. Excessively rare.
Silver	Halfpenny	Second coinage. First issue *c.* 1190–1194. Obverse has facing bust with DOM [for DOMINUS] in legend. Reverse has short double cross potent. i.e.
Silver	Farthing	Obverse has a Mascle with three pellets at end of each cusp. Reverse has cross potent with moneyer's name in the angles.
Silver	Halfpenny	Second issue *c.* 1196–1198. Similar to first issue but legend always contracted, and different moneyers.
Silver	Farthing	Similar to first issue, but different moneyers.
Silver	Halfpenny	Third issue 1198. Similar to first and second issue but double cross pommée on reverse. i.e.

John De Courcy, Lord of Ulster, 1177–1205

Unofficial Issues.

Silver	Halfpenny	First type. Obverse + PATRICIUS. Two beaded circles, within which is the head of a bishop's crosier. Reverse + IOH–S DE CURCI. Unique.
Silver	Halfpenny	Second type. Obverse CAPUT IONIS. Facing bust. Reverse Double short cross pommée. Very rare.
Silver	Farthing	Three different types. All very rare.

John, 1171–1216 [continued]

Metal	*Denomination*	*Remarks*
Silver	Penny	Third coinage, c. 1205–1210. Obverse has the legend IOHANNES REX and a facing bust, with a triangle. Fairly common.
Silver	Halfpenny	Similar. Very rare.
Silver	Farthing	Similar. Extremely rare.

Henry III, 1216–1272

Silver	Penny	Struck 1251–1254. Obverse. Facing bust in triangle. Only denomination.

Edward I, 1272–1307

Coins with name of Henry III, 1276–1279

Silver	Penny	As previous coins of Henry III, but with more realistic hair.

Coins with name of Edward I

Silver	Penny	Now arranged into six issues and dating from 1280–1302.
Silver	Halfpenny	Similar, struck only in the sixth issue 1296–1302.
Silver	Farthing	Similar to the halfpenny and struck only in the sixth issue.

Edward III, 1327–1377

Silver	Halfpenny	Similar in style to the coins of the previous reign. This is one of two Irish coins extant today which are considered to belong to this reign.

Henry VI, 1422–1461

Silver	Penny	Henry struck only one coinage for Ireland, and this penny [now in the B.M.] is one of two examples known to be in existence today.

Edward IV, 1461–1483

Metal	*Denomination*	*Remarks*
Silver	Groat	First issue, 1461–1463. Untitled crown on obverse.
Silver	Penny	Similar.
Copper	Farthing.	Similar.
Brass	Farthing	Bishop's legend PATRICIVS.
Brass	Half Farthing	Obverse. PATRIK and branch, crown in centre.
Silver	Groat	Second issue, *c.* 1463–1464. Similar to previous coins, but king's name and titles on obverse.
Silver	Penny	Similar.
		Cross Fourchée/Rose Coinage. c. 1464?
Silver	Groat	Cross fourchée on obverse, large rose on reverse. Very rare.
Silver	Penny	Similar.
Copper	Farthing	Obverse has shield bearing three crowns.

(*a*) *Heavy type. 45–35 grains. c.* 1465–1467

Silver	Groat	Facing Bust type, with English style reverse, *c.* 1465–1475. Similar to English groats, but cruder. Fairly common.
Silver	Halfgroat	Similar.
Silver	Penny	Similar.
Silver	Halfpenny	Similar.

(*b*) *Light type. c.* 1475

Silver	Groat	Similar to previous coins.
Silver	Halfgroat	Similar.
Silver	Penny	Similar.
Silver	Double-groat	The Double Groat issue. 1467–1470. Value 8d. Obverse. Crowned bust facing, curly hair. Reverse. Rose in centre of large sun.
Silver	Groat	Similar.
Silver	Halfgroat	Similar.
Silver	Penny	Similar.

Metal	*Denomination*	*Remarks*
Silver	Groat	Facing Bust Type/English Reverse. These coins have no initial marks and are all of the Drogheda mint. They are often called the fifth issue. Extremely rare.

Edward IV, Second reign. Final issue

Silver	Groat	Known as the Rose-on-Cross issue, this
Silver	Penny	device is on the reverse of both pieces.

Note. It should be borne in mind that Edward IV's reign still poses Irish numismatists some difficult problems. Briefly, there are a great many coins and it is not yet known where most of them fit in chronologically.

Richard III, 1483–1485

Silver	Groat	First issue. Similar to final issue of Edward IV.
Silver	Penny	Similar.
Silver	Groat	Second issue. The introduction of the '3-crowns' coinage. Obverse. Shield, arms of England. Reverse. Three crowns.

Henry VII, 1485–1508

Silver	Groat	First period 1485–1490. 3-crowns coinage [continued] As previous coinage.
Silver	Halfgroat	
Silver	Penny	

Lambert Simnel, 1467

Silver	Groat	Similar to previous coinage.

Henry VII [continued]

Silver	Groat	Further issues of 3-crown coinage. Similar to previous issues but different terminals to cross.
Silver	Halfgroat	

Metal	*Denomination*	*Remarks*
Silver	Groat	Second period. *c.* 1490. English style, both with open-crown and arched crown.
Silver	Halfgroat	
Silver	Groat	Third period. *c.* 1491–1502. First type. Similar to previous coins, but arms of reverse cross have elaborate ends.
Silver	Penny	
Silver	Groat	Second type. These coins have a strongly distinctive facing bust. In fact more of a portrait than an effigy.
Silver	Penny	

Again a series with many varieties within the main denominations. Such items as mint names, double and single-arched crowns, varieties of bust, annulets, pellets and so forth serve to divide many of the denominations into varieties and types.

The rare pieces of Lambert Simnel are of unusual interest. Simnel was crowned as Edward VI, King of Ireland, at Dublin on 24th May, 1487. His coinage, so called, was issued between late 1486 and 16th June, 1487. Simnel's story is bound up mainly with the history of England and the revolt against Henry VII.

Henry VIII, 1509–1547

Silver	Groat	Known as First Harp coinage. 1536–1541. Harp on reverse. hA (Henry and Anne Boleyn).
Silver	Halfgroat	
Silver	Groat	hI (Jane Seymour).
Silver	Halfgroat	
Silver	Groat	hK (Katherine Howard).
Silver	Halfgroat	
Silver	Groat	hR (HENRICVS REX). Two types. VIII omitted on second.
Silver	Groat	Second Harp coinage, 1542–1547. Three types, (i) reading hIBERNIE REX. (ii) and dated 37=year of reign, (iii) dated 38: with WS, struck at Bristol.

Edward VI, 1547–1553

(It will be remembered that the first coins of this reign in the English series had the bust and titles of Henry VIII.)

Metal	*Denomination*	*Remarks*
Silver	Groat	Various busts some of Irish workmanship, others originating from the Tower Mint.
Silver	Halfgroat	Similar.
Silver	Penny Halfpenny	

Mary, 1553–1554

Silver	Shilling	Dated MDLIII(I).
	Groat	No date, any with date are false.
	Halfgroat	The type for all three pieces is, obverse, bust to l., reverse, crowned harp dividing M R.

Philip & Mary, 1554–1558

Billon	Shilling	Busts, face-to-face, crown above, dated 1555.
	Groat	Similar, 1555–1558.

Elizabeth I, 1558–1603

Billon	Shilling	First coinage, 1558. Obverse, bust to l. Reverse, harp.
	Groat	Similar.
Silver	Shilling	Second coinage. Reverse, crowned shield with three harps dividing date, 15 61
	Groat	Similar.
Billon	Shilling	Third coinage, 1598–1602. Crowned harp reverse.
	Sixpence	
	Threepence	Both similar.
Copper	Penny	Issued 1601 and 1602. Obverse, shield dividing E R, reverse, crowned harp dividing date.
	Halfpenny	

James I, 1603–1625

Metal	*Denomination*	*Remarks*
Silver	Shilling	First coinage, Bust of king to right.
	Sixpence	Similar, 1602–1603
Silver	Shilling	Second coinage, 1605. Type similar.
	Sixpence	Similar.
Copper	Farthing	Similar type to the English series.

From Philip and Mary to James I the majority of the pieces are not so rare and expensive as those of the previous reigns.

Charles I, 1625–1649

Apart from the copper Farthing token pieces, struck in London, and being the same as the English series of James I and Charles I, no purely regal money was struck for Ireland during this reign. During the period of the Civil War official currency became so scarce that local issues appeared, usually known as 'Money of Necessity'. Of this money, Grueber, B.M.C., states:

'The issue of this 'Money of Necessity' in Ireland extended from 1642 to 1647, the period of the so-called 'Irish Rebellion'. It is very similar in character to the English siege money of the same period; much of it being mere pieces of metal of irregular shape, stamped with a value or other mark. They are of gold, silver, and copper; the gold is however the exception. The primary object in issuing this money was for the relief of the Government and the payment of the army, which was sent to suppress the rebels. The example set by the Crown was soon followed by the rebels, who also struck money for their own use.'

However there have been many re-attributions since the days of Grueber and the coins should be listed as follows: [This is mainly based on Philip Nelson's work on this series]

Kilkenny money, 1642.	Copper, Halfpenny, Farthing.
Inchiquin money, 1642. Silver issues.	First type. Crowns, Halfcrowns, Shillings, Ninepences, Sixpences.
	Second type. Ninepences, Sixpences, Groats, Threepences.
	Third type. Crowns, Halfcrowns.
1646 Gold issues.	Double pistole. Only two specimens known. Pistole. Excessively rare.

Ormonde money, 1642.	Silver, Crown, Halfcrown, Shilling, Sixpence, Fourpence, Threepence, Twopence. A Penny was catalogued by Ruding in his 'Annals', but no specimen is known. Named Ormonde Money on the supposition that it was issued during the viceroyalty of James, Marquis, and subsequently Duke of Ormonde, appointed in November 1643.
Rebel money, 1643.	Crowns, Halfcrowns. All rare.
Cork money, 1647.	Silver, Shilling dated 1647, Sixpence. Copper, possibly a Penny.

Copper pieces, possibly intended to pass as Pennies, were struck by the Parliamentary troops, at Bandon, Kinsale and Youghal, all of which places were in their hands at the time. The pieces from the latter place are dated 1646.

The majority of these pieces are rare and expensive.

Blacksmith's money, 1649	Silver halfcrown. [Copied from the English halfcrowns of Charles I.]
Dublin money, 1649.	[Issued by Ormonde to proclaim Charles II as King of Ireland] Silver crowns, halfcrowns.

Commonwealth, 1649–1660

No official money issued for Ireland. Trader's tokens appeared, exactly similar to those of the English Seventeenth century series.

Charles II, 1660–1685

Copper Farthing	1660, struck under patent by Sir Thomas Armstrong. Similar to the James I/Charles I English series.
Copper Halfpenny Farthing	Known as St. Patrick's money. Obverse, King David playing harp, reverse, St. Patrick, standing, to left.

James II, 1685–1691
(James II of England, 1685–1688)

Copper Halfpenny Struck 1685–1688.

The next part of this coinage consists of what is usually known as 'Gun Money', struck between 1689 and 1691, when James finally fled from the British Isles. It is so called because it was occasionally made from the metal of old brass guns, though bells and others objects are said to have been used.

The denominations consist of Crown, Halfcrown, Shilling and Sixpence. The Crown has the king on horseback, to left, on the obverse and on the reverse four crowned shields of arms, England, Scotland, France and Ireland with ANO DOM 16 90 in the angles, a crown in the centre. The smaller denominations have an English-type bust of James to l., while the reverse design is a crown in the centre above two sceptres in saltire, dividing J R in script. The date is at the top of the coin and the value in Roman figures below the date. (XXX=2/6d., XII=1/– etc.) Below the crown is the month of issue, Aug: Sepr:, abbreviated.

A small study of these not uninteresting pieces undertaken some years ago found many varieties of abbreviations, stops, dies, and so forth. A few pieces, presumably proofs, have been seen in silver, as well as a Crown in gold.

The coinage of the reign is concluded with a pewter Crown, Penny, and Halfpenny, circa 1689–1690, and some brass Farthings struck in Limerick, in 1691, after James had fled to France.

William & Mary, 1689–1694

Copper Halfpenny Busts to right.

William III, 1694–1702

Copper Halfpenny Bust to right.

George I, 1714–1727

Copper	Halfpenny Farthing	Issue by William Wood. Obverse, bust to right, Reverse, Hibernia with harp.

George II, 1727–1760

Copper	Halfpenny	(i) Young head, 1736–1746, (ii) intermediate head, 1747–1755, (iii) old head, 1760.
	Farthing	(i) Young head, 1737–1744, (ii) old head, 1760.
	Halfpenny Farthing	1760, called the 'Voce Populi' type because of the legend. Struck after the cessation of regal coins from 1755 till 1760.

This may be said to conclude the hammered Irish coinage. It will be noted that milled coinage was not introduced into Ireland at the restoration in the same way that it had been introduced in England. It is not till we come to the reign of George III, 1760–1820, that milled money proper was put into circulation.

The following mints as operated in Ireland. From the reign of Henry VIII most of the Irish coinage was struck in England.

Irish Mints

Bandon Bridge, Carlingford, Carrickfergus, Cork, Downpatrick, Drogheda, Dublin, Galway, Kilkenny, Kinsale, Limerick, Trim, Waterford, Wexford, Youghal.

The Milled Coinage of Ireland

George III, 1760–1820

Copper	Halfpenny	First coinage. (i) Short hair on king's head, 1766–1769, (ii) long hair, 1774–1783.
Copper	Penny	Second coinage. Struck 1805
	Halfpenny	Struck 1805.
	Farthing	Struck 1806.

There was also a series of silver Bank of Ireland tokens, similar to the Bank of England silver tokens of the same period. The denominations were Six shillings, Thirty pence, Tenpence, Fivepence.

George IV, 1820–1830

Copper	Penny	1822–1823. Obverse, bust to l., reverse crowned harp.
	Halfpenny	1822–1823
	Farthing	1822, known only as a pattern.

After 1823 the coinage of Ireland was entirely assimilated to that of Great Britain, and so remained till the formation of the Irish Free State in 1922. In 1949 the Free State became the Irish Republic. Northern Ireland is, of course, not a part of this State-Republic territory.

In 1928 the Free State had its own money, coined at the Royal Mint, and has continued to do so ever since. The attractive designs, local fauna, were some of the earliest of modern coins in this now popular field of coin design. The obverse of all denominations is the harp, while the reverses are:

Halfcrown: A horse, based on the Irish hunter.
Florin: A salmon, in Irish legend the emblem of wisdom.
Shilling: A bull.
Sixpence: The Irish wolf-hound.
Threepence: A hare.
Penny: A hen and chickens.
Halfpenny: A sow and litter.
Farthing: A woodcock.

To these designs by Percy Metcalf, which have remained unchanged ever since, there was recently added a Ten Shilling piece.

The only change in the coinage was in 1939, when the legend on the obverse was changed from SAORSTAT EIREANN=Irish Free State, to EIRE=Ireland. The Halfcrown, Florin and Shilling, originally silver, were changed to cupro-nickel in 1951 and the nickel Sixpence and Threepence were changed to cupro-nickel in 1952.

The following lists of dates of issue are taken from Jerome Remick's recently published *Guide Book and Catalogue of British Commonwealth Coins*, 1967. They do not agree, date for date, with those given in my own *British Commonwealth Coinage*. Remick's research is the later: my own lists did not take into account coins that might have been struck in one year but dated the year previously: not an uncommon occurrence at the Royal Mint if a contract over-runs the year-end.

Ten Shillings.	Halfcrown.	Florin.	Shilling.
AR	AR	AR	AR
1966	1928	1928	1928
	1930	1930	1930
	1931	1931	1931
	1933	1933	1933
	1934	1934	1935
	1937	1935	1937
	1939	1937	1939
	1940	1939	1940
	1941	1940	1941
	1942	1941	1942
	1943 RRR	1942	1951 Cu-ni
	1951 Cu-ni	1943	1954
	1954	1951 Cu-ni	1955
	1955	1954	1959
	1959	1955	1962
	1961	1959	1963
	1962	1961	1964
	1963	1962	1966
	1966	1963	
		1964	
		1965	
		1966	

Sixpence.	Threepence.	Penny.	Halfpenny.
Ni.	Ni.	AE.	AE.
1928	1928	1928	1928
1934	1933	1931	1933
1935	1934	1933	1935
1939	1935	1935	1937
1940	1939	1937	1939
1942 Cu-ni.	1940	1940	1940
1945	1942 Cu-ni.	1941	1941
1946	1943	1942	1942
1947	1946	1943	1943

Sixpence.	Threepence.	Penny.	Halfpenny.
1948	1948	1946	1946
1949	1949	1948	1949
1950	1950	1949	1953
1952	1953	1950	1964
1953	1956	1952	1965
1955	1961	1962	1966
1956	1962	1963	
1958	1963	1964	
1959	1964	1965	
1960	1965	1966	
1961	1966		
1962			
1963			
1964			
1966			

Farthing.AE.
1928
1930
1931
1932
1933
1935
1936
1937
1939
1940
1941
1944
1946
1949
1953
1959
1966

This brings the coinage of Ireland up to date. In 1970 decimal coinage is envisaged. If the opportunity is then taken to redesign the coins, it is hoped that the result will be as happy as was that of 1928. Not that the 1928 coins got away without comment. But over the years Percy Metcalf's designs, so well reflecting something of the pleasantness of the Emerald Isle, have become well liked, not the least among coin collectors.

Select Bibliography

DOLLEY, R. H. M. and SEABY, W. A. *Anglo-Irish Coins from John–Edward III.* Ulster Museum, Belfast. *Sylloge of Coins of the British Isles*, London, 1968.

GRUEBER, H. A. *Handbook of the Coins of Great Britain and Ireland in the British Museum 1899* (subject to the reservations at the head of this chapter). London.

NELSON, P. *The Obsidional Money of the Great Rebellion (1642–1649)*, 1905, reprinted 1968.

I am most grateful to Patrick Finn who rewrote the whole of the section dealing with Irish hammered coinage. This was done in the light of the yet unpublished book* on the series, mentioned at the head of this chapter, of which Pat Finn is co-author with Anthony Dowle.

CONCLUSION

This also brings us to the end of our story. It now only remains to sum up, and to try to see if this work has served any real purpose. As a working-book for the collector it is far from adequate, but this was not its prime purpose. As was said in the opening chapters, it was intended as a guide, both to the outline of our centuries of numismatic history and to other works, standard works, on which many students have laboured to give the collector of whatever interest the real meat.

Whatever you, the reader, may feel if you have succeeded in coming thus far: if you have obtained as much pleasure and help from these pages by reading them as the author has by writing them, then both are well rewarded.

* Now published. ***The Guide Book to the Coinage of Ireland, from*** **A.D. 955** ***to the present day.***

Index